Doing the Time Warp

Doing the Time Warp

Strange Temporalities and Musical Theatre

Sarah Taylor Ellis

methuen | drama
LONDON • NEW YORK • OXFORD • NEW DELHI • SYDNEY

METHUEN DRAMA
Bloomsbury Publishing Plc
50 Bedford Square, London, WC1B 3DP, UK
1385 Broadway, New York, NY 10018, USA
29 Earlsfort Terrace, Dublin 2, Ireland

BLOOMSBURY, METHUEN DRAMA and the Methuen Drama logo
are trademarks of Bloomsbury Publishing Plc

First published in Great Britain 2022
This paperback edition published 2023

Copyright © Sarah Taylor Ellis, 2022

Sarah Taylor Ellis has asserted her right under the Copyright, Designs
and Patents Act, 1988, to be identified as author of this work.

For legal purposes the Acknowledgements on pp. xi–xii constitute
an extension of this copyright page.

Cover design by Louise Dugdale
Cover photo © Stanley Bielecki Movie Collection/Getty Images

All rights reserved. No part of this publication may be reproduced or
transmitted in any form or by any means, electronic or mechanical, including
photocopying, recording, or any information storage or retrieval system,
without prior permission in writing from the publishers.

Bloomsbury Publishing Plc does not have any control over, or responsibility for,
any third-party websites referred to or in this book. All internet addresses given
in this book were correct at the time of going to press. The author and publisher
regret any inconvenience caused if addresses have changed or sites have
ceased to exist, but can accept no responsibility for any such changes.

A catalogue record for this book is available from the British Library.

A catalog record for this book is available from the Library of Congress

ISBN:	HB:	978-1-3501-5170-3
	PB:	978-1-3503-3319-2
	ePDF:	978-1-3501-5172-7
	eBook:	978-1-3501-5171-0

Typeset by Integra Software Services Pvt. Ltd.

To find out more about our authors and books visit www.bloomsbury.com
and sign up for our newsletters.

In memory of Michael Friedman (1975–2017)
The song makes a space.

Contents

Figures ix
Tables x
Acknowledgements xi

Introduction: 'I Would Like, Ah, if I May, to Take You on a Strange Journey ...' 1

1 A Funny Thing Happened ... to the Integrated Musical: Poetics and Politics of Queer Temporality 13
    Anxieties of integration: *A Funny Thing Happened on the Way to the Forum* (1962) 16
    In the meanwhile: 'The Miller's Son' (1973) 27
    No day but today: *Rent* (1996) 30

2 'Let's Do the Time Warp Again': Performing Time, Genre and Spectatorship 45
    Creatures of the night: *The Rocky Horror Picture Show* 48
    We'll make time stand still: *Dr. Horrible's Sing-Along Blog* 67

3 Ragging Race: Spectral Temporality in the American Musical 81
    Ragtime: The music 85
    Ragtime: The novel 90
    Ragtime: The musical 92
    Histories of integration 96
    Haunting me, just like a melody 102
    The player piano 105
    Ragging race 112

4	**'I Just Projected Myself Out of It': Rehearsing Identities in Youth Musical Theatre**	**115**
	Camping it up at *Camp*	120
	Finding *Glee*	129
	So what about *Hamilton*?	144
5	**'Just an Illusion': Identity and Musical Form**	**149**
	Performing the illusive 'I'	150
	Until now gives way to then: *Fun Home*	154
	The curious case of Bobby/Bobbie	168
	I am *A Strange Loop*	176
	Conclusion: 'Everything You're Feeling Is Appropriate'	**187**
	Flashback to 2016: A musical number	189
	Flashforward to 2021: Back to book time	199

Notes	202
Select Bibliography	247
Index	259

Figures

1	Marjory Stoneman Douglas High School drama students perform onstage during the 72nd Annual Tony Awards at Radio City Music Hall on 10 June 2018 in New York City	42
2	'Wild and Untamed Thing'	57
3	My first time. Or as I posted that night on Facebook, 'Rocky Horror Picture Show at the Nuart! This is what I like to call "research."' 13 November 2011	64
4	Cover of 'A Line of Rags' by D. Haworth, 1903	89
5	Cover of the theatre programme for Israel Zangwill's play *The Melting Pot*, 1916	98
6	Apollo Reproducing Piano advertisement	109
7	*Chapter 2*, an original musical written, composed and directed by Nightingale-Bamford School student Jordan Polycarpe	143
8	*Fun Home* – Alison Bechdel, Sydney Lucas, Emily Skeggs and Beth Malone	155
9	My unexpected appearance as 'Gloria' in the 24-hour *24-Decade History of Popular Music*	195

Tables

1	Length of the Show	21
2	Let's Do the Time Warp Again	55
3	Science Fiction/Double Feature	61

Acknowledgements

I started this research project about a decade ago as my doctoral dissertation at UCLA – but really, the project began when I was growing up as an artsy outsider in Albemarle, North Carolina. Small and Medium Sarah pop up throughout these pages. Since the journey to writing this book has been lifelong in many ways, I will inevitably miss several acknowledgements along the way. Please know how grateful I am.

Thank you to my interdisciplinary dissertation committee, particularly my co-chairs: Sue-Ellen Case challenged me to bridge my aesthetic interests into the politics of performance, while Raymond Knapp brought an infectious enthusiasm for musical analysis. Afternoon tea meetings with Ray and fellow grad students Samuel Baltimore and Arreanna Rostosky made the dissertation a much more gleeful process. Thank you as well to committee members Susan Foster and Gary Gardner, as well as the many other supportive professors and creatives with whom I collaborated at UCLA. Thank you to the undergraduate professors who laid the foundation for my life in the arts, particularly John Clum, Emanuel Azenberg, Anthony Kelley, Marianna Torgovnick and Jeff Storer. (Manny, the autobiographical bits are for you.)

Parts of this book have been previously published, including "'No Day But Today': Queer Temporality in the American Musical' in *Studies in Musical Theatre* and 'Let's Do the Time Warp Again: Performing Time, Genre, and Spectatorship' in *The Routledge Companion to the Contemporary Musical*. Thank you to the editors of these articles for helping refine my ideas and allowing them to be reworked and recontextualized in this monograph. Thank you to the peer reviewers, test readers and friends who provided invaluable feedback as I transformed the dissertation into a book, particularly John Clum, Ryan Donovan, Filip Holacký, Erica Meyer, Jenny Stafford, Sarah Whitfield, Zelda Knapp and my ever-reliable 'Giles', Raymond Knapp. Thank you to my editor Dom O'Hanlon and the team at Methuen Drama; it has been a particular joy to work with an editor who is an equally brilliant scholar, practitioner and fan.

Thank you to my colleagues and collaborators overlapping with and extending beyond the strange world of academia. Thank you to the talented teachers and staff at the Metropolitan Opera Guild, Roundabout Theatre Company, Harlem School of the Arts, the Nightingale-Bamford School, the University of Chester and ArtsEd. Moreover, thank you to my wonderful students at all these institutions. From original student musicals (shout-out to Jordan Polycarpe and Elliot Lee) to student-produced *Rocky Horror* shadowcasts (shout-out to Lee-El Bryan), I learned so much from building a music composition programme and growing with my student composers at Nightingale. Thank you to the ArtsEd Sixth Form Book Club (Greg Beavis, Julia Caldwell, Isabelle Haynes-Hopkins, Deborah Jardine, Eoin McCaul and Noah Thallon), who took the time in lockdown to be my first test readers, introduce me to TikTok and help me think through the final chapter before it ever hit the page.

Thank you to the brilliant writers, directors, choreographers, producers, stage managers, actors and collaborators on dozens of plays and musical projects through the years; I have learned so much by making music together. A particular thanks to my musical collaborator and demon sister Meghan Brown. Thank you to friends on tumblr, twitter and in real life who have avidly created, seen, fangirled and debated theatre with me; your names affectionately pop up throughout this text.

Thank you to my family. To my husband Ben and my cats E.L. Doctorow and Emma Goldman, who always supported my midnight writing sprees. Thank you to my little sister Mary Hannah; we have carried the banner through it all. And thank you to my parents, who didn't realize that extracurricular dance and piano lessons (thank you Miss Melissa and Mrs Harwood!) might be a way of dreaming myself into such a multifaceted, musical life – but have been ever supportive as I travel on my way.

Introduction: 'I Would Like, Ah, if I May, to Take You on a Strange Journey ... '

When their car breaks down one stormy night, newly engaged Brad and Janet find a beacon of hope at a nearby castle. They approach the Frankenstein place hoping to call a mechanic and resume their steady narrative drive towards marriage. But upon entering the castle, Brad and Janet encounter an odd assortment of characters performing a strangely seductive 'Time Warp'. In *The Rocky Horror Show*, 'The Time Warp' introduces Brad and Janet to the 'transsexual Transylvanians" alternative temporality and lifestyle. This participatory song and dance twists their perceptions of identity and reroutes their linear trajectory to marriage.

'The Time Warp' represents an extreme example of how musical performance can bend and even break normative narratives in musical theatre. Song and dance – sites of aesthetic difference within the musical – can complicate a linear, developmental plot by speeding, slowing, looping, layering and even stopping time; after all, musical numbers are called 'showstoppers' for a reason. The strange temporal deviation of a musical number has the potential to disrupt naturalized constructions of historical, progressive time and concordant constructions of gender, sexual and racial identities. A musical number can also implicate the spectator as a performer, actively involved in warping dominant ideologies by singing and dancing along; fans can embody a desire for difference by reperforming and recontextualizing extractable musical moments beyond the 'original' stage or screen production. This book employs the aesthetic principles of musical theatre to consider the genre's politics, which can cut against the grain of dominant ideology to establish identities and communities in difference. The musical, a bastion of mainstream theatrical culture, always and already contains a fan culture of marginalized and semi-marginalized outsiders who dream themselves into being in the liminal timespaces of song and dance.

Musical theatre is often considered to be pure entertainment: a commercialized genre offering escape and wish fulfilment for a generalized audience presupposed to be white, middle-class, heteronormative spectators.[1] To be sure, the plot lines of Golden Age musicals often tidily resolve in marriage; the wedding of a man and woman is frequently a synecdoche for the reconciliation of conflict in a broader community, and divergent parts are subsumed into a homogeneous whole – or violently excluded from this community – by the musical's narrative end.[2] Yet one of the musical's fundamental contradictions is the marginalized 'others' who have always been central to the creation of this popular art form: Jewish immigrants, African Americans, gay men and female divas.[3] Musical comedies of the early and mid-twentieth century created a space for performative assimilation by Jewish musical theatre actors and creators; the ruptures of musical numbers enabled the performance of difference and multiplicity by which immigrants wrote themselves into the narrative of mainstream America.[4] African Americans rarely featured as three-dimensional, narratively significant characters in early and mid-century musicals, but Black actors could temporarily steal agency in their virtuosic performances of musical numbers – which are, after all, the raison d'être for the genre.[5] Even when these Black bodies were absented from the stage, their aesthetic contributions – such as jazz music and tap dance – remained fundamental to the art form.[6] While the musical may have been carefully closeted in its Golden Age, coded dialogue and delightful releases into song and dance provided queer pleasures for the gay male 'show queen'.[7] For women, as well, musicals prominently feature divas with powerful, belting voices and fierce athleticism; female characters, though often narratively reined in to marriage by the end of the show, can have a performative presence that exceeds the plot for spectators desirous to see and hear difference.[8]

This book thus hinges on a consideration of the political and aesthetic 'integration' of the musical: are the diverse components of a musical subsumed into a homogeneous whole, or can the elements stand apart and offer a vibrant theatrical vision of difference and multiplicity? The answer is likely both: it depends on how the spectator desires to experience the genre. The aesthetically integrated musical reigned from 1943 to 1965, or from *Oklahoma* to *Fiddler on the Roof*. Pioneered by Rodgers and Hammerstein and modelled after Wagner's *Gesamtkunstwerk* (total work of art), the integrated musical aimed to progress the plot seamlessly through song and dance, rendering all theatrical elements subservient to the narrative drive.[9] The paradigm of integration has been invoked as a standard for judging musical theatre since mid-century, but whether musicals ever wholly elide the differences across divergent theatrical elements is questionable.[10] The poetics of the musical – a non-realist juxtaposition of multiple performance modes ranging from dialogue to song to dance – can open the genre to a wide range of identifications and interpretations, which can operate independent of narrative and character. While accounting for spectators' identifications and desires, I aim to critically re-view and recontextualize the musical with an eye towards dis-integration and difference.

This 'difference' can be most readily located in musical numbers and their temporal excess, or what I call the musical's 'strange temporalities'. 'Strange temporalities' is an umbrella term for diverse non-normative constructions of and relationships to time. Modern time consciousness is empty, homogeneous and disenchanted. It is epitomized by the mechanical clock, which subdivides time into equidistant, uniform intervals, and by the linear, horizontal timeline, which perpetuates a tidy progress-driven narrative (whether in a single life or over the course of human history). The standardized time of the clock exerts strict social, political and economic control over work and leisure; it obscures the plurality of our existence in time and erases cultural and racial differences in lived experience.[11] A linear, goal-oriented conception of time forms the basis of our understanding of human life on every systemic level, from medical practice to governmental policy.[12] But strange temporalities give rise to different conceptions of identity, alternative life trajectories and new forms of affiliation that ruffle these limiting and homogenizing myths.

Under the umbrella of strange temporalities, 'queer time' has been most extensively theorized and thus provides a vital lens onto the broader term; in fact, Jack Halberstam explicitly pinpoints queerness as an outcome of 'strange temporalities, imaginative life schedules, and eccentric economic practices'.[13] Queer temporality resists normative institutions of family, heterosexuality and reproduction, and it enables participants to imagine their lives outside of the paradigmatic markers of a heteronormative life: birth, marriage, reproduction and death.[14] Queerness is not exclusively about sexual identity, then, but about living a life in excess of the logics of labour, production and capitalism while seeking creative approaches to organizing time and constructing identity and community.

Halberstam theorizes queer temporality as emerging most vividly in the wake of the HIV/AIDS epidemic, which urged gay communities to reconsider a heteronormative emphasis on longevity and to instead embrace 'the here, the present, the now'.[15] Other conceptions of queerness reject this emphasis on the present, considering the here and now a prison house that can render time static and unchanging. For José Muñoz, queerness must be about critiquing the quagmire of the present and insisting on the concrete possibility of a queer futurity. He posits queerness as a horizon – 'not simply a being but a doing for and toward the future'.[16] Queerness as a verb actively pushes towards a luminous futurity of difference and possibility. Though this horizon is always just out of reach, it is sometimes palpable in the present; drawing on Ernst Bloch's theories of anticipatory illumination, Muñoz sees queerness as a modality of ecstatic time in which 'straight time' can be temporarily interrupted or stepped out of. Ecstatic, illuminating moments of recognition – whether announced in a scream of pleasure or a quiet contemplation of a past, present or future instant – can pleasurably lift one out of the present and point towards a queer futurity of unbound freedom.[17]

Strange new temporalities may arise when normative horizons of opportunity are diminished. Much as queer time locates new possibilities of life against the heightened pace of the HIV/AIDS epidemic, crip time rejects the notion of disability as a predetermined limit to life and imagines new ways of being for people with disabilities.[18] Postcolonial temporal critique considers how imperialism relied on a temporal strategy of deeming 'discovered' cultures 'primitive' or 'anachronistic', thereby relegating radical cultural difference to the past; these critiques make visible the cacophonous coexistence of multiple times, including nonsecular and supernatural times, in any given moment.[19] Black temporality seeks to free Black consciousness from a linear historical timeline of slavery and its traumatic aftermath, a reductive narrative that renders Black liberation an impossibility.[20] Key to these independent but interrelated strange temporalities is a vision of new futurities for marginalized subjects. These futurities are unbound from causal, progress-driven notions of time. Moreover, these futurities are envisioned not in the future tense as a distant, formless utopian hope, but in the *future real conditional*, as a future 'that hasn't yet happened but must' – a future that is actively beginning in the present. As Tina M. Campt explains, 'It's a politics of pre-figuration that involves living the future now – as imperative rather than subjunctive – as a striving for the future you want to see, right now, in the present.'[21]

Strangely enough, the crowd-pleasing genre of musical theatre can unravel limiting, linear notions of time and can spectacularly showcase strange temporalities and new horizons of possibility for willing spectators. In a seminal aesthetic consideration of the genre, *The Musical as Drama*, Scott McMillin differentiates between the progressive time of the musical's book and the repetitive time of musical numbers. For McMillin, song and dance inject a lyrical moment into the 'the cause-and-effect progress of the plot', suspending the linear book time in favour of a different order of time organized by repetition, circularity and accumulation.[22] To be sure, music does not unfold in 'real time', but imposes a suspended animation on intensified, emotional moments.[23] Musical numbers also have the potential to collapse time – memories of the past and dreams of the future – into a heightened here and now; the expansive present takes stock of time and makes multiple possibilities palpable, even proffering the potential of rerouting the narrative drive. Zachary Dorsey calls this sense of open possibility the musical's 'subjunctive mood', which sits adjacent to time and helps to connect character, actor and audience in a shared affective experience.[24]

This book does not attempt to codify every strange temporality that might exist in a musical, but it points to the many possible temporal manipulations – the speeding and slowing of time, time's arrest, circularity, repetition, collapsed and overlapping temporalities, syncopation, spectral temporalities, the temporalities of adaptation and pastiche, and so on.[25] Moreover, I aim to politicize the musical's time-warping aesthetics by considering their critical affective impact on those marginalized and semi-marginalized fans desirous to see, hear, perform and reperform difference. For many fans, the pleasures and possibilities of the musical often lie precisely in the genre's strange temporalities: in luminous moments of recognition that are experienced in an expanded present, and in the (re)performative potentialities generated by the inherently fragmented form. The musical's multifaceted temporalities can complicate a straightforward narrative drive and a normative arc of character development; it is in the exuberant, temporally divergent musical numbers that willing spectators can find release from conventional life structures and imagine different ways of spending time in the world.

After all, breaking into the repetitive time of song and dance not only alters the temporal landscape of the stage but also fundamentally shifts characterization. In an integrated musical, song and dance are often perceived to deepen character, but McMillin suggests that a musical number actually *doubles* a character, effecting a striking transformation into a new 'musical' self – and 'the incongruity is theatrically arresting'.[26] Bertolt Brecht is an essential guidepost in politicizing the diverse, incongruous theatrical elements of the musical, particularly the transformation that a character undergoes in song.²⁷ The purpose of the Brechtian *Verfremdungseffekt*, or alienation effect, is to defamiliarize what ideology makes appear normal and even natural: 'People's activity must simultaneously be so and be capable of being different.'²⁸ While the political goal of Brecht's praxis is to denaturalize structures of capitalism, his techniques of alienation, historicization and distanciation can be employed to denaturalize other cultural constructs such as gender, sexuality and race as well.²⁹ The 'crackle of difference' between book and musical number, between the character performed in dialogue and the character performed in song and dance, can spectacularly destabilize notions of essentialized identity and open up a space of difference within a 'self'.³⁰ Rather than identify with a singular protagonist on a narrative journey (as in an Aristotelian model), fans may be more attuned to the musical's transformations of time and identity, which can activate different structures of selfhood and community.

When attuned to the musical's strange temporalities, a spectator can locate, embrace and actively participate in the performance of difference, which is always and already embedded in the genre's dis-integrated form. The genre's participatory pleasures can offer a visceral experience of embodying alternatives to one's own life circumstances.³¹ As fans perform and reperform musical moments and incorporate musical stories, characters, songs and dances into their lives, musical theatre blurs the division between performers and audience members, between creators and consumers. Avid fans of the musical play on the tenuous borders between fiction and reality and locate agency in negotiating between scripted parts and their embodiment, between performativity and performance; they actively shape their worlds through the creation of new cultural fictions.³² Dreams and fantasies – temporal excesses to a linear life progression – are never pure imagination, after all, but forces that aspire to transform the 'real' world.³³

These musical numbers might be considered what Jill Dolan calls utopian performatives: 'small but profound moments in which performance calls the attention of the audience in a way that lifts everyone slightly above the present, into a hopeful feeling of what the world might be like if every moment of our lives were as emotionally voluminous, generous, aesthetically striking, and intersubjectively intense'.[34] Defining utopia less as a place than as a process of spending time, utopian performatives are indices to possibility: wormholes into the 'what if'.[35] Utopian performatives are close kin to Muñoz's 'ecstatic time', which points towards a horizon of strange new possibilities. While the musical does not present a model for a utopian world as in the classic literary models of Thomas More or William Morris, the genre provides a visceral sensation of how utopia might *feel*.[36] The very 'present-tenseness' of performance can bring the utopian possibility of communitas – a 'cohesive if fleeting feeling of belonging' – into the here and now.[37] These musical moments of recognition are always evanescent, performed in a fraught and conflicted present, yet they register the hopes, dreams and – most importantly – the survival of marginalized and semi-marginalized identities.

This book elaborates on moments of negotiating identities in difference in and through the musical's time-warping aesthetics. Rather than skimming the surface of many musicals in each chapter, I offer a 'wormhole' approach to analysis, digging deep into some of our favourite obsessions and the new horizons they illuminate. The text is designed to mirror the musical in form: rather than building a strictly linear, developmental argument, the structure is multifaceted. You will find moments of connection and flashes 'forward' and 'backward' across chapters, sometimes highlighted in the text or in the footnotes; the book's many divergent parts refract one another. I analyse a Frankensteinian crossing of media and performance practices throughout the text, from Broadway shows to shadowcasts, web series to player piano performances; I employ an array of research methods from archival work to musical analysis; and I combine performance studies and musicology with my praxis as a composer, music director, teaching artist, and unabashed fan of the genre and all its possibilities.

Chapter 1, 'A Funny Thing Happened … to the Integrated Musical: Poetics and Politics of Queer Temporality', locates the 'queerness' of musical theatre in the temporally divergent ruptures of the genre's musical numbers. I examine *A Funny Thing Happened on the Way to the Forum*, *A Little Night Music* and *Rent* in the context of pivotal events in the queer history of the United States to consider the ways in which the musical's aesthetics empower the gay male 'show queen' to imagine different ways of being in the world. This chapter lays a theoretical groundwork for the strange temporalities of the form by disrupting the mythology of the 'integrated' musical and exploring how musical numbers can speed, slow, stop and repeat time. Subsequent chapters expand from explicitly 'queer' time to an array of other strange temporalities, considering a broad range of marginalized and semi-marginalized fans who identify with the musical's poetics and politics.

Chapter 2, '"Let's Do the Time Warp Again": Performing Time, Genre and Spectatorship', identifies an affective link across non-realist, time-warping genres of science fiction/fantasy and musical theatre, as well as their dedicated and overlapping fan cultures. Defining genre as a performative structure rather than a set of aesthetic qualities, I explore how fans play on the borders of stage and screen, art and entertainment, art and 'fan art', and fantasy and reality in *The Rocky Horror Picture Show* and *Dr. Horrible's Sing-Along Blog*. Through shadowcasts and supervillanous creations, fans synchronize and syncopate time; they perform in counterpoint to the 'original' musical text to physicalize a strange, temporally divergent world in the here and now.

Chapter 3, 'Ragging Race: Spectral Temporality in the American Musical', explores a haunting in US popular culture: the under-acknowledged contributions of African Americans. Defining history as an always imaginative construction, I bridge from E.L. Doctorow's 1975 novel *Ragtime* and the 1998 musical adaptation – which posit ragtime music as a contradictorily violent and utopic crossing of African American, Jewish and Anglo American cultures – to historical performances of ragtime music at the turn of the twentieth century. Analysing late nineteenth- and early twentieth-century pianola advertisements, I reimagine the parlour piano as a spectral space of encounter between Black artists and white consumers in an attempt to uncover the fraught negotiations of race ragged across these eighty-eight black and white keys.

Chapter 4, '"I Just Projected Myself Out of It": The Excess and Economics of Youth Musical Theatre', considers the impact of marginalizing the arts in contemporary US public education systems in the early twenty-first century. Artistic disciplines are often allotted less class time than required subjects such as mathematics and the sciences, and they frequently receive less funding and public recognition than competitive sports and other mainstream extracurricular activities. Teenagers who identify with and participate in the arts are thus imagined as a community of outsiders, defined by alternative sexualities and other differences from the popular jock and cheerleader mould; these youth are often marginalized along with their artistic disciplines. Through an analysis of the cult movie *Camp* and the hit television show *Glee*, this chapter explores how musical theatre geeks project themselves into empowering musical anthems as a survival tactic to actively improve their challenging present.

Chapter 5, '"Just an Illusion": Identity and Musical Form', investigates how the disintegrated temporality of the musical lends itself to exploring the fragmented fiction of the self in *Fun Home*, *Company* and *A Strange Loop*. The theatrical technique of splitting a single character into multiple actors is used almost exclusively for roles that are female, LGBTQ+ and/or characters of colour; this multiplication of 'selves' can extend beyond the stage, as the authors of the musical or source text often autobiographically overlap with the protagonists. These musicals manipulate time and identity to make visible the illusions of integration in both human identity and in the identity of the musical as a genre.

The conclusion, 'Everything You're Feeling Is Appropriate', considers Taylor Mac's 24-hour-long *A 24-Decade History of Popular Music* as a flash of ecstatic time for queer communities, and as a critical and creative model of engaging with the quagmire of the present to reach strange new horizons of possibility, particularly in the wake of the Covid-19 pandemic.

Throughout these chapters, marginalized subjects find moments of coherence and connection in musical theatre's imaginaries of song and dance. A musical number can offer a luminous, liminal timespace of possibility for alternative constructs of identity and community. If only for a moment, the sensation of understanding self and being understood by others can grip the characters, performers and the audience, who collectively cling to the expansive present – breathless, longing, desirous of difference. At the end of a musical, the curtain may close and the fullness of the utopian moment may fade – but a melody can haunt, reprising the promise of communitas and performatively reaching for difference and transformation beyond the proscenium arch.

1

A Funny Thing Happened ... to the Integrated Musical: Poetics and Politics of Queer Temporality

EVAN: *Peter, you're reading a paper with a front page announcing the deadliest month in nine years for the soldiers in Afghanistan, and you're upset about theater? Don't you think that's a little ... narrow?*

PETER: *It's all of a piece, darling. See, that's what the computer-savvy greasers and soshes of your generation don't seem to understand. You flock to the interwebs for your fingerling snippets of news, and you call that 'being informed'. But, you whiz right past all the other awful shit that exists in the day's news. Now, me? I see all the awful. I hold it in my goddamn lap. Little awful smudges of it come off on my fingers. This paper is not a news bite, it is a news sandwich, an awful news sandwich made on awful bread with awful meat, awful lettuce, and sale-at-Penney's dijonaise. No page of this awful paper could have been possible without the inclusion of every other awful page, and it is nothing but farce to believe otherwise. So you see, dear, it isn't that I'm narrow, it's that I am concerned about everything via a very specific entry point.*

Philip Dawkins, *The Homosexuals*[1]

In *The Homosexuals*, 48-year-old regional theatre director Peter represents a familiar stereotype: the fabulously gay show queen. Playwright Philip Dawkins describes him as 'overtly and unapologetically flamboyant. If you cut him, he would bleed glitter.'[2] Peter thrives on

Broadway gossip and obsesses over the Tony Awards; his everyday rhetoric is rife with theatrical references, playfully poetic imagery and double entendre. Peter's boyfriend, an art history professor, loves how Peter's showy attire is a controversial work of performance art; Peter immediately unsettles fashion standards upon entering a room and boldly signifies his difference from the norm. For such a show queen, style is substance.

Like Peter, I am interested in reading style as substance, engaging the poetics of musical theatre as a 'very specific entry point' into processes of identification. The musical's very *musicality* paradoxically constitutes its mainstream popular appeal while also opening the genre to alternative appropriations; the song stuck in one's head after the curtain closes playfully pops out of the narrative, making it ripe for recontextualization.[3] Queerness and difference can always be located in this discontinuity between book and musical numbers, or what D.A. Miller calls the 'ecstatic release from all those well-made plots'.[4] The persistent binary between musicals and 'straight' plays further confers queerness on a genre that 'unnaturally' bursts into song and dance, rupturing the aesthetics of realism and its representations of normative identities. A musical's narrative can closet an alternate ideology that is always and already implicit in the rapturous song and dance of this art form; musical numbers can create an imaginary of identities in difference and new forms of affiliation.

It is notable that Peter's fashion sensibilities, his playfully self-aware rhetoric and his passion for musicals all sync with his idiosyncratic approach to time. 'The future is ambiguous. Like Capri pants', he explains. 'I'd much rather concentrate on the here and now, on all of the many this-very-moments that make up a life.'[5] Just as he signifies his difference from the norm with bold clothing, then, Peter bends time to a 'queer temporality' of his own creative self-fashioning. Queer temporality describes an array of alternative life narratives and relationships to time, embracing the here, the present and the now rather than a heteronormative, developmental progression of birth, marriage, reproduction and death. Jack Halberstam suggests that queer time 'flashes into view in the heart of a crisis', exploiting the potential of all that is transient, fleeting and contingent.⁶ Within the genre of musical theatre, the musical number's showstopping qualities frequently queer time; a song lyrically, musically and choreographically expands upon an evanescent moment, temporarily displacing the linear narrative drive. Animated by song and dance, bodies in musical performance can accelerate and decelerate time, foreground repetition and circularity, dip into memory and project into the future, and physicalize dreams in a narratively open present. The historical narrative of the formally 'integrated' musical insists that all elements, including musical numbers, linearly progress the plot, but re-evaluating the genre through a lens of strange temporalities illuminates the potential divergence of musical numbers from the narrative. Rather than read the musical as a homogeneously integrated *Gesamtkunstwerk*, I locate a shifting affective relationship among the book, music, lyrics, dance, design and other elements.⁷ The aesthetically charged and temporally distinct musical numbers emphasize performative self-invention that 'show queens' find ripe for reimagining identity and valorizing alternative lifestyles.

In the context of pivotal events in the LGBTQ+ history of the United States, this chapter explores queer temporalities and identification in *A Funny Thing Happened on the Way to the Forum* (1962) and *Rent* (1996), with a brief musical interlude from *A Little Night Music* (1973). The narratively closeted but stylistically queer musical comedy *Forum* opened on Broadway early in the decade that would culminate in the Stonewall Riots (1969), while *Rent* – featuring several 'out' characters and an avid queer fan base – opened towards the end of the first wave of the HIV/AIDS epidemic (1980s and early 1990s). *A Little Night Music*'s 'The Miller's Son' thus occupies a particularly fabulous and fleeting moment of rapturous promiscuity and excess in the 1970s and early 1980s.

While *The Homosexuals*' show queen Peter exults in musical theatre's time-warping moments of release from the normative narrative, I hesitate to essentialize the musical as an exclusively 'gay' genre.⁸ Many contemporary homosexuals, including characters in Dawkins's play, disidentify with the show queen stereotype; and while the musical has historically been a seminal point of identification for gay men, the genre can be a haven for a multiplicity of identities who feel 'other than'.[9] This chapter focuses on identification by the gay male 'show queen', but later chapters consider the musical as an identificatory site for other marginalized subjects; under the umbrella of strange temporalities, queer time has been most extensively theorized, and thus the temporal analysis herein provides a valuable lens onto the strange temporalities and identifications explored in subsequent sections.

Anxieties of integration: *A Funny Thing Happened on the Way to the Forum* (1962)

With book by Larry Gelbart and Burt Shevelove, music and lyrics by Stephen Sondheim, and original direction by George Abbott, the Tony Award-winning musical comedy *A Funny Thing Happened on the Way to the Forum* has been repeatedly mounted on the Great White Way, as well as in regional and school theatres, since its Broadway premiere in 1962. Sondheim claims that the show is almost foolproof; the play holds up whether performed by a professional company or a high school.[10] He attributes the show's success to the intricate plotting, witty dialogue and brilliant situational comedy of his collaborators. However, Sondheim's vibrant and radically disjunctive production numbers contribute just as much to *Forum*'s enduring success. Sondheim calls farces 'express trains' and musicals 'locals', making regular stops for their (literally) showstopping musical numbers.[11] Instead of progressing the plot or elaborating character, *Forum*'s production numbers bring the narrative to a thrilling halt; song and dance lift out of the linear, text-dominated plot into an exuberant performance of aesthetic difference.[12]

Yet these 'respites from the relentlessness of the comedy' were not always touted for their showstopping qualities.[13] The collection of Larry Gelbart's papers in the UCLA Performing Arts Collections includes a five-page typed document considering the 'Purpose of Songs' in *A Funny Thing Happened on the Way to the Forum*.[14] This detailed analysis of the function of songs in an early draft of the show demonstrates a palpable anxiety about whether the songs progress the book in the tradition of a Rodgers and Hammerstein musical drama, popularized in the 1940s and 1950s. 'Why does he sing this song?' the dramaturg asks. 'The resort to song has to be for a reason.' 'What is the purpose of this song? I can't see how this title and this spot for a song advances the story.' 'Could it be that this is incidental entertainment just interrupting here?' This anxiety about song and dance's 'integration' into *Forum*'s narrative is perhaps surprising since – following the show's Broadway success – critics and scholars, as well as the creative team, openly acknowledge that *Forum*'s songs do not progress the plot at all. This later admission of the production numbers' disjunction draws attention to complications in the historical narrative of the integrated musical and anxieties over how the hybrid genre of musical theatre always exceeds a straightforward story.

The integrated musical

Most histories identify Rodgers and Hammerstein's *Oklahoma!* (1943) as inaugurating the Golden Age of the sophisticated, integrated musical drama, in which 'all elements of a show – plot, character, song, dance, orchestration, and setting – should blend together into a unity, a seamless whole'.[15] Rodgers and Hammerstein marketed *Oklahoma!* as elevating the musical comedy to a musical play, commercial fodder to a work of art: 'Certainly the universality of the play's appeal cannot be doubted, but what makes it noteworthy to my mind is the fact that its appeal comes from its "art" qualities and its unwillingness to compromise with commerce', Rodgers explains. 'The result is a thoroughly integrated evening in the theater. The scenery looks the way the music sounds and the clothes look as though they belonged to the characters rather than the management.'[16] Adapting Wagner's concept of the *Gesamtkunstwerk* for the American musical stage, Rodgers and Hammerstein aimed for all theatrical elements to dovetail with character and seamlessly progress the story.

Integration theory stems from a desire to elevate the musical from its 'lower' roots in which book and numbers are separable (minstrelsy, extravaganza, pantomime, burlesque and vaudeville) to the supposed cohesion of art works within a higher cultural stratum; the musical also notably derives from Black performance practices, which can only achieve 'art' status through their integration by a white creative.[17] In the normative reading of an integrated musical, then, all elements are subordinated to a singular (white, masculine, heteronormative) 'Poetic Aim'. As evidenced in Rodgers's quotation above, this Poetic Aim stands in for the dubious claim to the 'universal'. The books of many Golden Age musicals promote a conventional, middle-class ideology along with a heteronormative marriage, explicitly or implicitly constructed in tandem with the United States' historical narrative of citizenship. *Oklahoma!*, for instance, ties two marriage plots – Curly and Laurey, Will Parker and Ado Annie – to the cooperation of the once-rival farmers and cowhands, as well as to Oklahoma's new statehood. The Western (re)productive body is united with the productive land, poised to become part of this great, forward-moving nation.

A third marriage is also of note: the Persian (coded Jewish) merchant Ali Hakim weds the silly Gertie Cummings; this marriage – and the musical's form – can be read as a performance of Jewish integration into the national community.[18] The integrated musical, or 'community musical', thus structurally unites opposites and imagines a tolerant American world in which heterosexual couples unite different groups.[19] For Bruce Kirle, the genre's happy or at least uplifting endings suggest that there are no class barriers in American society and 'that all ethnicities, races, and genders can triumph and transcend perceived notions of identity through will and desire'.[20] Such an evolutionary history elides the very real ruptures, limits and barriers to acceptance and implies the 'boundless' and 'irresistible' development of mankind itself: improvements in individuals' abilities and knowledge, as well as mankind's collective perfectibility over generations.[21]

Throughout the dramaturg's notes on *A Funny Thing Happened on the Way to the Forum*, several comments highlight a nervous need to advance the plot in the tradition of the 1940s and 1950s 'integrated' musical. That the dramaturg should be concerned with fitting this musical farce into an 'integrated' format is, in retrospect, rather farcical itself. In this intricately plotted musical inspired by the works of Roman playwright Plautus, a slave named Pseudolus strives for freedom by striking a deal with his young master Hero; Pseudolus will help Hero woo the beautiful courtesan next door, Philia, in exchange for his release from slavery. The comedy thrives on improbable situations, mistaken identities, witty wordplay, madcap pacing and other carnivalesque qualities of hyperbole and exaggeration. Farce provided Sondheim with the ideal atmosphere for stylistic 'cleverness, for list songs, for word-juggling: for playfulness' rather than straightforwardly presenting the plot.[22] But for the dramaturg, the song's primary function should be cleanly advancing the narrative; the most threatening criticism of a song – the criterion that puts a song on the chopping block – is its inability to progress the book. Handwritten comments in the margins of the document suggest that the creative team seriously contemplated this dramaturgical analysis as they made changes prior to the Broadway opening.

The dramaturg praises some songs for progressing the plot: Philia's 'When I Kiss Him, I'll Be Kissing You', for instance, 'advances the story nobly'. It is interesting to note, then, that this song was later renamed 'That'll Show Him' and moved to Act II; the ability to transpose the number to another narrative location casts doubt on whether the song was ever as closely tied to the plot as the dramaturg believed. Several songs critiqued in this document were cut before the Broadway opening, at least in part because they failed to forward the plot. The dramaturg questions the purpose of 'I Do Like You', an Act I number for Pseudolus and master slave Hysterium. 'I can't see how this title and this post for a song advances the story. Is it stuck in here just to give Hysterium a solo? If so, it stops the story', he concludes. A creative team member has emphatically underlined 'stops the story' in pencil. 'At the

Market Place', a song for Pseudolus, is similarly deemed 'incidental entertainment' that interrupts the plot's progression.

Yet several songs that openly delight in *stopping time* – such as 'Everybody Ought to Have a Maid' – remain. When Hero's father Senex unexpectedly returns from a trip, Pseudolus must invent an excuse for Philia's presence in his house; he quickly lies that Philia is his new maid. Delighted with this attractive new servant, Senex bursts into a bouncy song about maids, 'something no household should be without'.[23] The dramaturg suggests a particular order of characters that could make this raucous, repetitive song progress the story. 'If this song advances the plot, it can be only because it originates with Pseudolus, the plot advancer, or protagonist', he recommends. 'It seems to me that [Pseudolus] should be feeding each thought to Senex, until Senex has enough of it to carry it away with his own enthusiasm.' Handwritten to the side, though, is a small x – presumably a rejection mark. Not only was this showstopper kept in the Broadway production, but the creative team also ignored the suggested character order. If this song does not directly progress the plot, then what function does it fulfil?

Senex sings the first verse of 'Everybody Ought to Have a Maid' alone, while Pseudolus encourages his distraction by pantomiming a maid; following musical theatre conventions, Senex musically, lyrically and choreographically elaborates upon an imagined or hypothetical situation of a maid puttering all around his house. Having such a 'loyal and unswerving girl' becomes a collective daydream as Pseudolus and Hysterium join Senex in the first reprise. Lycus then enters to join the repetitive, rhyming crew for a second encore. Lycus has absolutely no narrative purpose in joining the song, but having heard the gleeful chorus from his house, he spontaneously enters the stage to join the fun:

LYCUS: A maid?
HYSTERIUM: A maid.
PSEUDOLUS: A maid.
SENEX: A maid![24]

This simple and repetitive exchange, set over a characteristic 'wrong note' vamp, launches the ensemble into an animated final encore, which is again structured by accumulative variation (in popular barbershop quartet style) rather than progress-driven narrative.

'Everybody Ought to Have a Maid' brings the house down with simple yet effective encores.[25] This tableau brings multiple perspectives to bear on the moment, mounting opinions – and humour – with every verse; by the end, even the audience could join the familiar refrain. Although the song contains its own progression in its additive technique, the production number flouts the rule of integration and the necessity of steadily progressing the plot through song, while delighting in the homosocial bonding of these motley characters. For the 1966 film adaptation directed by Richard Lester, the choreography of the camera manipulates the laws of time and space in this musical number, cutting from one location to another with increasing absurdity. Senex and Pseudolus wind up in bed together in the first verse; Hysterium flies away on the maid's broomstick in the second; and when Lycus joins, overhead shots organize the men in a parody of Busby Berkeley choreography.[26] Lycus's attempts to re-establish the narrative in the final chorus – 'Tell me, the virgin. I want to know how she – ' – are continually trumped by the exuberance of song and dance.[27] This showstopping and endlessly repeatable number carries the musical far away from the linear narrative drive.

At this point in the writing process, the creative team was attempting to condense the libretto. 'The script seems much too long. There is plenty of room for tightening it up', the dramaturg writes, urging the team to cut a good forty pages from the book (see Table 1).

Table 1 Length of the Show

First Act	78 pages	Cut 25 pages	Down to 53 pages
Second Act	52 pages	Cut 15 pages	Down to 37 pages
Script now	130 pages	Cut 40 pages	Down to 90 pages

Source: 'Purpose of Songs'. Larry Gelbart Papers (Collection PASC 22). Library Special Collections, Charles E. Young Research Library, UCLA.

Yet even as they try to tighten the plot, the dramaturg recommends expanding the musical with repetition – such as a musical medley ballet chase in Act II and several reprises of Pseudolus's motivating song 'Free'. It is significant that, even as this dramaturg advocates for songs that forward the story, he simultaneously highlights the importance of circularity to the musical's structure – and shows how this repetition can progress the story in its own way. Most prominent is the music suggested for a madcap chase in Act II, a common component of farce:

There should be some reprising of the earlier songs, no matter how briefly.

1. Hero should sing a few bars of 'Love, I Hear' to express the lone drive that is keeping him on this chase.
2. Pseudolus should belt out a few couplets of 'Free' to recharge his batteries during this pursuit of freedom.
3. Pseudolus, in desperation, should echo a snatch of 'In the Tiber There Sits a Boat' in his attempt to bring Philia into line with his plan. All he needs is a phrase, and he can take off on the run again, and we will be reminded of what all the running is about.
4. And, of course, Philia could stand up for her scruples with just singing the phrase: 'When I Kiss Him, I'll Be Kissing You.'
5. Whereupon, Miles, with drawn sword, should come through, wailing out a tabloid reprise of 'My Bride, My Bride.'
6. And Domina's musical theme during the pursuit is 'I Want Him.'

This musical medley, reprising all of the songs, could substitute for a lot of the dialogue and could bring up the action to the musical solution when Pseudolus overhears Philia driving poor Hero out of his wits with her song: 'When I Kiss Him, I'll Be Kissing You.' ... where Pseudolus could get the inspiration to push Hero up on the rooftop and make him impersonate a god.[28]

Repetition in this musical medley reminds the characters – and us, the audience – of 'what all the running is about': Hero's undying love for Philia, Pseudolus's desire for freedom, Philia's scruples in marrying the man to whom she is promised. This sequence certainly forwards the plot. Yet simultaneously, this medley *accelerates time* to a farcical frenzy; the chase scene creates a highly animated tableau that draws attention to the construction of time in its wild contrast to the book's normative narrative pacing.

Questioning formal integration

A wide array of temporal manipulations effected by music and dance exist between the extremes of showstopping standstills like 'Everybody Ought to Have a Maid' and the farcical acceleration of *Forum*'s chase scene. The musical articulates a more complex structure than one of well-integrated linear progress, the paradigm upon which musicals were judged throughout the 1940s, 1950s and beyond. An early article questioning integration theory's validity is Margaret M. Knapp's 'Integration of Elements as a Viable Standard for Judging Musical Theater' (1978), in which she points out the disjunction between book and numbers in not only pre-1943 musical comedies but also in an array of then-new 1970s musicals; Stephen Sondheim and George Furth's 1970 concept musical *Company*, for instance, employs musical numbers as commentary on the book's action. 'The variety of forms which recent musical comedies have employed makes the concept of integration, with its underlying assumption that all musicals should be created according to the same rules, an unreliable standard of judgment', Knapp concludes.[29] Like many other critics, Knapp fails to take into account Sondheim's earlier work in *A Funny Thing Happened on the Way to the Forum*, which had already begun to skew the straight Rodgers and Hammerstein narrative by stylistically evoking the musical comedies of the 1920s and 1930s.

Even as she advocates for an expanded understanding of the relationship between book and numbers, Knapp maintains integration theory as a viable rubric for understanding Rodgers and Hammerstein-era musical plays, which place musical numbers in service of the book's progression. More recent scholarship challenges this paradigm of integration in *all* musicals, including those from the Rodgers and

Hammerstein era that seem to wed book, music, lyrics, dance and other dramatic elements together so seamlessly. Temporality is one of the grounds on which the musical's seamless integration can be most questioned.

Scott McMillin addresses the temporalities of the musical most extensively in *The Musical as Drama*, one of the first aesthetic considerations of the genre. Fighting staunchly against integration theory, McMillin posits the musical as an art form reliant on the 'crackle of difference' between two orders of time: the progressive time of the book and the repetitive time of the song and dance numbers.[30] He argues that these disparate elements are held in a relationship of 'coherence' rather than seamless integration.[31] The integrated musical aims to create seamless flows between scenes and songs, a cause-and-effect structure of historical or dramatic inevitability; the relationships between elements cannot be actively reconfigured as in vaudevillian comedies or revues, but must occur in the designated narrative order. An integrated musical appears to progress the book by easing the transitions between storytelling modes – for instance, by employing underscoring or rhyming dialogue to lead into a song. Contemporary musicals sometimes even eschew applause following production numbers; songs trail off into an instrumental underscoring that elides a break between shifting temporalities and, again, gives the impression of seamlessly progressing the plot through the production number. But even when a musical number forwards the plot, the number's primary function is to elaborate 'in the spirit of repetition and the pleasure of difference'.[32]

If a work of art can bring forth another world, then a second mode of storytelling within that artwork – namely, song and dance within a musical – may enact a second layer of distanciation with complex and contradictory effects: distancing the spectator from the forward motion of the plot while entrancing the spectator in the pleasurable, temporally alternative universe of a musical number.[33] Could this layering open the potential for a simultaneous distanced and immersed response, a critically affective engagement with the artwork? Music and dance can in fact negate directional time and space, opening up a 'presentic', unoriented space that is liberated from a straight, directional progression.[34] Unmoored from the goal-oriented trajectory of the narrative, can the strange temporality of the musical number enact imaginaries of alternative subjectivities and modes of relation? And what might make this temporality particularly 'queer'?

Queer temporalities

Like 'Everybody Ought to Have a Maid', 'Lovely' provides another exuberant example of a song that remains in *A Funny Thing Happened on the Way to the Forum* although it fails to advance the narrative. As the dramaturg notes, this song 'does not really advance the story and is not strictly necessary' – yet it is deemed 'fun', which seems enough to secure its place in the musical. 'Lovely' was originally planned for Act II, but it was moved to Act I in the original Broadway version to provide a musical moment just after Hero and Philia first meet. Rather than progress the plot, 'Lovely' deepens character and heightens the youthful romance in effusive lyrical variations on Philia's innocence and physical beauty.[35]

> I'm lovely,
> All I am is lovely,
> Lovely is the one thing I can do.
> Winsome,
> What I am is winsome,
> Radiant as in some
> Dream come true.[36]

'Lovely' cleverly 'deepens' Philia's character by revealing her shallowness. Rather than a deep interiority, Philia is all style, all surface – and Hero is enraptured.

A showstopping tableau similarly 'does' lovely by crafting a stylistically stunning elaboration of a fleeting instant; music can create a sense of 'suspended animation' that amplifies select moments.[37] A musical theatre showstopper draws on a tradition of tableau in nineteenth-century grand opera, which 'freezes' the plot to musically elaborate on emotional heights; such a tableau forms a layered, acoustic image that is affectively intelligible even without the text.[38] While such smothering, multivoiced excesses are often theorized as dangerously disillusioning,[39] Wayne Koestenbaum provides a compelling counterargument for queer identification with the stylistic excesses of opera and musical theatre. 'Is opera queendom or immersion in an original-cast album a dreamland from which the body never returns, a narcotic space separate from companionship and speech, or do self-exposure and self-knowledge take root inside that moment of solitary, naked listening?' he wonders.[40]

These stylistic pleasures open to a particularly queer temporality when repetition unmoors 'Lovely' from its original heterosexual context; an Act II reprise features Pseudolus and Hysterium – dressed in Philia's 'virginal gown and wig'.[41] Musical reprises often delineate a narrative progression, such as Curly and Laurey's 'People Will Say We're in Love' becoming 'Let People Say We're in Love' when the couple is united in *Oklahoma!* But repetition also enables pleasurable sites of recontextualization – both in and out of the theatre. The drag reperformance of 'Lovely' in Act II of *Forum* warps the song to suit the performers at hand; a simple change in key, context and costume queers the song's 'original' function of solidifying a heteronormative pair.[42] Even the most integrated musical can be queered when reprised by a fan in a piano bar such as Marie's Crisis, at Musical Mondays in West Hollywood, or in the intimate confines of a suburban bedroom.[43] Stephen Sondheim suggests that 'Lovely' brings the house down not only because of its queered recontextualization but also because of its unexpected affect: 'In the midst of a farce there occurred a sudden and weird emotional moment: Hysterium, initially reluctant at having to get into drag, begins halfway through the song, and clearly for the first time in his life, to feel attractive. As with the best of Chaplin, this *humanity peeking through the silliness* made for radiant comedy.'[44]

'Lovely' thus tugs in two directions simultaneously: towards outrageously playful theatricality and deep emotional interiority. Raymond Knapp writes that this camp dimension is precisely what opens the musical to affective reappropriation by fans:

> Musicals have proven to have an extraordinary capacity to overlap significantly with the lives and souls of their various constituencies, who learn to express themselves, to act, to conceive of themselves and the world around them, and often even to *be* themselves more fully and affirmatively by following their rhythms, living out versions of their plots, and singing their songs.[45]

Punctuating a progress-driven narrative, musical numbers offer a visceral experience of rhythmic alternatives to the present, in the present – and the particular queerness of the musical lies in these numbers. For the fleeting moment of song and dance, a politicized imaginary of identities in difference and new forms of affiliation can expand beyond a musical's narrative expectations to musically and choreographically embody alternate structures of feeling in the here and now.

In the meanwhile: 'The Miller's Son' (1973)

In a queer genealogy of the Broadway musical, composer/lyricist Stephen Sondheim offers a compelling link between a musical with openly gay characters (such as Jonathan Larson's *Rent*) and its narratively closeted predecessors.[46] Larson is the protégé of Sondheim, and Sondheim is the protégé of Oscar Hammerstein II, who pioneered the 'integrated' musical of the 1940s and 1950s with composer Richard Rodgers. Yet Sondheim cites Rodgers and Hammerstein's first flop *Allegro* (1947) as a greater aesthetic influence than their canonized classics such as *Oklahoma!* In addition to its fluid cinematic staging, *Allegro*'s innovative attempts 'to break down the sheer plot-telling chronology, to make an epic style out of a series of scenes' indelibly impressed the seventeen-year-old Sondheim, who served as a gofer for the production.⁴⁷ This musical's episodic structure and Greek chorus temporally manipulate the show's linear narrative, dis-integrating the plot and commenting on the musical's action. Sondheim even jokes that his career has been spent trying to 'fix' *Allegro* through storytelling with different concepts of time.⁴⁸ Sondheim employs Brechtian choruses in *A Little Night Music* and *Sweeney Todd*; collapses of time in *Sunday in the Park with George* and *Assassins*; ghosting in *Follies*; and an episodic framework unfolding entirely in the mind of the main character in the concept musical *Company*.⁴⁹

Ravishing triple metre rhythms and scandalous waltzes drive the narrative of Hugh Wheeler and Stephen Sondheim's *A Little Night Music* (1973), a sophisticated musical romance of uncoupling and recoupling – or, more simply, a sex comedy.⁵⁰ But the powerhouse 11 o'clock number, which is often a turning point for the protagonist, is assigned to a surprisingly minor character: the wildly promiscuous maid Petra, who tumbles onstage with manservant Frid towards the end of Act II. 'The Miller's Son' embodies the tension between a plodding, normative life trajectory and the ecstatic pleasures of living 'in the meanwhile'. Although her life will end in marriage and children, Petra presently celebrates every rapturous rustle in the hay. By embracing every 'meanwhile', Petra lives in a queer temporality – which, for Sondheim, is of central significance to the show. The song 'is about how you waste time through flirtation', he explains. 'The Bergman film ends with Petra and Frid fucking in the grass!'⁵¹ With *A Little Night Music* premiering in 1973, Petra can be read as a symbol of gay men's rights to sexual pleasure with multiple partners in the short-lived post-Stonewall and pre-AIDS period of the 1970s and 1980s.⁵²

Many 11 o'clock numbers revel in excess to the narrative, but 'The Miller's Son' goes far beyond the stylistic bounds of propriety.⁵³ The song constructs a freewheeling multiplicity of potential life rhythms, and the promiscuous maid sees no reason to be stuck with just one. The song's continually shifting metres and tempos contribute to its temporal excess in relation to the linear narrative:

Slow 3/4	I shall marry the miller's son,
	Pin my hat on a nice piece of property.
	Friday nights, for a bit of fun,
	We'll go dancing. Meanwhile …
Quick 2/4	It's a wink and a wiggle and a giggle in the grass
	And I'll trip the light fandango,
	A pinch and a diddle in the middle of what passes by.[54]
Quick 3/8	It's a very short road
	From the pinch and the punch
	To the paunch and the pouch
	And the pension.
	It's a very short road
	To the ten thousandth lunch
	And the belch and the grouch
	And the sigh.
	In the meanwhile,
	There are mouths to be kissed
	Before mouths to be fed,
	And a lot in between
	In the meanwhile.
	And a girl ought to celebrate what passes by.[55]

Petra oscillates between deadening dreams of marriage and thrilling, licentious indulgence in the present moment throughout the song. Although she will eventually resign herself to the measured 'Slow 3/4' of wedlock, she presently embraces the rapturous joys of the 'Quick 2/4' and 'Quick 3/8'. The 'Quick 2/4' doubles the rhythms of the laboured first verse; this eruption into an energetic patter song then gives way to a sweeping, swirling chorus that luxuriously lingers 'in the meanwhile'.

In *Losing the Plot in Opera*, Brian Castles-Onion calls this 11 o'clock number 'one of opera's strangest star spots'.[56] David Craig also considers 'The Miller's Son' to be a problem song of unwarranted length for such a minor character. 'One can do little more than sing the devil out of it (and the role is always cast to make that a certainty) while paying lip-service to post-coital positioning', he elaborates.[57] The disproportionate length of this rollicking musical number and its loose relation to the plot is directly tied to Petra's performative and sexual excess. Promiscuity is not inherently negative, but its definition as a 'disorderly mixture – whether sexual or otherwise' is often interpreted adversely.[58] In fact, many critics attempt to rein in this excess by 'integrating' Petra's strange star turn into *A Little Night Music* and focusing on her inexorable narrative conclusion: 'I shall marry the miller's son'. Stephen Citron, for instance, theorizes the number as a quasi-operatic aria that 'builds up the servant girl's fantasy about her future husband'.[59] Thomas Adler similarly focuses on the narrative destination of marriage, analysing the song for 'more than simply a hedonistic, *carpe diem* attitude'. After all, Petra will ultimately 'submit herself to the rhythms of life and, through the ritual of marriage, assume her proper place in the social and cosmic orders'. The promiscuous servant's recognition of her rightful place in wedlock extends to her superiors in the musical's concluding waltz, which Adler asserts, symbolizes proper coupling and restoration of the natural order: 'Nature's pattern, seen even in the temporarily unsettling condition of perpetual sunlight, becomes, therefore, the real hero of the play'.[60]

Yet the 'temporarily unsettling condition of perpetual sunlight' should not be so quickly dismissed. The sun is visible for a continuous twenty-four hours in Sweden's summer months, and this warping of time facilitates the destabilization and reconfiguration of relationships during Act II's weekend in the country; this fantastically queer 'meanwhile' actually reroutes the narrative drive. Similarly, this four and a half minute 11 o'clock number extends an ecstatic moment just before *A Little Night Music*'s conclusion. Even as a narrative of 'integration' aims to reign in the excess, the musical's pleasurably prolonged siren song calls out to identities in difference and offers ravishing imaginaries of the manifold possibilities of the present: 'a girl has to celebrate what passes by'.[61]

No day but today: *Rent* (1996)

American theatre of the early 1990s addressed a rising epidemic that seemed to hit hardest within the Broadway community itself: AIDS. As a generation of theatrical writers, composers, choreographers and performers succumbed to the disease, dramas such as Tony Kushner's *Angels in America* (1993) and Terrence McNally's *Love! Valor! Compassion!* (1995) played side by side with musicals such as James Lapine and William Finn's *Falsettos* (1992) and Jonathan Larson's long-running hit *Rent* (1996). Although Larson was not gay, this young, struggling artist was part of the impacted East Village community of the late 1980s and early 1990s,[62] and queer temporality extends to those living in the shadow of the HIV/AIDS epidemic: those who 'live outside of reproductive and familial time as well as on the edges of logics of labour and production'.[63] Larson never saw the acclaim and commercial profit that his rock musical ultimately won. Rather, this composer witnessed his friends struggle with HIV/AIDS and died from an aortic aneurysm shortly before the New York Theatre Workshop previews of *Rent*.

Much scholarship criticizes this popular musical for normalizing or banalizing HIV/AIDS as just another aspect of *la vie bohème*. In an article surveying the field of theatre and performance studies, for instance, David Savran offers a scathing critique of *Rent*'s economic, cultural, social and symbolic contexts:

> The gentrification of the East Village; the commodification of queer and queer wanna-be culture; the mainstreaming of hip-hop; the prolonged economic boom that has particularly benefited the Broadway theater-going classes; the transubstantiation of high into low, *La Bohème* into rock opera, as the occasion for slumming by members of these affluent classes; the romance of miscegenated cultural forms; the romance of miscegenation; the tragic mulatta updated as Latino drag queen in the wake of *Paris Is Burning*; [and] the Disneyfication of Times Square, in relation to which the Nederlander Theater, gussied up to look dilapidated, becomes a theme park of abjection.[64]

John Clum echoes these sentiments in *Something for the Boys*,[65] as does Helen Lewis in a dissertation on the commodification of queerness in *Rent*.[66] For Lewis, *Rent*'s identity as a queer, fringe musical dissolves with its Broadway opening; this once-subversive event becomes a piece of cultural capital on the Great White Way, and it further degenerates into a piece of nostalgia, devoid of its radical queerness, in the 2005 film adaptation.[67]

While these critiques are warranted, Lewis's personal reaction to her first Broadway viewing of *Rent* complicates her thesis. 'To many of us coming out in mid-1990s America, who also doubled as musical theater queens, Jonathan Larson's rock opera *Rent* was a declaration of rebellion, a call to a new generation', she writes.[68] Although highly commercialized, *Rent* provided a point of identification for young queer spectators like Lewis, as well as a space for both gay and straight audience members to consider the gravity of the AIDS epidemic. Indeed, popular culture can create meaning that exceeds or contradicts its commodification; regardless of the venue, the strength of ensemble performance in *Rent* is a vital embodiment of community in the face of crisis.[69]

Popular media began heralding the end of AIDS with the proven success of protease inhibitors in 1996, and as AIDS became a manageable rather than a fatal disease, the subject slowly slipped from discourse in the United States.[70] Yet *Rent* was one of the few popular entertainments to repeatedly raise the issue of HIV/AIDS on Broadway, winning four Tony Awards and a Pulitzer Prize for Drama, then continuing its run at the Nederlander for twelve years. Even the Broadway closing in September 2008 feels open-ended, as this rock opera lives on in national tours, local productions (including often controversial high school productions of *Rent: School Edition*[71]), multiple cast albums, a 2005 film adaptation that reunited much of the original Broadway cast and a live recording of the final Broadway performance.

In its various incarnations over the years, *Rent* has garnered a dedicated young fan base of 'Rentheads'. During its original Broadway run, *Rent* became the first show to offer a limited number of $20 tickets on the day of the performance; Rentheads would camp out overnight to secure these seats in the first two rows of the orchestra. This rush and lottery policy, particularly popular with students and young adults, has since extended to most Broadway musicals and plays. The marketing strategy not only develops young audiences who will hopefully continue to go to the theatre later in life, but it also queers the Broadway theatre-going crowd in the present by enabling younger and less affluent audience members to attend at a more affordable price. Michael Riedel observes that seating these raucous, obsessive fans in the front rows 'seems to perplex the people behind them, some of whom paid scalpers $500 for their seats'. Rentheads attend the theatre in a queered form of repetitive cultural consumption; in March 1997, less than a year after *Rent*'s Broadway premiere, Riedel interviewed fans who had seen the show as many as fifty-seven times. More actively engaged than one-time audience members, Rentheads 'notice the slightest variations in performances, nudging each other when, say, Wilson Jermaine Heredia, who plays a transvestite, tries out a new shade of lipstick'. The very act of 'camping' out in front of the Nederlander creates a tight-knit community of enthusiasts who embrace the musical's affective and even therapeutic powers of presentism: the philosophical belief summed up in the repeated lyric, 'No day but today'. 'When I saw "Rent" for the first time, I was going through a difficult period in my life', one self-proclaimed Renthead explains. 'I'd just broken up with someone and I'd lost four friends to AIDS. "Rent" gave me hope.'[72]

By Halberstam's definition, queer temporality 'emerges most spectacularly, at the end of the twentieth century, from within those gay communities whose horizons of possibility have been severely diminished by the AIDS epidemic'.[73] Queer time thus embraces each fleeting and evanescent moment. Paradigmatic of the shifting temporalities accessible in the genre of musical theatre, *Rent* is simultaneously concerned with the swift passage of time and the possibility of time's arrest; the show advocates a powerful, communal 'no day but today' mentality as a response to a crisis. This musical's queering of the linear timeline offers an alternative lifeline of identification that is particularly resonant for socially marginalized subjects and communities. *Rent*'s showstopping anthems extend a fleeting sense of communitas that expands the luminous possibilities of the present and blurs the boundaries among characters, performers and spectators.[74]

Temporality of the HIV/AIDS crisis

Jonathan Larson's friend Victoria Leacock Hoffman calls HIV/AIDS an 'apocalyptic disease'. The diagnoses of several friends had a profound impact on the composer's temporal perception of life in the late 1980s and early 1990s. 'It would accelerate everything, because, I believe, it started an invisible stopwatch. Time could run out', she writes.[75]

Time is accordingly of central importance as *Rent* opens – established before the characters are introduced by name or the setting is elaborated. 'We begin on Christmas Eve, with me, Mark, and my roommate, Roger', Mark narrates. 'We live in an industrial loft on the corner of 11th Street and Avenue B, the top floor of what was once a music publishing factory.'[76] *Rent* structurally plays out the apocalyptic acceleration of time in the bohemian East Village. Act I covers a succinct span of Christmas Eve through Christmas Day, but sets in motion a dynamic series of intertwined storylines. The fiery relationship between performance artist Maureen and her new girlfriend Joanne begins to crack; HIV-positive Roger meets and eventually admits his feelings for fellow diagnosee Mimi; Collins falls for Latino drag queen Angel, both of whom have AIDS; and Mark stands by to document every moment on film – including the pivotal performance 'Over the Moon' and the subsequent protest at the Life Cafe. From this concentrated sequence of events, Act II then covers a sprawling span of time: New Year's Eve through Christmas Eve of the following year. Relationships flounder, but ultimately revive as the community learns to embrace the present moment against this apocalyptically quickened pace of life.

The title *Rent* is often read as a play on two definitions: the noun describing Mark and Roger's looming financial deadline on the first of the month, as well as the verb 'to tear apart with force or violence, an apt metaphor for the turmoil in the community'.[77] We can also read the word 'rent' as a tear in the fabric of linear time: an attempt to intervene in time's progression by embracing the present moment. Individuals and communities impacted by the AIDS epidemic sought to counter the heightened speed of life by celebrating 'the here, the present, the now', seemingly bringing time to a standstill.[78] Although *Rent* is a sung-through musical, temporal manipulations are still palpable throughout the piece. Recitative marks the quickened linear passage of time, while anthems, reprises, combination songs and other repetitive frameworks take stock of time and attempt to capture a luminous and showstopping *communitas*.

'Another Day' establishes this structural contrast between recitative and anthem as the agitated and isolated Roger continually recoils from Mimi's attempts to engage him in the present moment. Roger's dynamic dialogue-like verses tactically seek to drive Mimi away: 'Who do you think you are? / Barging in on me and my guitar / Little girl – Hey / The door is that way / You better go, you know the fire's out anyway.' Occurring in linear time at a quickened progressive pace, Roger defers any potential romance to 'another time – another place'.[79] In contrast, Mimi's anthemic chorus employs heightened rhetoric and is rife with simple lyrical and musical repetition:

There's only us
There's only this
Forget regret
Or life is yours to miss
No other road
No other way
No day but today.[80]

Melodically circling within the small range of a fifth, Mimi echoes the presentist credo that has been prefigured in an earlier Life Support meeting, a support group for those diagnosed with HIV/AIDS. Against Roger's harried quaver rhythms (continued in the accompaniment), her mantra slows time to strong, stilled half notes. After alternating between these competing temporalities, 'Another Day' collapses the two in a combination song conclusion: as Roger persistently pushes Mimi away, Mimi – now vocally backed by the Life Support group – pleads with Roger to embrace the expanded here and now. Roger's anxious deferral to 'Another time, another place / Another rhyme, a warm embrace / Another dance, another way / Another chance, another day' is continually met – and eventually trumped – by the resounding collective assertion: 'No day but today.'[81] This takeaway message for the audience is repeated throughout the show, including as the final refrain of the entire musical.

Embracing the circular 'Seasons of Love'

'Seasons of Love' is a paragon of a showstopping anthem embracing the 'No day but today' mantra; at the top of Act II, this song takes stock of time while bringing it to an expansive pause. The actors meander to the front of the stage, slowly forming a stalwart line of bodies – each standing awash in a spotlight, a visually vibrating standstill. The spotlight often accompanies showstopping moments in the genre of musical theatre; the scenic background fades into darkness and characters uninvolved in the number may freeze in place or exit the stage. Similarly, the surrounding narrative context may fade as the focus shifts to the performer(s) in the prolonged present moment. Coupled with breaking the fourth wall, a showstopping number creates a heightened, Brechtian tension between the performer and the character being portrayed.[82] Anthony Rapp (who originated the role of Mark) even recalls that director Michael Greif encouraged the actors 'to strip yourselves of your characters a bit, and let yourselves be exposed' in this 'presentational' song, which lies outside the bounds of straightforward storytelling.[83] The doubleness in this staging of 'Seasons of Love' consciously extends the song's applicability beyond the theatrical narrative.

Musical structures in 'Seasons of Love' work by circularity and repetition, rather than a progressive linear temporality. A simple piano vamp – the immediately recognizable undercurrent of the song's verse – begins the tune. This two-measure chord progression creates a quasi-inversion around the tonic triad (F major). Chords are notably ambiguous, open and widely spaced in their initial iterations, filled in and full-bodied with vocal and instrumental elaborations only later in the song. The opening two chords (labelled in the score as an open B-flat major suspension with an added second and an A minor seventh) are particularly incomplete, with multiple directional implications. Rather than instantiating a linear, goal-oriented tonal trajectory, these gapped chords play up the openness, uncertainty and possibility of the present moment. The open B-flat major suspension that completes the sequence simultaneously begins the next iteration, making the vamp never-endingly circular, and allowing it to function as a harmonic ostinato figure.

In harmonic analysis, the chorus ('How about love?') can be reduced to a common pop/rock music progression: IV–I–IV–V. However, this progression is rendered *un*common by its lush arrangement. Each iteration of the chorus is a site of sensuous difference in vocal and orchestral elaboration; the chorus works by circularity and sedimented accumulation in the soundscape rather than directed, linear progress. Just as the opening piano vamp harmonically feeds into itself, the chorus harmonically collapses into the verses; the chorus' final lyric, 'Seasons of love', is underpinned by the verse's vamp, making the entire song structure open and circular. In fact, 'Seasons of Love' ends not on the expected consonance of the central chord I, but on a deceptive arrival on vi that maintains the unfinished quality of the anthem.

Significantly, this song's lyrics and repetitive, modular melody also focus on circularity rather than progress: on the repeated rituals that bring meaning to the 525,600 minutes in a year, rather than the linear timeline of life. Echoing the sparse opening chords, the vocal line is riven with gaps. Much of the melody is arpeggiated, and quaver rests break up the verses:

> In | daylights [rest], in sunsets [rest], in | midnights, in cups of coffee,
> | [rest] In inches, [rest] in miles, in | laughter, in strife.
> In | [rest] five hundred twenty-five thousand | six hundred minutes [rest]
> How | [rest] do you measure a | year in the life.[84]

These audible gaps echo the absence of loved ones in a community wracked by AIDS. Even as rests break up the phrasing of the verse, though, rests also provide space for collective breaths – another of the repetitions by which one can measure a life. Chests rise together on the downbeat of the chorus, a full crotchet breath: 'How about **[breath]** love?' A breath is an affirmation of continued life in the community, even as it marks a melodic absence. Singular events in the life of an individual – birth and death – are sites of repetitions in the ongoing, collective life of the ensemble.

An organ joins the accompaniment towards the end of the song, introducing a gospel quality to the final iterations of the chorus. Using musical tropes of religious transcendence, 'Seasons of Love' seeks to transcend life's linear progression through an embrace of the repetitions of life – and to transcend the life of any one individual by pointing to the ongoing life of the community. Two African American soloists, a female followed by a male, improvise on the melody of the second verse while backed by choral harmonies. The company rejoins the soloists in the second chorus and erupts into offbeat clapping, filling some of the previous rests with a powerful, embodied ensemble presence:

> It's | time now [**clap**] to sing out [**clap**],
> Tho' the | story ne[**clap**]ver ends [**clap**].[85]

The audience often joins this celebration of life by clapping in solidarity with the characters/performers, both the dramatic and the real-life communities affected by the HIV/AIDS epidemic. These communities overlapped significantly, as the disease affected a wide range of theatrical talents in the 1980s and 1990s.

Repeating with a difference, accumulating meaning

When 'Seasons of Love' is reprised later in Act II, an empty beam of light marks Angel's former position in the line of actors. Even as the linear narrative trajectory of *Rent* hurls Angel towards her death, she is one of the few characters to live fully in a queer temporality throughout the musical – embracing every here, present and now – and her light lingers beyond her time onstage. The repetition of 'Seasons of Love' with a difference draws the audience back to earlier iterations of the song – and, thus, outside of the strictly linear plotline of events; in the genre of musical theatre, repetition can contain and transform the past. Rather than being emptied out as a mechanical refrain, the chorus can expand into accumulating, and possibly even conflicting, meanings. Through leitmotif, reprise, combination songs and other repetitions, the musical enters the realm of sedimented history, complexly layered rather than strictly linear. In fact, the character of Angel can be read as a Benjaminian 'angel' of history:

> Where we perceive a chain of events, [the angel] sees one single catastrophe which keeps piling wreckage upon wreckage and hurls it in front of his feet. The angel would like to stay, awaken the dead, and make whole what has been smashed. But a storm is blowing from Paradise; it has got caught in his wings with such violence that the angel can no longer close them. The storm irresistibly propels him into the future to which his back is turned, while the pile of debris before him grows skyward. This storm is what we call progress.[86]

Although her body is absented from the stage, Angel's spectral presence lingers to 'awaken the dead' – by awakening Mimi to hear Roger's song – and to 'make whole' this community in crisis by continually urging them to live in the present moment.[87]

After Angel passes away, friends hold a memorial service where they recount stories of her life, culminating in a reprise of 'I'll Cover You' – a song that resonates in the memory of the characters as well as audience members. This song originates as an Act I duet in which Angel and Collins vow to protect one another as they musically and choreographically envision their life together. This musical act of projection, realized in a faithful though brief relationship, now exists only as a memory. Yet Angel is a 'new lease' on life for Collins and his queer community, who learn to embrace the here and now against the apocalyptic speed of the HIV/AIDS crisis. Reminiscent of 'Seasons of Love', the reprise of

'I'll Cover You' opens to sparse piano accompaniment beneath Collins's embellished, soulful remembrance of the song he shared with his lover. As instrumentation builds and Collins's voice gains strength, the company supports Collins with choral backup vocals, again echoing the gospel quality in the second verse of 'Seasons of Love'. Joanne and another soloist soon begin filling in Angel's missing vocals in a soaring, harmonized elaboration of her line, 'So with a thousand sweet kisses, I'll cover you.'[88] Like the empty beam of light, this act of surrogation fails to fully fill the gap left by Angel, but vitally memorializes her and calls the past into the present.[89] The company finally erupts into a full reprise of 'Seasons of Love', overlaid with Collins's continuing reprise of 'I'll Cover You'. Temporally collapsing these once-separate strands of the musical, this combination song again points towards transcendence of a linear timeline; the elevated gospel vocals at the end of this reprise invoke religious transcendence as well as the transcendence of an individual life through the ongoing life of the community.

Throughout *Rent*, repetition and surrogation seek to awaken and enliven collective memory. In fact, the names of the Life Support group change every night to 'honor actual friends of the company who have died of AIDS'.[90] Like 'Seasons of Love' breaking the fourth wall, this act of surrogation merges the cast members' fiction and reality – and even if the names are 'fixed' in a cast recording or film version, fans can read their own friends and family into the never-ending round. The Rentheads interviewed in Michael Riedel's 1997 article identify the anthems 'Seasons of Love' and 'Will I?' as the most emotional moments in the show because of their layered reach from characters to performers to audience members.[91] It is not the recitative or the quickened linear passage of time that lingers in the audience's collective memory, but the repetitive frameworks that disrupt time's relentless forward progression. Cracking open the linear timeline, these dense and sedimented moments of collective memory resound with characters, performers and audience members alike.[92] In these fleeting and fragmentary moments of connection, or what Jill Dolan might call utopian performatives, *Rent* is a vitally present invocation to memory;

extracted into our own repertoire to be reprised and recontextualized, such songs can extend a message of communal hope in the wake of a crisis.⁹³

Richard Dyer has most fully explored the utopianism of musical theatre in *Only Entertainment* (1992). Defined as a culturally and historically specific performance produced for profit, entertainment offers escape, wish fulfilment and a release into 'something better'. 'Alternatives, hopes, wishes – these are the stuff of utopia, the sense that things could be better, that something other than what is can be imagined and maybe realized', he writes.⁹⁴ For Dyer, narrative contradictions are seamlessly resolved in musical numbers: space is alternatively animated as scarcity gives way to abundance, exhaustion to energy, dreariness to intensity, manipulation to transparency and fragmentation to community. These tidy, harmonious and spectacularly capitalist resolutions consistently elide issues of class, race and patriarchy: 'While entertainment is responding to needs that are real, at the same time it is also defining and delimiting what constitute the legitimate needs of people in this society.'⁹⁵

As illustrated earlier, much criticism waged against *Rent* rightfully focuses on the rampant commercialization and commodification in this musical's transfer to the Broadway stage and adaptation to Hollywood film. Still, Dyer points back to the powerful contradictions underwriting musical theatre's production and reception, including the potential oppositional quality of '*almost all aspects of dance and music*'.⁹⁶ Dyer finds particular promise for contesting normative structures in the musical's peculiar mix of two modes – 'the historicity of narrative and the lyricism of numbers' – foreshadowing Scott McMillin's distinction between linear narrative time and repetitive lyric time.⁹⁷ Elaborating on this temporal excess of the genre, Dyer also posits a link to Ernst Bloch's theories of anticipatory illumination. Bloch seeks to locate concrete moments in history that point the way towards an actual transformation of the material world. The luminous aesthetic quality of these moments, even though they are fragmentary, allows them to be used and reused for realizing what has not yet become, but can become.⁹⁸

'Seasons of Love' is certainly one of the most extracted and reperformed musical theatre songs of the 1990s, from high school graduations to concerts benefitting an array of local, national and international causes. Songs such as 'Seasons of Love' have also served to solidify the queer fan culture of Rentheads, who 'came out' during an era in which musical theatre was distinctly uncool.[99] And while the HIV/AIDS epidemic in the United States may have subsided beginning in 1996 for those with access to good health insurance, the disease has not been eradicated; the musical theatre community lost composer Michael Friedman to HIV/AIDS-related complications as recently as 2017. *Rent* can thus serve as a vital invocation to memory and to present action (Figure 1).

Musical numbers do not strictly progress the plot, but engage in a narratively open present. Even in a sung-through musical such as *Rent*,

Figure 1 Marjory Stoneman Douglas High School drama students perform onstage during the 72nd Annual Tony Awards at Radio City Music Hall on 10 June 2018 in New York City. Photograph by Kevin Mazur. Courtesy of Getty Images for Tony Awards Productions.

anthems, reprises and other repetitive frameworks can queer time and capture a fragmentary sense of communitas that valuably blurs the lines among characters, performers and audience members. While the genre of musical theatre may seem steeped in abstract idealism, then, performers can step out of character and spectators can join the anthem, appropriating the formal difference and the utopian openness of the musical number to articulate concrete desires and needs.

2

'Let's Do the Time Warp Again': Performing Time, Genre and Spectatorship

1. *(It's just a) JUMP TO THE LEFT, with hands UP.*
2. *A STEP TO THE RIGHT (Time-Warper ANNETTE FUNICELLO suggests a very WIDE step.)*
3. *(With your hands on your HIPS) YOU BRING YOUR KNEES IN TIGHT.*
4. *(Then) THE PELVIC THRUST (if repeated FIVE times, it nearly drives you insa-a-ane)*
5. *HIPSWIVEL (if not driven insa-a-ane by step four)*
6. *LET'S DO THE TIME WARP AGAIN!*
                   The Rocky Horror Picture Show: The Official Fan Site[1]

In *The Rocky Horror Show*, 'The Time Warp' – an exuberant participatory song and dance – reroutes Brad and Janet's linear trajectory to marriage and twists their perceptions of identity. The 'transsexual Transylvanians'' seductive, strange temporality and lifestyle is predicated on the rapturous joys of repetition and circularity, rather than a numbingly predictable narrative drive from birth to marriage to death. A choreographed jump to the left and a step to the right very nearly ends where it begins, with the dancer then enjoying a rocking pelvic thrust into a rollicking hip swivel: fun and simple moves that are ready to be repeated again and again.

In speculative fiction, a 'time warp' enables rapid and radical time travel; it permits discontinuities and irregularities in a linear narrative by jump cutting across time and space. A time warp is not a narrative destination unto itself, but a liminal timespace of projection into an alternative: a wormhole of open-ended possibilities, much like a musical number. Although often criticized for being escapist, speculative fiction imaginatively explores the possibilities of and alternatives to the present, both utopian and dystopian. Anti-quotidian genres such as science fiction, fantasy and musicals probe the limits of what is objectively present by physicalizing a temporally divergent world in the here and now.[2] These non-realist genres can disintegrate the notion of a homogeneously unified present and make palpable alternatives to a normative life trajectory. This chapter locates an affective link between the time-warping genres of musical theatre and science fiction/fantasy through an analysis of *The Rocky Horror Picture Show* and *Dr. Horrible's Sing-Along Blog*. Dedicated fan engagement with these fabulous 'genre' creations draws attention to the tenuous borders between stage and screen, art and entertainment, art and 'fan art', and fantasy and reality.

Genre studies are not without their detractors, especially as postmodern trends towards blending and blurring modes of discourse can cause genre studies to be perceived as an 'idle' and even 'anachronistic pastime'.[3] Yet genre is a persistent reality that structures bookstores, Netflix queues and university modules today. Genre is an important intersection of poetics and history: a codification of discursive properties that works as a horizon of expectation for readers and as models of writing for authors.[4] The construct of genre does not disinterestedly classify cultural texts, but establishes hierarchies of value. Michael Chabon points out that genre fiction – constructed in opposition to literary fiction, or simply 'fiction' – is 'a thing fundamentally, perhaps inherently debased, infantile, commercialized, unworthy of the serious person's attention'.[5] Graphic novels, horror, mystery, romance, science fiction and fantasy, thrillers and Westerns are physically separated from 'fiction' or 'literature' in bookstores, and rarely does a genre work receive a major artistic award. Often considered to be inferior and formulaic products targeted to a specific and passive consuming audience, genre works inhabit a paradoxical position of mass popularity and critical dismissal. Although genre films increasingly reign at the box office, the Academy Award still typically goes to dramas, social problem films, biopics, literary adaptations and big-budget epics.⁶ Meanwhile, musicals consistently outsell straight plays on the Great White Way, but critical reception can cut these flashy entertainments down to size. When rock musical *Next to Normal* received the Pulitzer Prize for Drama in 2010, for instance, *LA Times* theatre critic and chairman of the Pulitzer board Charles McNulty advocated for more deserving 'dramatists' of the legitimate stage 'who care about theater as an art rather than as an expensive diversion'.⁷

Socially constructed hierarchies of literary fiction and genre fiction, 'straight' plays and musicals, classical and popular music, illustrate that genre is not an atemporal formal structure but a historically contingent and culturally embedded discourse that is intimately intertwined with an imagined distinction between art and entertainment. Pleasure and profit are the primary factors defining this binary. While entertainment produces pleasure for a price, art is imagined as challenging audiences with edifying and refined works created beyond the boundaries of capitalism.⁸ Despite these class-based prejudices, popular forms of entertainment have held millions spellbound and deserve our critical attention.⁹

'Spellbound' may suggest consumers' passive reception of popular culture, but multiple parties interplay in producing any genre's meaning. What's more, a text has no single, stable meaning; rather, its meanings mutate and multiply depending on its audience and interpretive community.¹⁰ Rather than analyse 'the text itself', we should consider the world brought into being by the text. The concept of a self-contained text, as well as broader definitions of genre and artistic form, lose stability if we refocus on the diverse interpretative communities that 'perform' them.¹¹ Although the musical's aesthetic is always determined by its commodity status, the uses and meanings produced by fan cultures can warp a commodity's exchange value to unpredictable identifications.¹²

In considering the time-warping hybridization of musical theatre and sci-fi/fantasy fan cultures in *The Rocky Horror Picture Show* and *Dr. Horrible's Sing-Along Blog*, I am particularly interested in the ways that their exaggerated aesthetics exude a cult and camp sensibility that attracts a (broadly defined) queer audience. In different ways, each film digs through the sci-fi detritus of the past to create new narrative mash-ups of outrageously alien situations; the plots' artificiality is then further heightened by song and dance. Characters are intentional caricatures: drag queens with luscious red lips and supervillians with oversized lab coats and goggles. Behind these comical costumes, actors wink at the camera and welcome the audience into a strange, stylized universe that continually draws attention to its own fabulous, low-tech construction. In such blatant theatricality and intentional gaps between character and actor, both *The Rocky Horror Picture Show* and *Dr. Horrible's Sing-Along Blog* point to sites of negotiation between a scripted part and its embodiment, or between performativity and performance.[13] These films illustrate the possibilities of reiterating cultural norms with a difference; they locate agency in the potential to reconfigure a role from within.[14] Fans of these Frankensteinian texts play on the tenuous borders between fantasy and reality, rapturously embracing the wormholes of imaginative alternatives to a normative identity and life trajectory.

Creatures of the night: *The Rocky Horror Picture Show*

British writer/composer/actor Richard O'Brien's *The Rocky Horror Show* met with both critical and popular acclaim when it premiered at the Royal Court Upstairs in 1973. The nine- by twelve-metre rehearsal room above London's prestigious Royal Court Theatre had been converted into a club for experimental new work only a few years earlier. Although the fringy first season of shows in 1969 was 'a critical disaster', the space soon exploded into an acclaimed 'in-yer-face' venue for theatre artists such as Sam Shepard, Caryl Churchill, Sarah Kane and Danny Boyle. As *Guardian* critic Michael Billington recalls, audience members 'had nowhere to hide from the sex and violence that inevitably loomed large' in this intimate space, and the crowd's visceral involvement in the show contributed to *Rocky Horror*'s early success.[15]

The Rocky Horror Show soon transferred from the Court to the Classic Cinema (a converted movie theatre) and the King's Road Theatre for a combined total of 2,960 performances in London. Beginning in March 1974, Rocky Horror also achieved a successful nine-month run at the Roxy Theater, a concert venue and former strip club on the Sunset Strip in Los Angeles. These alternative venues catered to a queer audience eager for an evening of campy pleasure, poking fun at the mainstream while creating a world of difference.

The Rocky Horror Show opens at the height of heteronormative bliss: a wedding. Wedding guests Brad and Janet are set on the fast track to marriage when Janet catches the bridal bouquet, but this couple's subsequent love duet 'Dammit Janet' strikes a critical and ironic attitude towards their impending union. In the now-iconic film adaptation of the stage show, a man and a woman (later identifiable as Riff-Raff and Magenta) dress as the dull and weathered couple of Grant Wood's *American Gothic*; they punctuate each of Brad's sung professions of love with a flatly spoken 'Janet'. In the second verse, attendants carry a coffin into the church, transforming the event directly from a wedding to a funeral. Brad and Janet's kiss at the end of the song even takes place in a graveyard. The song openly mocks the clichéd, confining and ultimately deadening social institution of marriage, as the vocals and visuals collapse the heteronormative trajectory of 'cradle, wedding, [and] coffin: the socially-ordained milestones of life which, it would seem, we must inexorably reproduce'.[16]

Perhaps Brad and Janet are fortunate that their car breaks down, side-tracking their predictable wedding plans. Once they are swept into the 'transsexual Transylvanians'' 'Time Warp' at the Frankenstein place, the straightforward linear plot is rerouted; *The Rocky Horror Show* spins into an episodic musical adventure, dominated by the powerhouse performance of 'sweet transvestite' Dr Frank-N-Furter (Tim Curry). In a glittering corset and fishnets, the Transylvanians' cool and confident leader brings to life a new creation: a muscular man with blond hair and a tan named Rocky. He bludgeons wayward rocker Eddie (Meatloaf in the film) and serves him for dinner. Most importantly, he strips the baffled Brad and Janet down to their underwear and seduces them into increasingly outrageous fantasies, culminating in an orgy of fluid gender and sexual identities.

It is perhaps no surprise that in March 1975, then, *The Rocky Horror Show* flopped at the symbolic pinnacle of mainstream musical theatre culture: Broadway, where it played only four previews and forty-five performances at the Belasco Theater. Although *Hair* had brought a hippie subculture of sex, drugs and rock 'n' roll to the Great White Way in 1968, *The Rocky Horror Show*'s sexual confusion and sci-fi fusion marked a lifestyle too extreme.[17] Frank's monstrous creatures and cannibalism bothered Broadway critics less than his gender-bending sexual perversity. AP drama critic William Glover writes, 'The key to "The Rocky Horror Show" is that third word. Horror, as in vile.' His review exudes anxieties about the performance of sexuality, especially in such an interactive theatre space. 'When not displaying explicit boy-girl and boy-boy conjunctions on an enlarging shadow screen, Curry and his gang caress and grope individually or at each other while screaming purported songs downstage, along a lighted runway or up on balcony structures', he complains.[18]

In 'Taking a Camping Trip on Broadway', *Wall Street Journal* writer Edwin Wilson conveys even more explicit concerns about camp aesthetics that advocate for – and perhaps even indoctrinate audience members into – alternative (read: homosexual) lifestyles:

> When Camp reaches this point it is no longer emphasizing style and aesthetics, as Ms. [Susan] Sontag insisted it was in the beginning, it has become an instrument for exploitation, a means to deliver a message. [...] In its original conception Camp was sophisticated but it also seemed innocent and fun. As we encounter it in 'The Rocky Horror Show', however, there is little about it that is innocent. It has become didactic to the core.[19]

The Rocky Horror Show's carnivalesque inversion of compulsory heterosexuality may indeed be didactic, but the Brads and Janets of the world could perhaps benefit from a playful interrogation of their sexual norms. Camp's style is its substance, and queer spectators may actually desire to be absorbed into glam mad scientist Dr Frank-N-Furter's unconventional convention of 'transsexual Transylvanians'. This musical's alternative ideology can be a liberatory fantasia for marginalized identities.

Like the Broadway production, the film adaptation *The Rocky Horror Picture Show* flopped in mainstream movie houses in its first general release on 29 September 1975. *Chicago Tribune* critic Lynn Van Matre gave the film a mediocre 2.5-star rating: 'It's not exactly a great movie, but more often than not it's great fun, provided your heart belongs to drag parodies with overtones of dementia', she writes. Her review is tellingly titled '"Rocky Show" Bumps to a Different Beat', tying the film's alternative sexualities to a demented pulse, out of sync with the mainstream.[20]

The mythology of *Rocky Horror* is thus intimately bound up with the queer art of failure.[21] *Rocky Horror* fan culture constitutes itself as reclaiming (what was once) an abject commodity; the musical's roots are decidedly located in subcultural fields that were immiscible in the 1970s mainstream. Richard O'Brien's Frankensteinian musical is itself an anachronistic reclamation of earlier lowbrow commodities: a patchwork homage to low-budget science fiction, horror and other B-films of the early twentieth century, particularly the 1930s and 1950s. The opening number, 'Science Fiction / Double Feature', pays tribute to genre films, which were often billed as the 'excess' of a double feature picture show. Motion picture studios' focus on big-budget features meant that B-films were both less marketed and critically disdained, if not entirely ignored; these movies were considered formulaic fodder preceding an artistically superior (and more expensively produced) feature film. Yet paradoxically, the studios' predominant focus on features meant B-films could experiment in style and content, pushing moral boundaries with less systematic censorship. Although *The Rocky Horror Picture Show* and many of its constituent B-films initially played in mainstream culture, their ongoing subcultural attachments are intimately intertwined with histories of their initial abjection, as well as their stylistic and ideological excess to the mainstream. Creators, producers and fans had to locate alternative commercial structures in which these strange texts could thrive artistically, financially and affectively.

In the early 1960s, film-makers such as Kenneth Anger, Gregory Markopoulos, Stan Brakhage, Maya Deren and Ron Rice began late-night screenings of their independent films in alternative movie houses. Jonas Mekas's New American Cinema Group offered a pioneering structure for these artists; drawing inspiration from the Free Cinema in England, the Nouvelle Vague in France and the young movements in Poland, Italy and Russia, the New American Cinema Group explored alternative modes of financing, promoting and distributing films.[22] A central part of the group's manifesto was a cooperative distribution centre and partnerships with theatres such as the Charles Theater in New York's East Village, which held the first weekend midnight programme in 1961. 'Bizarre sexual extravaganzas' by Ron Rice, Ken Jacobs, Jack Smith and Andy Warhol soon dotted the late-night underground cinema scene.[23]

This subcultural practice became more firmly established by the 1970s. Alejandro Jodorowsky's *El Topo*, a brutally bloody Spanish-language Western, scared off distributors until Ben Barenholtz introduced it as a midnight film in New York City's Elgin Theater on 18 December 1970. The evocative and incongruous imagery of *El Topo* quickly drew a crowd of fascinated repeat theatregoers; after the first showing, word of mouth packed the cinema each weekend. Particularly following the success of *El Topo*, theatre owners 'saw that [they] could create a world around the concept of midnight', according to Larry Jackson of Boston's Orson Welles Theatre, 'that at 12 o'clock, a different world of movie-going took place'.[24] Midnight screenings became an alternative business model for experimental and independent genre films that were immiscible in the mainstream, and theatres in urban centres such as New York and Los Angeles, as well as college towns, began consciously seeking the next great midnight hits. Midnight movies both embraced and commercially exploited the liberatingly liminal age between childhood dependency and adult subsumption into normative life patterns to create a temporally dissident world around midnight theatregoing.

'It's the audience that creates the cult, it's not the film', says Barenholtz.[25] Yet following *El Topo*, mainstream failure and a rerelease at an alternative screening time undeniably primed and positioned certain films to become cult classics. George A. Romero's black-and-white indie horror *Night of the Living Dead* developed a midnight following after a critically disastrous mainstream release in 1968, and gay spectators flocked to John Waters's flamboyant *Pink Flamingos* in 1972. Queer audiences embraced the shocking cinematic experience of films that deferred a singular meaning; these films' unconventional narratives elevated experimental style over coherent content. Midnight movies accrued an aura of opposition to mainstream values, overlapping with countercultural protests against the Vietnam War, racism, and gender and sexual norms in the 1970s.

This midnight mythology laid the groundwork for *The Rocky Horror Picture Show*'s first midnight showing at New York City's Waverly Theater on 2 April 1976. In fact, both *El Topo* and *Night of the Living Dead* had already achieved cult success at this same theatre. *Rocky Horror* soon became a popular midnight happening, pushing on the tenuous boundaries of this fantastical film as a stable and self-contained text when repeat theatregoers began interacting with the movie; this performative phenomenon continues at theatres across the world today. Late on a Friday or Saturday night, life's regimented rhythms loosen their grip, and leisure time drags and suffuses into a pleasurably elongated present. Costumed crowds wrap around urban cinemas, waiting for earlier feature films to conclude. As fans dressed in fishnets and corsets shiver with anticipation, the queer time of a midnight movie slips into queer space. *The Rocky Horror Picture Show* is a local and embodied practice of creative world-making for these time-warping fans; participatory midnight screenings model a subject's performative navigation of cultural norms through complexly layered acts of synchronizing and syncopating time, creating a queer world in and through queer temporalities.

Syncing time

I would like, if I may, to take you on a strange journey: a queer, anachronistic jump to Gertrude Stein's American lecture circuit from 1934 to 1935. In 'Plays', Stein explores theatre 'from the standpoint of sight and sound and its relation to emotion and time, rather than in relation to story and action'.[26] In short, Stein is concerned with whether an audience member can keep time with a play. Her dramaturgical model for synchronization with the drama's emotional time – which she calls landscape – is suffused with circularity and repetition rather than a linear narrative drive. This queer temporality maps onto the stage much as the operatic stop-time examined in Chapter 1; an audience member does not follow a linear plotline, but indulges in the layered elaboration of a moment. After all, Stein believes the purpose of art is 'to live in the actual present, that is the complete actual present, and to completely express that complete actual present'.[27]

Stein's landscape is a spatialized queer temporality; it 'is exciting and it moves but it also stays'.[28] When fans play within and across *The Rocky Horror Picture Show*, the ensuing performative landscape is similarly exciting, moving but also staying, intertwining a present performance with the repetition of a familiar film. Although it is impossible to pinpoint precisely how performative interaction with *The Rocky Picture Show* began, 'The Time Warp', while perhaps not the very beginning of the phenomenon, is a very good place to start. This song and dance explicitly invokes audience participation, and instruction is built into the lyrics for 'virgins' experiencing a midnight *Rocky Horror* for the first time: 'It's just a jump to the left and then a step to the right'. As mentioned previously, a jump to the left and a step to the right makes the choreography circular, essentially ending where it begins. Perhaps more important is the song's advocacy for repetition after these simple steps have been taught: 'Let's do the Time Warp again!' The chorus maintains a 'tight, quasi-hysterical circle of control' in the melody, underpinned by a strangely jolting, non-linear chord progression: almost an all-major-key circle of fifths progression in reverse (see Table 2).[29] This 'again'-ness of the 'Time Warp' is inherent to the number's musical and choreographic structure,

Table 2 Let's Do the Time Warp Again

Lyrics:	Let's	do the	Time	Warp	again!	Let's	do the	Time	Warp	again!
Melody:	F	E	G	F#	F#-E	| F	E	G	F#	F#-E
Chords:	F	C	G	D	A	| F	C	G	D	A

Source: *The Rocky Horror Picture Show*, dir. Jim Sharman (Twentieth Century Fox, 1975), DVD. Table by Sarah Taylor Ellis.

as well as to the audience itself: fans who return week after week to the same theatre's midnight showings. The participatory invocation of 'The Time Warp' enables O'Brien's kaleidoscopic musical landscape to sprawl beyond the movie screen; *Rocky Horror* becomes a localized participatory playground built upon intimate familiarity with and repetition of the film.

In West Los Angeles, performance troupe Sins o' the Flesh has Time Warped at the Nuart Theatre since 'late '87 / early '88 (there was soo much alcohol consumption, no one from the era is quite sure!)'.[30] Each Saturday night, the cast of rotating performers generates a party atmosphere by pumping pop music and dancing as crowds pour into the theatre; they sell *RHPS* T-shirts and buttons created by local artists; and, following an elaborate pre-show ritual of reciting rules and sacrificing the *Rocky Horror* virgins in an orgy of newbies, they sync with the screen in a live shadowcast performance. Although audiences often consist of dozens of virgins, Sins o' the Flesh represents *Rocky Horror*'s raucous and repetitive theatregoing cult(ure); when troupe members are not performing with the shadowcast, these fans attend anyway to participate from the audience and support their friends. Sins o' the Flesh solidifies their fan community by hosting theme nights around other geeky intersections with genre entertainment; they have previously crossed *Rocky Horror* with zombies and superheroes, *Austin Powers* and *Animal House*. They delight in premiering shadowcast productions of other cult classics such as *Clue*, *Romy and Michele's High School Reunion* and *Shock Treatment* – Richard O'Brien's ill-fated sequel to *Rocky Horror*. Sins o' the Flesh emerges at the intersection of these marginalized popular entertainments, with *Rocky Horror* as the group's dominant organizing landscape.

I have previously explored how repetition is an act of performative place-making in *The Sound of Music*; across time, musical reprises constitute a nuclear family, a value system and a transportable sense of place for the displaced von Trapps.[31] However normative this Rodgers and Hammerstein classic may be as a 'self-contained' text, cultural phenomena like the annual *Sing-A-Long Sound of Music* at the Hollywood Bowl constitute (and reconstitute, year after year) a musical fan culture surprisingly in excess of an expected white, heteronormative, middle-class fan base.[32] Syncing with the musical does not mean direct interpellation into its authorially intended ideology; rather, the audience and interpretive community can perform a horizon of meanings in excess of the creators' expectations. While not as campy as cult classics such as *Mommie Dearest* or *Reefer Madness*, *Sound of Music* fans sing along and dress up as everything from girls in white dresses to Academy Awards in head-to-toe gold lamé. Like *Rocky Horror* fans, they delight in the plural possibilities of mimesis and explore the creative possibilities of the landscape. Fans perform in fluid synchronicity with the film, theatrically navigating between self and other in mimetic acts that sometimes soar in an uncanny likeness to their cinematic counterparts and sometimes fail to step in time, disclosing how all identifications are fragmentary and partial.

Rocky Horror cast members invest both time and money in elaborate costumes, wigs, makeup and props to performatively subsume themselves in the filmic landscape of *The Rocky Horror Picture Show*. Though Fox began producing flimsy mainstream Halloween costumes for the film's major characters in 2001, fans pride themselves on obsessive detail; whether rummaging thrift shops for adaptable costume pieces or ordering custom sequined material to make Columbia's bustier, fans emphasize the time and labour spent in the 'DIY' (do it yourself) act of reconstruction. Costume construction is even a side business for particularly skilled fans. Former Sins o' the Flesh cast leader Liz Stockton rose to 'Rocky Horror Legend' status not only for her multifaceted performances but also for her wig designs, which feature in *Rocky Horror* stage productions and shadowcasts around the world.[33] Nina Minnelli, who frequently plays Frank for Sins o' the Flesh, can whip up a stunning replica costume not only for one's *Rocky Horror* shadowcast needs but also for crossovers with

Clue and *Cry-Baby*.³⁴ Functionality is always as essential as accuracy for *Rocky Horror* costumes; a hidden side zipper on every corset can help ensure that quick changes, particularly the pesky transition into the floor show, run as smoothly as possible.³⁵

For LA's Sins o' the Flesh as with most shadowcasts, actors are not typecast by gender, sexuality, race or other physical attributes, and an actor may specialize in several roles. Performing since 1991, Liz Stockton has played everyone from a Transylvanian to Janet to Frank-N-Furter; Stockton even played Frank in an all-star shadowcast filmed at the Wiltern for the thirty-fifth anniversary Blu-ray. Yet the frequent casting of 'women' in 'men's roles' both conceals and reveals the gender binary at work in *Rocky Horror* fan culture; *Rocky Horror*'s playful affront to traditional masculinity attracts few men – and particularly few straight men – to the Sins o' the Flesh cast. While Tim Curry's husky-voiced, cross-dressing Frank-N-Furter seduces a beautiful blond man onscreen, a corseted female Frank-N-Furter (such as Nina Minnelli, fabulously pictured in Figure 2) may seduce a male Rocky Horror

Figure 2 'Wild and Untamed Thing'. Photograph by Abby Mahler. Courtesy of Abby Mahler and Sins o' the Flesh.

onstage; the homoerotic relationship of the film is erased in this specific shadowcast embodiment, although a woman is placed in a pleasurable position of power. When a female Janet is paired with a female Brad, the filmic parody of this couple as a 1950s ideal of heteronormative bliss is instantly upended. Shadowcast performers sync with the screen in a kaleidoscopic array of gender and sexual patterns, shifting from week to week and cast to cast; all gender is revealed as performance. Yet the lack of 'men' – and the even more notable absence of racial diversity – point to potential limits of *Rocky Horror*'s carnivalesque fan landscape.

As the film is mapped into the 300-seat Nuart Theater, the shadowcast performance also draws attention to the disjunctive time and space of the filmic medium. Although editing can create the illusion of a seamless and integrated flow, the live performance of a film discloses its radically disintegrated temporality; film editing enables quick cuts across time and space, not to mention camera angles and special effects that cannot be replicated onstage. Having originated as a live performance, *Rocky Horror* creates fewer staging complications then would, for instance, a shadowcast of a Busby Berkeley spectacular or a fast-cutting Baz Luhrmann movie musical such as *Moulin Rouge*. Still, Sins o' the Flesh must creatively navigate character entrances and exits, often using the theatre's double aisles for a more encompassing interactive experience, and performers must imaginatively fill in the cuts of each scene with appropriate (and sometimes impishly inappropriate) action for their character.

The final scenes of the film present a wide array of problems for live performance. After Dr Frank-N-Furter uses his sonic transducer to freeze Brad, Janet, Rocky Horror and Columbia into nude statues, he dresses them in corsets and fishnet tights, then unfreezes them to perform the floor show: a highly choreographed performance of alternative sexualities. Performers have only a short interlude – slightly over a minute of narration from the Criminologist – to scramble into position for 'Rose Tint My World'. As The Fantasie Factory Players advise in the Transylvanian University online manual for shadowcasts, floor show makeup is nearly impossible: 'Don't even try when you're first starting out. You'll have a hard enough time getting changed into costumes.'[36] Layered costume components and corsets with side zippers are invaluable, as are helping hands from fellow cast members and techies, to effect this quick transition. As Frank-N-Furter enters to croon 'Don't Dream It, Be It', he plunges into a foggy pool of fluid identities: a scenic impossibility for the movie theatre stage. Although Sins o' the Flesh has conducted an underwater photo shoot to replicate this scene, the weekly shadowcast embraces the theatricality of Frank 'floating' vertically in a Titanic lifesaver and of characters 'swimming' across the stage with exaggerated arm movements to embrace one another. The ensuing orgy is deliciously low-tech; the 'impossibilities' and 'failures' of live performance become rich sites for creative synchronicity. Shadowcast performances do not simply replicate the film, then, but play in the margins of a gapped and incomplete artefact; they shift and shape the landscape through intimate, embodied mimesis.

Syncopating time

Gertrude Stein theorizes that the theatre causes nervousness because an audience member's emotional time is never precisely in sync with the emotional progression of the play:

> The thing that is fundamental about plays is that the scene as depicted on the stage is more often than not one might say it is almost always in syncopated time in relation to the emotion of anybody in the audience. What this says is this. Your sensation as one in the audience in relation to the play played before you your sensation I say your emotion concerning that play is always either behind or ahead of the play at which you are looking and to which you are listening. So your emotion as a member of the audience is never going on at the same time as the action of the play.[37]

Stein wonders whether what is seen or what is heard dominates an audience member's perception; whether hearing replaces seeing; whether the audible interferes with the visual.[38] Theatrical elements do not fuse together into a seamless narrative, for Stein, but create an unnerving sensation of syncopation. How is an audience member to keep pace with the drama?

Perhaps the better question is whether the audience *desires* to keep time with the drama, to be seamlessly interpolated into its narrative progression. Elin Diamond locates postmodern possibilities in the very concept of syncopated time that causes Stein such anxiety; for Diamond, this 'visceral and cognitive sense of temporal otherness' can dislodge myths of a unified time and a unified subject.[39] Synchronization with the film is always a fluid and creative act that elaborates on the film's landscape. Yet participatory audiences at *The Rocky Horror Picture Show* also delight in syncopating time with the film: speaking back to the movie in cacophonous counterpoint to the original text.

Louis Farese first began speaking back to the screen on Labor Day weekend of 1976, according to fan club president Sal Piro's history of the participatory phenomenon.[40] As the narrating Criminologist opened the story – 'I would like, ah, if I may, to take you on a strange journey' – Farese spontaneously called back, 'How strange was it?' If the film is a self-contained object, then the Criminologist's story proceeds oblivious to Farese's question; the narrator pulls a black book from the shelf and continues, 'It seemed a fairly ordinary night when Brad Majors and his fiancée Janet Weiss, two young, ordinary, healthy kids, left Denton that late November evening to visit a Dr Everett Scott, ex-tutor, and now friend to both of them.' But if the audience gives weight to Farese's interjection, then the remainder of the film can be a response to that query: 'How strange was it?' Having seen the film multiple times, Farese's question anticipates the narrative proceedings with glee and rips into the temporal fabric of the 'finished' text.

Counterpoint dialogue, which has emerged over years of collective midnight movie improvisation, syncopates with and against textual authority. Each audience's script defers a singular meaning, alternatively underpinning and undermining Richard O'Brien's original script. The film seems ready-made for participatory interjections since the pacing of the acting often drags, filled with awkward pauses at the end of lines and expansive rests at the end of musical phrases. Take, for instance, the chorus of the opening number in Table 3, 'Science Fiction/Double Feature'. The grey

Table 3 Science Fiction/Double Feature

1	2	3	4	1	2	3	4
		Sci-	ence	fic-	tion		
		Dou-	ble	fea-	ture		
		Doc-	tor	X			
	Will	build		a	crea-	ture	
See	an-		droids	fight-	ing		
		Brad	and	Ja-	net		
	Anne	Fran-	cis	stars		in	
		For-	bid-	den	Pla-	net.	
Oh		Ohhh	hhhh	hhhh	hhhh	Oh	oh oh
		hhhh	hhhh			At	the late
	Night		Dou-	ble	Fea-	ture	
Show						Pic-	ture

1	2	3	4	1	2	3	4

Source: The Rocky Horror Picture Show, dir. Jim Sharman (Twentieth Century Fox, 1975), DVD. Table by Sarah Taylor Ellis.

portions in the table represent rests, available for interjections. Although the script of counterpoint dialogue shifts from location to location, audiences often fill the temporal gap after 'Doctor X' with the rhyming chant 'Sex sex sex sex', making the film's eroticism more explicit. 'See androids fighting' is frequently followed by '*and fucking and sucking on*' 'Brad and Janet'. Both the authorially intended line ('See androids fighting Brad and Janet') and the modified meaning ('See androids fighting and fucking and sucking on Brad and Janet') can be simultaneously upheld. Why settle for a single meaning when one can read double at the late night 'anal friction' double feature 'Rocky Horror' picture show?

When the host theatre allows, fans also physically participate in the film; they pelt virgins with rice during the wedding scene, literalize the lyric 'You're a hot dog' by throwing wieners, and toss 'cards for sorrow' and 'cards for pain' during Dr Frank-N-Furter's heartwarming 'Going Home'. Such audience participation multiplies the tracks of signification at play, creating a heterotopia of temporalities that are never fully subsumed into one another.[41] The counterpoint dialogue and prop usage complicate the relationship between text and frame; the boundaries between what lies inside and outside the text become pleasurably porous.

This interpenetration of frame and text can trace its lineage to the horror hosts of late-night B-films, televised in the 1950s. In the fall of 1957, when Universal Pictures released their library of 1930s and 40s horror films to television, local stations across the country signed vampires, mad scientists and other campy costumed personalities to frame the late night proceedings.[42] With cheap costumes and shabby sets, horror hosts improvised intriguing material to liven up these low-budget movies at the midnight hour. The witty frameworks soon surpassed the films in popularity. John 'The Cool Ghoul' Zacherle, for instance, became an enduring personality as the vampire Roland – accent on the second syllable. While hosting horror films for Philadelphia's WCAU, Roland inhabited a dungeon with his coffin-dwelling wife and assistant Igor. He conducted gruesome experiments in his laboratory, played with his fuzzy pet amoeba made of jello and occasionally sang a monster tune; his debut album *Dinner with Drac* launched the second leg of his career on New York's WABC. At Channel 7, Roland became known as 'Zacherley' and enjoyed an elaborate set with more realistic props, as well as a live band; one episode featured Transylvanian folk music, while another premiered the new opera *Il Draculare*.[43]

Film critic Leonard Maltin reflects on Roland's antics as silly and sophomoric, but also exciting and spontaneous: 'Looking back now, you know, as a film buff and something of a historian and a purist, I shudder to think at the idea of interrupting the movie or mocking the movie, dismantling the movie in some cases. But to a kid it was just a lot of fun.'[44] This 'fun' fundamentally shifted the shape of the movies for spectators, particularly as horror hosts began intentionally confusing frame and film. Zacherley developed a technique at WCAU for inserting himself into the movie. During a broadcast of *The Black Cat*, Roland's face appeared among a series of close-ups for participants at a devil worship ceremony; and during a broadcast of *The Raven* at WALB, Zacherley injected his own name into the film: 'Who's on the case?' 'Zacherley and Gasport.' These 'break-ins' or 'jump-ins' pleasurably disrupted the film's temporality, and fans often tuned in to the worst B-films just to see Roland's affectionate antics. Across the country, other local horror hosts – Elvira, Vampira, Svengoolie, Ghoulardi, 'Chilly Billy' Cardille and more – were independently experimenting with similar acts of synchronizing and syncopating with the screen. Numerous horror host fans became *Rocky Horror* devotees, including *RHPS* fan club president Sal Piro.

Within *The Rocky Horror Picture Show* itself, the narrating Criminologist inhabits the tenuous borders of the filmic frame much like a television horror host – although he was more directly modelled on Edgar Lustgarten, a host of popular British crime programmes syndicated for airing in the United States.[45] From his leather-bound library, the Criminologist guides the audience through the action of the film with a British accent and quasi-academic distance. As the investigator of Frank-N-Furter's crime, he strives for a detached and objective perspective even as he himself is imbricated in the proceedings. His narrative reconstruction of the events unfolds through a massive collection of evidence, from a dense black book of photographs and victims' statements to a pull-down diagram of 'The Time Warp'. But his academic analysis of the proceedings, verging on voyeurism, breaks down in – what else? – 'The Time Warp'. Although the Criminologist typically provides transitions between disparate scenes and settings, he is pleasurably interjected throughout this musical number in increasing states of disarray; by the end of the song, the Criminologist shimmies on the top of his mahogany desk in time with the 'transsexual Transylvanians'. This series of Roland-like jump-ins complicates his distanced authority and discloses his pleasure in the fantastical, circuitous story.

The Criminologist embodies the crisis of the scholar-fan, who transgresses the norms of both (distanced) academic and (immersed) fan subjectivities (see, for example, Figure 3).[46] The

Figure 3 My first time. Or as I posted that night on Facebook, 'Rocky Horror Picture Show at the Nuart! This is what I like to call "research."' 13 November 2011. Courtesy of Sarah Taylor Ellis.

scholar-fan is often excluded from both academic and fan circles; academics imagine that his critical eye is blinded by immersion in the fan landscape, while fans imagine that a critical distance blunts the ecstasies of pure and unadulterated fandom. Yet *Rocky Horror*'s participatory experience thrives on double meanings and upholds contradictions. Like the repetitive theatregoers who simultaneously sync and syncopate with the time of the film, the Criminologist can be read as both a part of and a counterpoint to the narrative. He crosses and confuses the binary between intellectual and embodied knowledge, giving himself over to physical pleasure even as he analyses these 'insects called the human race, lost in time, and lost in space – and meaning'.

Anything can happen on Halloween?

The Rocky Horror Picture Show may have had its midnight premiere on April Fool's Day of 1976, but today the movie is more readily associated with the carnivalesque and costumed culture of Halloween. In fact, West Hollywood's Annual Halloween Carnaval in 2010 was Rocky Horror themed; 8,239 people danced 'The Time Warp', breaking the Guinness Book Record in honour of the film's thirty-fifth anniversary.

Decades after the film's premiere, as thousands of fans do 'The Time Warp' in a gay friendly Los Angeles neighbourhood, critics may question the ongoing identificatory charge of *The Rocky Horror Picture Show*. This once maligned subcultural object has entered into – and wildly succeeded within – the mainstream media. Young fans increasingly consume *Rocky Horror* in a setting far from the charged alterity of a midnight movie; *Rocky Horror* was released on VHS for the first time in 1990 and had its US television premiere on the Fox network in 1993, complete with an edited audience participation track.[47] When fans attend a midnight movie, the event rarely holds the same countercultural charge as in the 1970s. Mainstream films often premiere at midnight, drawing a youthful but not necessarily 'queer' audience for the latest summer blockbuster.[48] *The Rocky Horror Picture Show* arguably contains little more than a nostalgic memory of its past immiscibility into cultural norms.

How, then, can we reconcile the persistent shock of contemporary fans' first encounter with *Rocky Horror* – whether at a midnight movie, on television or on DVD? Perhaps the hybridity of this 'horror-rock-transvestite-camp-omnisexual-musical parody' still marks a limit to our aesthetic frames of reference; its charged 'otherness' induces a complex crossing of anxiety and intrigue.[49] A hint of immiscibility is further encoded in the film's censorship for the small screen; provocative scenes are carefully cut away and curse words are dubbed over, but traces of these erasures remain in the asynchronous movement of those lush red lips. An entire episode of the hit television series *Glee* debates issues of censorship and the musical's appropriateness for teens.[50] And no matter how many times a fan has seen the film on TV, attending a midnight movie 'in the flesh' becomes an important rite of passage; the resulting fan community can imagine itself in excess of the mainstream, even as the film becomes increasingly accessible.

What's more, *The Rocky Horror Picture Show* maintains its identificatory power for a queer fan base because it persists in such a contradictory, frayed and fragile present. The acceptability of queer lifestyles is an uneven flux across times and spaces; hate crimes can (and do) arise on topsy-turvy Halloween or a more mundane day, in West Hollywood or a Bible Belt suburb. *Rocky Horror* insists on the cacophonous coexistence of these times and spaces. Within the film itself, Frank-N-Furter's sexually liberated reign is only a flashing, fleeting moment. Deeming his lifestyle too extreme, the mad scientist's own followers Riff-Raff and Magenta ultimately kill Frank and rocket back to Transylvania, leaving cracked and confused remnants of human culture in their wake. Yet Dr Frank-N-Furter is resuscitated as his fans do 'The Time Warp' week after week, co-creating another utopian moment of cultural acceptance.

We'll make time stand still: *Dr. Horrible's Sing-Along Blog*

Warping time is the ultimate power for supervillain/countercultural heroes Dr Frank-N-Furter of *The Rocky Horror Picture Show* and Dr Horrible of the viral web series *Dr. Horrible's Sing-Along Blog*. While Frank uses a sonic transducer to stop time and manipulate his guests into performing the floor show, Dr Horrible invents a Freeze Ray to stop time, get the girl and rule the world: an undoubtedly ambitious mission. In fact, *Dr. Horrible's Sing-Along Blog* was born of equally ambitious aims during the Writers Guild of America (WGA) strike against the Alliance of Motion Picture and Television Producers (AMPTP) from 5 November 2007 to 12 February 2008. Wielding their Freeze Rays on film and television studios, writers sought to explore alternative methods of artistic production and distribution during this work stoppage.

In a blog post addressed to his friends (i.e. fans) in spring 2008, Joss Whedon cast himself as the protagonist in a horribly familiar fantasy:

> Once upon a time, all the writers in the forest got very mad with the Forest Kings and declared a work-stoppage. The forest creatures were all sad; the mushrooms did not dance, the elderberries gave no juice for the festival wines, and the Teamsters were kinda pissed. (They were very polite about it, though.) During this work-stoppage, many writers tried to form partnerships for outside funding to create new work that circumvented the Forest King system. Frustrated with the lack of movement on that front, I finally decided to do something very ambitious, very exciting, very mid-life-crisisy.[51]

While time stood still for the studios, Whedon gathered writers Zack Whedon and Maurissa Tancharoen, composer Jed Whedon and a stellar cast and crew to self-produce a three-act web series: *Dr. Horrible's Sing-Along Blog*. When Act I debuted on 15 July 2008, free and without adverts, traffic to drhorrible.com crashed the servers. *Dr. Horrible* was subsequently released as an affordable iTunes download, as well as a DVD loaded with extras created for – and sometimes by – the web series' devoted fans. As a 'Sing-Along', *Dr. Horrible* explicitly invites fans to be supervillainous co-conspirators, collectively navigating new methods of artistic creation that circumvent the corporate studio system.

Dr. Horrible's Sing-Along Blog emerges from a field of parallel fiction that explores familiar texts and genres from alternative perspectives. Gregory Maguire's *Wicked* – adapted into the wildly popular Stephen Schwartz and Winnie Holzman musical in 2003 – recasts *The Wizard of Oz*'s Wicked Witch of the West as a misunderstood, green-skinned outcast and political activist.[52] John Gardner's novel *Grendel* similarly skews *Beowulf* to the sympathetic monster's side. This flipping of a familiar narrative can even be traced back to Greek satyr plays, which employed a chorus of hairy, horny goat men in a carnivalesque retelling of a favourite story to close the annual Festival of Dionysus. The only fully intact satyr play is Euripides' *The Cyclops*, adapted into a Pulitzer Prize-nominated rock opera by Psittacus Productions in 2011; this play lampoons Odysseus' heroism by recounting one episode of his epic odyssey through Polyphemus' eye.[53]

Dr. Horrible's Sing-Along Blog upends the superhero genre by flipping narrative focus to the supervillain; the straightforward story of good vs evil is reconfigured to reveal a more complicated range of perspectives, continually deferring moral certainty and closure.[54] In *Dr. Horrible*, the 'hero' Captain Hammer is actually a cheesy corporate tool who grows hilariously insufferable over the series. With a bombastic baritone voice and ripped body, the hypermasculine Hammer may convince the Mayor to convert an old building into a homeless shelter, but his underlying motive is always to boost his own ego and bash his competition. The nightly news lavishes praise on this political crusader and the newspapers cover his every triumph, but the mainstream media's portrayal never coincides with the reality; the airheaded Captain's advocacy for the public good is a by-product of advocacy for himself. Captain Hammer is all surface: a comic caricature drawn in bold and brash strokes.

Audiences are more apt to align themselves with the sympathetically awkward anarchist Dr Horrible.[55] Like Clark Kent and Superman, or Bruce Wayne and Batman, Neil Patrick Harris's character uncomfortably straddles two identities: boy-next-door Billy and supervillain Dr Horrible. Both Billy and Dr Horrible are nerdy misfits marked by failure; an oversized eggshell lab coat and rubber gloves can never wholly transmute this geeky boy into a triumphant anti-hero. 'May I suggest a drinking game where every time I do a ridiculously awkward long blink, someone does a shot of some alcohol?' Harris proposes in the DVD commentary.[56] In his everyday life, Billy longs for recognition by Penny, the soft-spoken girl from the Laundromat, but he stumbles over words and struggles to make a 'real, audible connection' with her.[57] Meanwhile, Dr Horrible plots how to gain acceptance to the elite Evil League of Evil. He may not be as mediocre a supervillain as Moist, who wields the questionable power of making objects damp, but Dr Horrible's career is also tainted by failure. His overlapping operations in love and supervillainy are continually thwarted by Hammer.

Dr Horrible becomes a particularly charismatic and queer countercultural hero when a third identity is layered onto the character by Neil Patrick Harris himself: a beloved theatre, film and television actor. Harris's career began with the title role of *Doogie Howser, M.D.*, a teenage doctor with a boyish charm that still accrues to the actor today. Following an expansive range of roles including a parody of himself in *Harold & Kumar Go to White Castle* (2004) and the womanizing Barney in *How I Met Your Mother* (2005–14), Harris came out as 'a very content gay man' in an exclusive November 2006 *People* article.[58] His popularity subsequently soared; 'NPH' became a gay icon, showcased most spectacularly in the realm of musical theatre. Only a few months after the web debut of *Dr. Horrible's Sing-Along Blog*, Harris was featured in Marc Shaiman's 2008 viral web short *Prop 8: The*

Musical, advocating for gay marriage in California.⁵⁹ Harris played the questionably heterosexual Bobby in the 2011 New York Philharmonic concert production of *Company,* as well as Hedwig on Broadway in 2014.⁶⁰ He also hosted the Tony Awards in 2009, 2011, 2012 and 2013; the 2011 awards show featured an opening number that proclaimed, 'Broadway: it's not just for gays anymore'. Harris's public persona as an out and proud song-and-dance man is perhaps his most charmingly popular character yet – and indelibly linked to his portrayal of Dr Horrible.

Dr Horrible would never be the subject of an exclusive magazine story like NPH or make headlines like Captain Hammer. Instead, this 'low-rent super villain' projects himself into the world via 'alternative' media; Dr Horrible updates viewers on his latest heists and answers fan email from a webcam set up in his home laboratory.⁶¹ Thwarting expectations for a big opening musical number, *Dr. Horrible's Sing-Along Blog* abruptly leaps into one of the supervillain's amateur webcam posts. From his lair, Dr Horrible announces a new weapon designed to solve all his problems: 'So transmatter is 75% and more importantly, the Freeze Ray is almost up. This is the one. Stops time.' Dr Horrible then reaches out to his viewers, implicating them in his villainous master plan: 'Freeze Ray. Tell your friends.'⁶²

The utopian moment: 'My Freeze Ray'/'Strike!'

'My Freeze Ray' was the first song to be written for *Dr. Horrible's Sing-Along Blog* and neatly encapsulates the time-warping spirit of the entire artistic endeavour. Light, staccato C major chords sneak into the background as Dr Horrible reads an email from long-time watcher DeadNotSleeping: 'You always say in your blog that you will show her the way, show her you are a true villain. Who is "her" and does she even know that you're … '⁶³ Dr Horrible stares into the webcam and trails off into a musical dream world. With endearingly simple music and lyrics, 'My Freeze Ray' expands the space of the supervillain's vlog (video blog) beyond the four walls of his secret lab and into the Laundromat, where

Penny tosses her underthings into the wash. The supervillain's multiple identities coexist in this song: the scheming Dr Horrible on his webcam, the awkward Billy at the Laundromat and – most importantly – the debonair supervillain anarchist he dreams of becoming.[64]

'My Freeze Ray' employs a short and simple popular song structure: verse, chorus, verse, chorus, bridge, verse and truncated chorus. In the choppy and short-breathed phrases of the verses, Billy fumbles for words that always fall short of describing how Penny makes him feel: 'What's the phrase? / Like a fool / Kinda sick / Special needs / Anyways'. Fortunately, Penny cannot hear him shuffle through these embarrassing and even offensive compliments. Caressing his Freeze Ray on his webcam, Dr Horrible plans to stop time, elongating it into a present of open-ended potential; in the best of all possible worlds, he will finally 'find the time to find the words' to eloquently express his feelings for her.[65]

Music and lyrics already empower this supervillain with greater verbal coherence than he has in everyday conversation, and in the chorus, his idealized self – which Whedon calls the 'one where he's actually freezing things and being awesome' – finally takes cool and confident control of the Laundromat.[66] The idealized Dr Horrible presses an imaginary pause button that suspends Penny in the midst of dumping laundry into the washing machine; free from his typical nervous tics, he relaxes onto a nearby machine to admire her. He musically elongates phrases and explores a greater melodic range through the chorus, with the bridge expanding into his most articulate and lyrical confession of emotion yet: 'I'm the guy to make it real / The feelings you don't dare to feel / I'll bend the world to our will / And we'll make time stand still.'[67] This prolonged utopian moment reveals that the supervillain is a softy at heart. Dr Horrible's Freeze Ray is not a weapon of mass destruction, but an enabler of alternatives to the present; he is intent less on 'destroying the status quo' than on bending it to discover its multiple potentialities.[68] What's more, Dr Horrible's ideal world relies on collaboration with a partner in crime: Penny.

'[Penny] *is* fighting "the man"', albeit in her own quiet way, according to Zack Whedon; her method of putting power in different hands involves volunteering to serve meals and collecting signatures to support a new homeless shelter, rather than enacting supervillainous plots.[69] While Captain Hammer's triumphs are broadcast in the mainstream media and Dr Horrible wields the power of the web, Penny's labours often go unrecorded and unrecognized. In fact, as the web series continues, Captain Hammer usurps credit for Penny's work, and her selfless, collaborative labour is crushed between two increasingly competitive male egos. In the battle between selfish 'supers', everyone loses. Dr Horrible grows dark and destructive when his nemesis gets the girl; he ultimately uses his Freeze Ray in tandem with a Death Ray, which backfires and kills the innocent Penny in the hotly debated Act III.[70]

Yet, for the utopian moment of 'My Freeze Ray', Dr Horrible and Penny peacefully warp the world together. During a light-hearted instrumental break after the bridge, the idealized supervillain and Penny dance in a sunny dream version of the Laundromat in which only they exist; Billy twirls and dips his partner with the perfect poise that he lacks in everyday life. 'That's the plan / Rule the world / You and me / Any day', Dr Horrible croons to the webcam.[71] Though that 'any day' is not today, 'My Freeze Ray' physicalizes the possibility of a partnership between this sympathetic supervillain and dedicated local activist, dancing their way towards subversion of the status quo together.

Joss Whedon explicitly connects Dr Horrible's subversion of the status quo to his own exploration of alternatives to the studio system in a DVD special feature, *Commentary! the Musical*. Like the counterpoint dialogue that creates a layered range of meanings for *The Rocky Horror Picture Show*, *Commentary!* reframes the popular web series with an array of behind the scenes stories. This additional audio track bends the genre of film-makers' commentary into a heightened, campy and memorable musical form. After a densely self-referential opening number ('Commentary!'), Whedon contextualizes the creation of

Dr. Horrible's Sing-Along Blog with a workers' anthem: 'Strike / For all the writers / Strike / For a living wage / Until these wrongs are righted / We won't write another page.'[72] The juxtaposition of visuals from 'My Freeze Ray' with the unified patter and percussive drive of the new audio track – 'Strike!' – encourages audiences to read the writers' strike as a utopian moment of creative solidarity, akin to Dr Horrible's own dream collaboration with Penny.

While freezing work on mainstream projects, writers sent the studios scrambling to fill the gaps in the television schedule and redirected their imaginative energies to blogs and viral videos. Maurissa Tancharoen, Jed Whedon and Zack Whedon primed themselves for *Dr. Horrible's Sing-Along Blog* by creating clever web shorts throughout the strike. Their YouTube hit 'WGA v AMPTP' even foreshadowed the battle between Dr Horrible and Captain Hammer by exaggerating the binary between poor, well-meaning writers and wealthy, heartless studio heads. Executives at CBS, FOX and NBC worried that the WGA would win the public relations battle through their compelling storytelling strategies and Dr Horrible-like command of new media.[73] As it turned out, the mix of new shows and repeats during the three-month strike hardly changed television viewership, but cable and internet viewership increased during the strike, and viral videos such as 'WGA v AMPTP' seem to have swayed public opinion. In a survey for the April 2008 Nielsen Report on the strike's impact, 100 per cent of respondents knew about the strike, and 77 per cent supported the writers either strongly (55 per cent) or somewhat (22 per cent).[74]

Despite audience support, the writers' supervillainous mission was at least partially a failure; many studios took advantage of the strike to sever existing contracts, replace scripted shows with reality television and pull back on developing pilots.[75] Still, the writers won residuals for digital media, and *Dr. Horrible's Sing-Along Blog* emerged as 'our small proof not only that things can be done differently in this business, but that the greatest expression of rebellion is joy', according to Joss Whedon.[76] How better to rebel than by singing along?

All art is fan art

'Strike!' comes across as 'a really, really long history class' in comparison to the wonderfully wacky array of songs in the rest of *Commentary! the Musical*, which freely converge on – and, more often, diverge from – the expected film-maker's commentary. The cast and crew play scripted versions of 'themselves', and no backstage anecdote is too small to be elaborated into song, even the iPhone game that bonded the cast and crew ('Ninja Ropes'). The songs are rarely about the web series and more often self-contained gems about the creators themselves. 'That's like breaking the ninth wall. It's pointless', Zack Whedon complains.[77] Yet precisely by diverging from the typical behind-the-scenes narrative, these songs give voice to the diverse writers, actors and fans who conspired in this web series' success. If *Dr. Horrible's Sing-Along Blog* focuses on a marginalized supervillain, then *Commentary! the Musical* pays gleeful homage to the margins of the margins in another fantastic genre flip.

Felicia Day's character Penny may be continually overshadowed by the competing supers in the musical, but *Commentary!* gives Day time to shine – and to publicize her pioneering web series *The Guild*, one of the inspirations for *Dr. Horrible's Sing-Along Blog*. In quick patter verses of her solo 'The Art', Day admits to using surface-level performance strategies during *Dr. Horrible*, stumbling and stammering simply "cause that's what it says to do in the script'.[78] Everything from a live horse to a soldier-boy extra seems destined to distract Day from her serious acting process. Only in the song's slow and serene chorus, tinged with Eastern instrumentation, does Day find creative zen. In this oasis, Felicia Day elevates her own web series to the mystical realm of 'art': 'Memory, method, primal and deep / All Stanislavsky, Strasberg and Streep / Truth, Mr. Lipton, that's how you build / *The Guild*.'[79]

In fact, Day's episodic comedy *The Guild* is delightful, unpretentious entertainment; the web series follows the intersecting online and offline lives of the Knights of Good, a diverse group of MMORPG (massively multiplayer online role-playing game) players. Although Day originally scripted the show as a television pilot, studio producers 'loved it, but said it was too "niche."'[80] So Day and her friends decided to self-produce the series, entertaining their fellow geeky gamers with easily digestible YouTube webisodes. Launched on 27 July 2007, *The Guild* was endearingly 'DIY' but had smart writing and high production values, which Joss Whedon particularly respected.[81] Actors worked for free during the first season, which was funded by family, friends and a rapidly expanding legion of fans. By October 2007, *The Guild*'s first episode had been featured on YouTube's front page, garnering over 850,000 hits and 18,000 channel subscribers.[82]

Yet even as Felicia Day's song lampoons a sacred conception of art, it points to a gap in the recognition of web video as a legitimate medium of artistic production in the early 2000s. Similar to a hierarchy of genres, a hierarchy of media initially privileged film and television above media produced for the internet. Joss Whedon's crossover to the World Wide Web with *Dr. Horrible's Sing-Along Blog*, as well as web shorts from the writers of *The Office*, began to productively complicate this distinction. In fact, Day credits *Dr. Horrible* for 'legitimizing' web video; Whedon's work within the studio system on cult shows such as *Buffy the Vampire Slayer* and *Firefly* brought credibility to his own web series and, by extension, to others' online productions. Although *The Guild* had racked up recognition among gamers since its inception, Day's web series soared in popularity as it extended to a pre-existing Whedon fan base post-*Dr. Horrible*.[83] *Dr. Horrible*'s success opened the door for recognition of web series' entertainment value and even artistry; in fact, *Dr. Horrible's Sing-Along Blog* won a 2009 Emmy Award in a new category recognizing the merit of 'alternative' media: short format live-action entertainment programmes.[84]

Dr Horrible hijacked that year's Emmy ceremony to proclaim, 'The future of home entertainment is the internet!' – and in making this announcement, the supervillain symbolically crossed the line from 'alternative' media to the 'mainstream'. Today, that line is increasingly blurry and perhaps even non-existent as digital platforms including Netflix, Hulu, Amazon Prime and Disney+ regularly release original shows and movies direct to their streaming channels. Flexible cross-media content proliferates across computers, smartphones, tablets and web-connected televisions, and corporate presence is increasingly palpable across them all. In theory, a movie or web series can skirt the film and television studio system, captivate an audience and go viral on the 'alternative' platform of the internet; in practice, the most enduring strike a balance between creative experimentation and corporate sponsorship and marketing. By its sixth and final season, for instance, *The Guild* was sponsored by Sprint and distributed by Xbox Live and Microsoft; production quality improved with corporate funding, but writer/actor Day always strove to uphold the web series' homespun collaborative community by using fan art for the opening titles and interacting with fans and fellow creatives on her web forum Geek & Sundry.[85] A more recent example is the TikTok musical adaptation of Disney/Pixar's *Ratatouille*, which emerged under the hashtag #RatatouilleMusical in November 2020; hundreds of TikTok creatives, nostalgic for live theatre during the Covid-19 pandemic, began posting sixty-second clips of songs, costumes, puppets, playbills and more from this hypothetical Broadway show. *Ratatouille: The TikTok Musical* took flight when it partnered with Seaview Productions and TodayTix; a pre-recorded, pay-what-you-can digital benefit performance in January 2021 starred Broadway luminaries including Tituss Burgess, Mary Testa and André De Shields and raised over $2 million for the Actors Fund.[86]

Similarly, *Dr. Horrible's Sing-Along Blog* set out not to overturn the film and television studios, but to question their dominance and to make space for new, artist-driven methods of production; Joss Whedon recognizes fandom as key to this endeavour. Whedon fans are often established in and through his blockbuster studio work (he achieved unprecedented success writing and directing Marvel Studios' *The Avengers* in 2012) – but the expansive 'Whedonverse' subsequently becomes a springboard for artwork, short stories, comics, blogs and other fan engagement that can break down artificial hierarchies of artistic production and shift the status quo. Fans accordingly pop into the frame at every textual and paratextual level of *Dr. Horrible's Sing-*

Along Blog. Beginning with the opening number of Act III, a campy chorus of groupies interject in the web series; dressed in homemade Hammer T-shirts, they stalk the superhero, promise weird sexual favours and collect creepy memorabilia like clippings of Captain Hammer's hair and his laundry list ('Four sweater vests!').[87] The fans swoon and croon along with their hero in 'Everyone's a Hero', although Captain Hammer insists on a hierarchy of heroism that places him at the top. *Commentary! the Musical* then amplifies these fans' voices exponentially, to the point that superstar Neil Patrick Harris grows frustrated at his lack of air time, which has been turned over to 'people who don't matter'. The groupies share a song entitled 'All About Me', with each groupie (#1, #2 and #3) insisting that the web series is actually all about their marginal character. Each fan also receives a full-length solo in *Commentary!* A lisping homosexual named Steve (Groupie #3) wonders whether he was hired for his linguistic quirks or his legitimate talents; Stacy (Groupie #2) buys herself a '$10 Solo' (that NPH duly interrupts); and Maurissa (Groupie #1) laments that her Asian ethnicity condemns her to stereotypical sidelined roles. Within the frame of the film, Maurissa Tancharoen is a writer cross-dressing as a groupie; but Tancharoen could equally be considered a fan cross-dressing as a writer.

In both *Dr. Horrible's Sing-Along Blog* and *The Rocky Horror Picture Show*, the textual poaching of sci-fi films and musical conventions creates a palimpsest of cultural references culled from the creators' own diverse and obsessive fandoms. Their Frankensteinian creations embrace the fact that all artistic labour is fan labour, warping a sweeping array of influences into a tentatively 'original' creation. It is perhaps no surprise, then, that Whedon's work has become a mainstay of sci-fi/fantasy conventions like Comic-Con. At these unconventional conventions, alternative worlds pleasurably mix and mingle; although a hierarchy of fame is still palpable, creators and fans overlap significantly. The real triumph of *Dr. Horrible's Sing-Along Blog*, according to the writers, is not the 'finished product', but the physicalization of their product's ever-expanding *potentialities* through the fans who dress and perform as Dr Horrible, Captain Hammer, the Bad Horse cowboy chorus – and their own supervillainous creations.[88]

Dr. Horrible's Sing-Along Blog epitomizes a type of creative consumerism that does not deny its imbrication in capitalism, but refuses to reduce its product to its exchange value. Warping time and genre, *Dr. Horrible's Sing-Along Blog* not only acknowledges but actively encourages fans' immersion in and commentary on its ever-expanding world. In fact, the Evil League of Evil began accepting online applications for membership in autumn 2008; ten new members were awarded with inclusion in the DVD's special features. Over a thousand supervillainous fans produced short YouTube and Vimeo video applications to be considered by the League and its designated agents. Winning spin-offs of the original singing supervillain included the clever Tur-Mohel and his Minyan, Mr Terrible and Lord Stabbington; their 'fan labour' garnered recognition alongside Whedon's 'legitimate' web series.

One ELE winner embraces the 'Sing-Along' spirit of *Dr. Horrible's Sing-Along Blog* unlike any other. Miss Broadway Dork is a frighteningly exuberant fangirl whose weapon of choice is a performative act rather than a physical object: she sings showtunes. With a girlish giggle, the high-spirited Miss Broadway Dork admits that showtunes may seem to inspire jazz hands more than fear and terror. But the strangeness and alterity of song and dance can stop time, much like Dr Horrible's Freeze Ray. 'Have you ever gone out in the middle of a crowded street and just started singing at the top of your lungs? People stop. People stare. People look at you like you are horrible and have done the worst thing in the world', she explains. Miss Broadway Dork views this stoppage of time as a potential enabler of chaos; showtunes can snap out of the time of capital, as well as out of a heteronormative genealogy, by distracting people from looking after their cash registers, their children and their elderly. Miss Broadway Dork concludes her Evil League of Evil application with a sinister smile, 'Showtunes. They're not all happy and cheery. And even when they are, they can be used ... for evil'.

Miss Broadway Dork realizes that the use of any cultural text hinges not on an authorially intended meaning, but on its performative deployment and redeployment by a specific interpretive community. Open and unfinished, packed with wormholes of possibilities, sci-fi/fantasy and musical theatre are particularly ripe for a time-warping, embodied subversion of the status quo.[89] And when the status is not quo, fans will act. Just as fans have recently distanced *Harry Potter* from its author in the wake of transphobic remarks, many fans have now firmly removed Joss Whedon from the centre of the Whedonverse. In a 2017 guest blog on *The Wrap*, Joss Whedon's ex-wife Kai Cole revealed Whedon's serial cheating and called him a 'hypocrite preaching feminist ideals'.[90] While this revelation did some damage to his reputation, mounting evidence of Whedon's abusive behaviour towards actors, writers and other creatives hit a tipping point when Charisma Carpenter tweeted on 10 February 2021 how Whedon had threatened and harassed her when she was pregnant. Carpenter's allegations were swiftly followed by messages of solidarity from fellow (mainly female) actors including Michelle Trachtenberg, Amber Benson and Sarah Michelle Gellar, who wrote on Instagram, 'While I am proud to have my name associated with Buffy Summers, I don't want to be forever associated with the name Joss Whedon.'[91] Whedon's misconduct has prompted some fans to no longer engage in his work at all, while other fans are now laying claim to the Whedonverse's empowering characters and worlds as independent from their 'creator'. After all, these stories never belonged solely to Whedon, but also to all the writers, actors, designers and other collaborators on the shows, movies and web series – as well as to the fans. This 'death of the author' potentiality is one that Whedon, previously hailed as a feminist superhero, likely never foresaw. But consider it our small proof that things can and must be done differently in this business.

3
Ragging Race: Spectral Temporality in the American Musical

Books are acts of composition: you compose them. You make music: the music is called fiction.

E.L. Doctorow, *The Paris Review*[1]

And by that time the era of Ragtime had run out, with the heavy breath of the machine, as if history were no more than a tune on a player piano.

E.L. Doctorow, *Ragtime*[2]

At the turn of the twentieth century, the syncopated sounds of ragtime captured the bustling American city in its increasing industrialization and ethnic diversity. In musical terms, syncopation displaces a regular metrical pattern by placing accents off the strong beats; this alternate rhythmic pattern is a common feature of African-derived music including ragtime, jazz, reggae, funk, rap and other percussive dance music. Ragtime maintains a basic 2/4 beat in the left hand with an embellished, syncopated melody in the right; the coordination and balance of the competing rhythmic components is essential. For Scott Joplin, the foremost composer and performer in this idiom, syncopation was 'no indication of light or trashy music'; ragtime was a dynamic modern invention, and it was here to stay.[3] As with the syncopated spectatorship described in Chapter 2, the ability to play within and against a regimented rhythm constitutes ragtime's pleasures and politics of difference.[4] The music's 'weird and intoxicating effect' is achieved 'by giving each note its proper time and by scrupulously observing the ties' in the accented melody. 'Play slowly until you catch the swing, and never play ragtime fast at any time', Joplin advises.[5]

The burgeoning businesses of sheet music publication and the manufacture of player piano rolls transported the racialized urban sounds of ragtime from Harlem nightclubs to the parlours of white middle-class Americans in the early 1900s. In this process, the music's African American roots were increasingly elided, and Black composers' essential contributions to American popular culture were rendered spectral; ragtime began to be promoted as a national rather than a racial sound. Yet the player piano's heavy breath and invisibly pounded keys persistently pointed to the layers of human labour embedded in the machine. The temporally and spatially distant composer/arranger of the piano roll, the machine manufactured by an array of hands and the human operating the machine collaborated in a present act of producing new music. Though the machine's breath would run out at the end of a song, all it took was the push of a button or a pump of the bellows to revivify the phantom fingers. What ghostly collaborations were being performed across these eighty-eight black and white keys?

Haunting is a peculiar manifestation of strange temporalities. Drawing on Henri Bergson, Bliss Cua Lim posits that the spectral time of haunting and return, 'in which the dead are alive and the past, fully preserved, "lean[s] over the present" and "gnaws" at the future'.[6] A ghostly presence can unsettle the homogeneous, empty present by being simultaneously past and present, visible and invisible, dead and yet very much alive; these apparitions can fantastically disclose the limits of historical time. This chapter explores the spectral translations of ragtime music across history and media. I employ E.L. Doctorow's 1975 novel *Ragtime* and its 1998 musical adaptation by Lynn Ahrens, Stephen Flaherty and Terrence McNally as a lens through which to revisit the music popularized in the United States in the late nineteenth and early twentieth centuries. Much as the musical fan cultures in Chapter 2 probe the boundaries between reality and fantasy, this chapter explores how creative reconstructions of the past play on the borders of the historical and fictional; imaginative and embodied histories generated in literature and musical theatre can operate as spectres, ruffling the present and gnawing at the future by enabling the restless ghosts of our past to flicker into view.

My work on ragtime follows from David Savran's analysis of jazz as a structure of feeling and emblem of the cultural revolution of the 1920s. As the culture of racialized and working-class citizens emerged in the burgeoning white middle-class mainstream via new technologies such as the phonograph, the ensuing culture wars pitted jazz against classical music, 'legitimate' theatre against vaudeville and musical comedy, Jews and African Americans against Gentiles, the old middle class against the new, advocates of the machine against its adversaries.[7] Many of the musical, moral, racial and class-based anxieties of jazz in the 1920s – which were later echoed in controversies about rock 'n' roll in the 1950s and hip-hop in the 1990s – can trace their roots to the tensions circulating around the production of ragtime only a few decades earlier. This chapter structurally syncopates *Ragtime* on the page and the stage with historical performances of ragtime music, locating the piano as a spectral site of working through social tensions of unacknowledged labour, artistry and collaboration in the white middle-class US American household. Performing ragtime tunes on this instrument enabled a mediated performative encounter between Black artists and white consumers in the antebellum parlour.

By juxtaposing the historical phenomenon of ragtime with works of fiction that riff on these syncopated sounds, I conceive of art as a social relation and show the imbrication of the 'historical' and the 'fictional'. Narrative is the predominant mode of discourse for both history and fiction. Whether or not the content of a narrative account is factual, the discursive form is always a creative and ideological construction, employing imagination in the production of human truth.[8] In a historical account, the narrative form is often perceived to be a transparent simulacrum of real events.[9] In actuality, historians actively shape the story by dictating the perspective from which events are told, as well as which events and personages merit inclusion. In the United States' historical narrative, racialized identities are often sidelined; histories of slavery and social injustice riddle the historical record with shameful truths and tragic gaps in our knowledge. In fact, race can be conceived of as a melancholic formation in US culture. Racialized others have been constitutionally integrated into the United States, yet they are still marginalized in the national narrative due to their difference from the dominant, imagined white ideal.[10] These 'hyphenated' Americans (African-Americans, Asian-Americans, Mexican-Americans, et al.) occupy a liminal space between citizenship and persistent difference from the norm. Their essential contributions to US American culture are often derealized; the cultural impulse is to devalue products of a racialized origin, to devalue the contribution of the specific group to the product or to claim that racial difference is irrelevant to the work.[11]

This racial melancholia extends to the formation of artistic canons as well. Toni Morrison considers African American presence to be a 'formative but denied ghost' in American literature,[12] while Susan McClary notes the refused centrality of African American contributions to popular music around the globe, from ragtime to hip-hop to musical theatre.[13] This problem of racial exclusion in historical content is also intertwined with a problem of form; narrative histories cannot represent African American music making traditions in all their embodied, participatory complexities. Historians have traditionally constructed narratives from an archive of newspapers, correspondence and tangible objects of analysis while disregarding corporeal systems of knowledge. The past should be conceived of not only as a linear timeline of documented work but also as a multilayered sedimentation incorporating events and processes, performances and repeated rituals.[14]

Particularly since African American history has gone 'unrecorded, dismembered, [and] washed out' in the United States, playwright Suzan-Lori Parks perceives the iterative and embodied nature of performance as a quintessential mode of rewriting and creating history anew.[15] Parks considers it her responsibility to dig through the sedimented layers of the past to recover and write her ancestors' stories:

One of my tasks as playwright is to – through literature and the special strange relationship between theatre and real-life – locate the ancestral burial ground, dig for bones, find bones, hear the bones sing, write it down. The bones tell us what was, is, will be; and because their song is a play – something that through a production *actually happens* – I'm working theatre like an incubator to create 'new' historical events. I'm re-membering and staging historical events which, through their happening on stage, are ripe for inclusion in the canon of history.[16]

Parks's theatrical techniques depend upon a manipulation of a linear, calendrical sense of time that derives from the improvisational traditions of jazz. Repetition and revision, or Rep&Rev, allows her work to expand beyond a linear timeline, to vitally re-embody the past, and to play like music in a dense 'drama of accumulation'.[17] What spectral histories can be imaginatively unearthed by repeating and revising ragtime?

Ragtime: The music

The African American origins of ragtime were a significant source of anxiety in the early 1900s. Many US cultural leaders were disquieted by this 'savage' music's intrusion into popular culture. 'Can it be said that America is falling prey to the collective soul of the negro [*sic*] through the influence of what is popularly known as "rag time" music?' Walter Winston Kenilworth asked in the *Musical Courier* in 1913.[18] A few early writings attempted to claim European origins for ragtime, but more often, critics aimed to obscure the music's Black roots by describing ragtime as quintessentially American – although not explicitly *African American*. Hiram Moderwell, for instance, defined ragtime as the 'folk music of the American city' at the turn of the century:

> As you walk up and down the streets of an American city you feel in its jerk and rattle a personality different from that of any European capital. This is American. It is our lives, and it helps to form our characters and conditions our mode of action. It should have expression in art,

simply because any people must express itself if it is to know itself. No European music can or possibly could express this American personality. Ragtime I believe does express it. It is to-day the one true American music.[19]

Irving Berlin similarly connected the 'speed and snap' of ragtime to a country moving at a faster pace, particularly in this burgeoning era of industrialization; ragtime captured 'the hum of an engine, the whirr of wheels, the explosion of an exhaust' from the Model T Fords rolling off the assembly line and on to the city streets.[20]

Technologies of mass production – an expanded publishing industry, piano rolls and phonograph records – certainly engendered a new national homogeneity in popular music at the turn of the century.[21] Jewish songwriters employed ragtime styles to perform their way into America – foreclosing the perpetually 'othered' African Americans in the process. Tin Pan Alley publishers developed the style into big business, and middle-class Americans gradually adopted and adapted the music into their social life.[22] Black cultural critic James Weldon Johnson grapples with this brazen appropriation of ragtime into white culture. 'Before the Negro succeeded fully in establishing his title as creator of his secular music, the form was taken away from him and made national *instead of* racial', he writes.[23] But despite attempts to occlude its African American roots, ragtime often remained a stubbornly racialized style.

While most studies of ragtime focus on the rowdy and male-dominated music halls, this racialized music was also performed in the antebellum parlour, such as the parlour of the white family's 'house at the crest of the Broadview Avenue hill in New Rochelle, New York' in *Ragtime*.[24] The house described in Doctorow's novel is the actual home in which the author lived while writing *Ragtime*; Doctorow and his family had inhabited this six-bedroom Victorian-Colonial home since 1964.[25] The author recalls struggling with writer's block while working on a new novel based on the life of James Pike, an outspoken Episcopal bishop who disappeared in the Judean Desert in 1969. Staring at the blank walls of his study, he began imagining

Pike's childhood in the early twentieth century. 'Suddenly I made the connection: "Hey! This house!" And all these images came to me. I was off on my book and it had nothing to do with James Pike.'[26] Through the blank walls, Doctorow began to chronicle the changing demographics of the surrounding city: the waves of immigration, industrialization and artistry that shifted the landscape of New York and its suburbs at the turn of the century, and the spectral negotiations of identity in this new world.[27]

The sheet music that would have been played in these parlours offers a rich, multifaceted site of cultural criticism, extending from the actual musical scores to the cover images, from systems of publication and distribution to performance practices. In the Victorian cult of domesticity that pressed into the early twentieth century, the parlour was a stage for middle-class families to perform their refinement and '[offer] "proof" that they understood how to be polite'.[28] 'We cannot imagine a model New England home without the family Bible on the table and the family piano in the corner', said Vice President Calvin Coolidge in the early 1920s.[29] Most families flaunted a parlour instrument and at least one accomplished (female) pianist, around whom husband, wife, sons and daughters gathered to act out the 'emerging national identity of family'.[30] The parlour piano symbolically aggregated middle-class values of a strong work ethic, as well as spiritual and moral fortitude, performed through the burgeoning genre of American popular song.[31]

Beginning in the 1830s and well established by the Civil War, blackface minstrel songs thrived in the market of US sheet music, positing race as a central cultural anxiety to be negotiated in musical performance. In popular minstrel numbers, white composers such as Stephen Foster (often considered the father of American music) constructed musical counter-images of Black family relations.[32] These songs lyrically suggested that African Americans were incapable of respectable familial bonds; they positioned Black relations in striking contrast to the normative white middle-class family gathered at the parlour piano.[33] The earliest sheet music explicitly labelled as 'ragtime' also consists of 'coon songs', which overlap and interact with the minstrel tradition. In the late nineteenth and early twentieth centuries vocal rags spread detrimental tropes of Black 'violence (especially with a razor), dishonesty, greed, gambling, shiftlessness, cowardliness, and sexual promiscuity'.[34] Denigrating musical portraits of African American life assured white families of their own propriety and superiority by comparison; only in nostalgic musicalizations of plantation life were African Americans characterized as noble and virtuous.

These persistent stereotypes played an active role in barring African Americans from full citizenship – particularly in the antebellum South. In fact, the state and local laws that maintained discriminatory practices into the twentieth century were nicknamed after the minstrel character Jim Crow. Originating among Black performers in the 1820s, Jim Crow was initially an emancipatory folk trickster, an 'agent for tribal Africans exploring their black mutualities within American unfreedom'.[35] Yet in the 1830s, Jim Crow was appropriated by white blackface performer Thomas 'Daddy' Rice. With racial anxieties heightened in the decades immediately preceding the Civil War, Rice's blackface routine swept the nation, and the popular song 'Jump Jim Crow' joined the domestic repertoire of racial stereotypes. After 'Jump Jim Crow' was published in 1832, an array of sheet music trading on the character followed. Persisting into the antebellum era, Jim Crow became a paradoxical icon, representing at once a liberated trickster and a clampdown on African American citizenship. The first published reference to the oppressive 'Jim Crow laws' date from the 1890s, towards the beginning of ragtime's reign.

Even in 'pure' instrumental compositions, the titles and cover images of ragtime sheet music perpetuated racist ideology. The word 'rag' was employed to simultaneously describe the 'ragged' or syncopated time of the music, the rags worn by the music's racialized originators and the rag-picking vocation. The cover of a 1903 composition by D. Haworth, for instance, contrasts the servile African American woman hanging her family's ragged laundry – which forms the title 'A Line of Rags' – to the pristine domestic space of the white family playing the song (Figure 4). And yet the sheet music

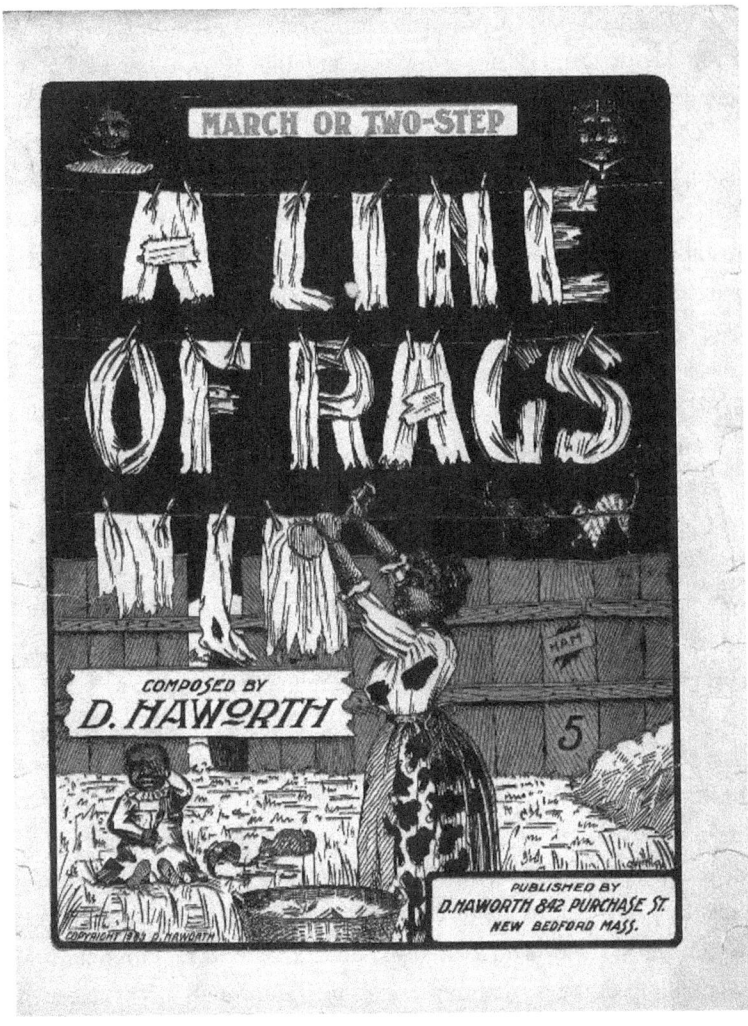

Figure 4 Cover of 'A Line of Rags' by D. Haworth, 1903. Courtesy of Historic American Sheet Music, David M. Rubenstein Rare Book & Manuscript Library, Duke University.

inside – a collection of black notes arranged in striking patterns across the white page – suggests a more complex relation being performed at the parlour piano. Much as the music articulates a syncopated melody within and against a regular metrical accompaniment, a ragtime song can pit racist lyrics, titles and cover images against a tune that stems from African American spirituals, plantation work songs and other African folk sources.[36]

African American composers strove to define ragtime as distinct from, and even in opposition to, 'coon songs', minstrel numbers and other stereotyped representations. Scott Joplin was a particularly key figure for instilling pride in the new musical style. Sheet music publisher John Stark purchased Joplin's 'Maple Leaf Rag' for $50 plus royalties in 1899; selling over a million copies, this piano rag catapulted Joplin to greater fame, praise and respect than any other ragtime composer, Black or white.[37] Stark & Son soon began advertising their sheet music as 'classic ragtime': a designation intended to elevate the art form and distance the music from racist representations, but not from its racial origins. Stark's 'House of Classic Rags' promised music that rivalled the European classics, fusing Black folk melodies and art music into an 'American' sound that was increasingly acceptable in the white middle-class home. A trend towards milder lyrics, downplayed dialect and fewer racialized titles and cover images developed with the rise of Joplin's classic rag style.[38]

No wonder Coalhouse Walker selects 'Wall Street Rag' and 'Maple Leaf Rag' by 'the great Scott Joplin' to showcase his piano skills for the white family in E.L. Doctorow's novel *Ragtime*.[39] Rather than cater to desires for a degrading 'coon song' to be played on their parlour piano, Coalhouse promises the white family an 'authentic' performance of a racialized music in which he can take pride. *Ragtime* the novel centres ragtime music in African American bodies and performs cross-cultural negotiations at the turn of the century in and through this syncopated sensation.

Ragtime: The novel

When *Ragtime* was published in 1975, E.L. Doctorow's panoramic American novel was awarded the National Book Critics Circle Award and became the bestselling novel of the year. Its experimental form intertwined historical and fictional characters in a cross-cultural tapestry of life in the United States in the early twentieth century. The book centres on three archetypical families: a white upper-class family in New Rochelle (Father, Mother, The Little Boy, Grandfather and Mother's Younger Brother); poor Jewish immigrants in pursuit of the American dream (Mameh, Tateh and The Little Girl); and a set of urban African Americans (ragtime pianist Coalhouse Walker Jr., his fiancée Sarah and their son). As these families' lives become indelibly intertwined, the fictional characters intermingle with historical symbols: the escape artist Harry Houdini, ex-chorus girl Evelyn Nesbit, anarchist Emma Goldman, psychoanalyst Sigmund Freud, industrialist Henry Ford and others. '"Ragtime" works – and works so effortlessly that one hesitates to take it apart', wrote the awestruck Christopher Lehmann-Haupt in *The New York Times*. 'Still, the questions persist: How does it work? Why do these historical images – half documentary-half invented – seem truer than the truth?'[40]

While many readers were entranced by Doctorow's imaginative history, other critics accused the author of wilfully confusing historical fact through a mongrel hybridization of fiction and non-fiction. Doctorow's 1977 essay 'False Documents' does not explicitly address *Ragtime*, but nonetheless defends the author's genre-bending style. Doctorow identifies two types of power in language: the power of the regime, which has a factual attachment to the real world, and the power of freedom, which imaginatively discloses 'what we threaten to become'.[41] These designative and evocative functions of language are not a strict binary; literature, for instance, blends and blurs the two. Yet in a technologically developed society that privileges empirical thought, fact and fiction are more firmly differentiated,[42] and literature is rendered ornamental rather than useful:

> Our primary control of writers in the United States [...] operates on the assumption that aesthetics is a limited arena where, according to the rules, we may be shocked or threatened, but only in fun. The novelist need not be taken seriously because his work appeals largely to

young people, women, intellectuals, and other pampered minorities, and, lacking any real currency, is not part of the relevant business of the nation.[43]

Doctorow yearns for a (perhaps mythical) ancient time when storytelling wielded social power, when 'it bound the present to the past, the visible with the invisible, and it helped to compose the community necessary for the continuing life of its members'.[44]

Yet for contemporary readers willing to ascribe truth value to fiction, Doctorow's work radiates something more penetrating and perceptive than historically established facts. Using the syncopated rhythms of ragtime as its organizing structure, *Ragtime* stages cross-cultural connections that wield the power of imaginative truth; his impressionistic history enlivens negotiations of class and ethnic identity during a period of heavy immigration and rapid industrialization at the turn of the century. In the end, Doctorow's work even obliterates the distinction between fact and fiction: all is narrative. Whenever a reader approaches Doctorow to ask, 'Did it happen? Did J.P. Morgan ever really meet Henry Ford?', he simply replies, 'He has now.'[45] These fantastical encounters are vitally re-embodied in the musical adaptation.

Ragtime: The musical

Producer Garth Drabinsky approached E.L. Doctorow with the idea of turning *Ragtime* into a musical in 1994. After being disappointed with the film adaptation in 1981, Doctorow hesitated at first, but he recalled the success of a few public readings he had performed with musical accompaniment – 'programs with excerpts from the book punctuated by musical interludes' – and he began to contemplate how music could contribute to a theatrical adaptation.[46] Doctorow agreed to a stage adaptation only if he had approval of the creative team and input throughout the writing process. Bookwriter Terrence McNally (*Love! Valour! Compassion!* and *Master Class*) was secured first, then Drabinsky invited composers and lyricists to audition for the job; from the demo tapes of eight teams, Drabinsky and Doctorow chose lyricist

Lynn Ahrens and composer Stephen Flaherty, whose previous work had included *Once on This Island* and *My Favorite Year*. Frank Galati, whose epic-scale Steppenwolf production of *The Grapes of Wrath* had impressed Doctorow in 1988, was signed as the director. It is notable that *Ragtime* stems from a white and Jewish creative team; even as Black music is centred in the musical, Black creatives are absent. (See Chapter 5 for further discussion of how the musical theatre industry is even more predominately white than 'straight theatre'.)

For Doctorow, the genre of musical theatre would mean a fundamental stylistic shift from the novel, which maintains a critical emotional distance through the use of third-person narrative and never differentiates what the characters say from what is narrated. Rather than subsuming the reader into a character's psychology, the book sweeps across subjectivities in short and simple sentences. Doctorow points out that, in contrast, 'it's not in the nature of musicals to keep their distance from the characters – where everyone sings how they feel. They love or hate or they're upset about something, and they'll sing it.'[47] Although McNally's libretto uses direct audience address and has characters speak in the third person, the theatrical adaptation also employs an 'integrated' emotional release into song as per generic convention. The musical nonetheless 'registers very clearly the American allegory that's implicit in the book', Doctorow believes.[48]

To be sure, the musical – considered a quintessentially 'American' art form – has been central to the construction of the United States' national mythos; national identity is even arguably the central theme of American musicals.[49] While European nationalism privileges a 'pure' strain of citizenship with a deep history tied to a specific landscape, the younger American nation promotes a melting pot model by which – in theory – anyone can become a citizen and attain the American dream of fame and fortune. The diverse components of this melting pot are spectacularly musicalized in the opening number of *Ragtime*. 'Prologue: Ragtime' introduces each of the story's intersecting ethnic groups – upper-middle-class whites, African Americans and Eastern European immigrants – sharing the same ragtime melody, but with divergent physicality, vocal styles and orchestration.

The original Broadway production begins with an oversized wooden stereopticon – a magic lantern or slide projector that dissolves between two projected images to create the illusion of depth – suspended in front of the proscenium. As this lens onto fantastical images of the past rises, a slow and simple piano rag floats from the orchestra pit, and The Little Boy enters the stage. He peers into a small stereopticon viewer of his own; images of a Victorian house appear on scrims upstage left and right, then cross and travel off to disclose the three-dimensional house upstage. The Little Boy narrates in direct address to the audience with a line adapted from the novel's first chapter: 'In 1902 Father built a house at the crest of the Broadview Avenue hill in New Rochelle, New York, and it seemed for some years thereafter that all the family's days would be warm and fair.'[50] 'Fair' links the pleasant atmosphere of the neighbourhood to the monolithic fair skin tone of its residents. In front of the mansion, the white upper-middle-class residents of New Rochelle pose for a photograph. Dressed in crisp cream costumes, the poised Victorians sing the gentle chromatic melody and syncopated ragtime rhythms with vocal reserve and propriety. Their 2/4 tune verges on a patriotic march, with chimes and light big band orchestration. Ragtime is still a 'distant music' for the white families of New Rochelle; the new music permeating the air is 'simple and somehow sublime', yet safely detached from their physical existence.[51]

After all, ragtime music originates not with these New Rochelle WASPs (white Anglo-Saxon Protestants), but with the urban African Americans who bound onstage in the next verse. This ensemble immediately signifies difference through earthen-coloured costumes, brash vocals and bold physicality. Coalhouse Walker thumps out the ragtime music with panache at an upright piano in a New York City nightclub. He narrates, 'In Harlem, men and women of color forgot their troubles and danced and reveled to the music of Coalhouse Walker, Jr. This was a music that was theirs and no one else's.'[52] The syncopated sounds vibrate in and through the African Americans' bodies; the orchestration mounts in liveliness and colour as the men punctuate the cymbal hits with high kicks and the ladies swing their hips and swirl their skirts in rhythm. Their jazzier sound and open movement exhibit greater improvisational freedom over the controlled musical structure established by the white chorus.

The third group to enter the stage is a group of Eastern European immigrants, dirty and weary, yet filled with hope as they board a rag ship bound for the United States. In this opening number, the immigrants are as dark and different from the pristine white Victorians as the African Americans; the Jews' heavy black coats and thick accents set them apart both visually and vocally. Their underscoring is additionally tinged with a Jewish klezmer sound; the violins voice a particularly sombre, straining melody (à la *Fiddler on the Roof*) as Tateh dreams of a brighter future for his Little Girl. 'It would be a long journey, a terrible one. He would not lose her, as he had her mother', he tells the audience.[53] The Latvian immigrants sway to the ragtime even as they are burdened with babies and luggage to transport to America.

After each ethnic group's distinctive style is introduced, differences in orchestration begin to be subsumed into one another and the ensembles sing together with increasing force:

> And there was music playing,
> Catching a nation in its prime …
> Beggar and millionaire,
> Everyone, everywhere
> Moving to the ragtime![54]

The last syllable of 'ragtime' lands on an F major chord, the V of the Bb major key signature. While the melody remains on the same pitch, the harmonic grounding is suddenly destabilized; the foundation is ripped away from this stable note and the tonality drastically shifts to an Ab^7 on the next downbeat – the V chord of the new Db major key. The performers' awareness of space shifts with this musical cue; while the ethnic groups have previously occupied their own imagined separate spheres of New Rochelle, Harlem and Latvia, Graciela Daniele choreographs a sudden change in focus by which these diverse communities (and the audience) realize that they share the same (national) stage.

A carnivalesque instrumental rag follows the key change, full of hemiolas that rhythmically spill over the barlines and spin into a series of uncomfortable encounters; the unassimilated groups find themselves in awkward moments of contact and confrontation. In this 'tense, tremulous dance', the whites, Blacks and Jewish immigrants cling to their own kind; the separate choruses weave around one another, testing boundaries of proximity but never mixing.[55] Even as they harmonize and occupy the same stage space, the groups remain stubbornly separate at the number's conclusion: the white ensemble commands centre stage, framed by the ethnic others with whom they will increasingly find themselves in contact and conflict over the course of the show.

Let us now set up our own stereopticon and fade across fiction and history, *Ragtime* and ragtime, to make visible the spectral negotiations of racial identity being worked out in and through this new music at the turn of the twentieth century.

Histories of integration

In his review for *Theater Journal,* Rick Simas calls *Ragtime* 'arguably the most perfectly structured and integrated musical play ever written'.[56] The choice of 'integrated' is notable, since this musical adaptation employs a formally integrated structure to consider the politics of racial integration at the turn of the century. Terrence McNally rightly traces the lineage of *Ragtime* to Jerome Kern and Oscar Hammerstein II's *Show Boat* (1927) and Rodgers and Hammerstein's *South Pacific* (1949), 'stories with a lot of plot, a moral fabric to the center of them and a real involvement with the society we live in' – that is to say, questions of national and racial identity.[57] These shows were also pioneers in the formal integration of the musical; both adapt a respected literary work (Edna Ferber's novel *Show Boat* and James A. Michener's short stories *Tales of the South Pacific*, respectively) into a 'seamless' *Gesamtkunstwerk* for the American stage.

As explored in Chapter 1, the 'integrated' musical is often hailed as the height of this artistic form. With the aim to minimize sensations of difference and disjuncture between theatrical elements, however, the formally integrated musical is a contentious model for considering racial integration on a narrative level. The form seems to promote a homogenizing melting pot: a model popularized by Israel Zangwill's *The Melting Pot*, first produced in 1909. In this play, music is an organizing metaphor for harmonizing ethnic differences. Russian-Jewish immigrant David Quixano, survivor of a pogrom, aims to occlude his past by imagining a bright American future in a symphony that blends ethnicities into a harmonious whole of the new American. Yet the symphony's title – 'The Crucible' – foretells the violence of this assimilation. One playbill illustration shows diversely coloured people streaming past the Statue of Liberty into a fiery crucible emblazoned with an eagle and American flag; swirling, separate strands of immigrants disappear into the sizzling pot, which will melt their differences into a normalized American citizen (Figure 5).

For numerous Jewish composers, writers, directors, actors and other musical theatre creators in the early twentieth century, this melting pot form of assimilation was a viable political option. By pushing the biological notion of race into a performative notion of ethnicity, first and second generation European immigrants such as Irving Berlin, George and Ira Gershwin, Jerome Kern and Leonard Bernstein performed their way into popular American culture. These artists pioneered a genre of musical theatre that grappled with anxieties of difference and offered opportunities for imaginative self-invention; the Broadway stage enabled Jews to envision an ideal nation and write themselves into that imagined community.[58] 'Jews' had disappeared from view onstage by the late 1930s, having effectively 'become white' by performing themselves into the culture; since Jews' 'otherness' was not tied to skin colour, adopting alternate personas in mainstream white culture was a distinct possibility.[59] Yet this mode of performative assimilation notably foreclosed African Americans, Asian Americans,

Figure 5 Cover of the theatre programme for Israel Zangwill's play *The Melting Pot*, 1916. Courtesy of Special Collections, the University of Iowa Libraries.

Latin Americans and other divergent races that were visually marked as different from the imagined white ideal.

In E.L. Doctorow's *Ragtime*, Tateh embodies this American dream of assimilation – although his path to cultural acceptance, fame and fortune is tumultuous. Upon first arriving in America with his wife and daughter, Tateh peddles silhouettes on the streets of New York and struggles to make ends meet. He disowns his wife after learning that she is prostituting herself for additional money, and his sickly daughter nearly dies in the crowded tenements of the Lower East Side; she is nursed back to health by celebrity Evelyn Nesbit, who temporarily sustains the family by commissioning dozens of silhouettes of herself and The Little Girl. After years of backbreaking labour and increasing disillusionment with the American dream, Tateh finally begins to turn a profit by binding his silhouettes into movie books, and he later becomes a director in the burgeoning film industry. Like the escape artist Harry Houdini, and like the Jewish composers, playwrights and performers of the Broadway stage, Tateh navigates his assimilation into America through the entertainment industry; by producing new fictions, he and other Jewish immigrants performatively negotiate their way into the culture.[60]

Tateh's new American persona requires reframing his identity and erasing his past as a working-class immigrant. He dyes his hair and beard to conceal his world-weary looks. He renames himself the Baron Ashkenazy, inventing an exotic and royal lineage that allows his Yiddish accent to pass as an elevated foreign inflection, rolling off his tongue 'with a flourish'.[61] Even more importantly, Tateh incorporates himself into the American capitalist system by founding a new film company: Buffalo Nickel Photoplay, Inc. 'He was a new man', Doctorow writes. 'He pointed a camera. His child was dressed as beautifully as a princess. He wanted to drive from her memory every tenement stench and filthy immigrant street. He would buy her light and sun and clean wind of the ocean for the rest of her life.'[62]

When *Ragtime* was adapted for the musical stage, issues of formal and racial integration were compounded precisely by the 'Inc.' – the commercialization of the art form and the increasing vertical integration of the theatrical industry in the early 1990s. Rather than an 'organic' writing process originating with the authors, *Ragtime* originated with the production company Livent – the Live Entertainment Corporation of Canada, Inc. – which primed spectacular mega productions such as *Kiss of the Spider Woman, Fosse* and a wildly successful revival of *Show Boat* for Toronto, the West End and Broadway. Livent represented a new corporate presence on the Great White Way, pioneered by Disney Theatricals in 1994 with *Beauty and the Beast*. The musical adaptation of *Ragtime* had been in the public eye since 1995 with public readings, workshops, a cast recording, a 1996 production in Toronto, and a 1997 production at the Ahmanson Theater in Los Angeles. This systematic development of the show contributed to an early critical backlash, and its slick corporate production values seemed particularly at odds with the story's socialist leanings.[63] For Ben Brantley, the carefully constructed spectacle resulted in 'less a celebration of theater per se than of theatrical technology and its smooth manipulation'. He even compared *Ragtime*'s production process to that of a Model T Ford – fresh off the assembly line and loaded with mechanical wonders, but lacking heart and humanity.[64]

The musical's deradicalization of Tateh's path to success is another cause for concern; it partakes in a sentimental understanding of the immigrant experience that reinscribes the American dream while eliding the realities of racial injustice and the limitations of the social class system in America.[65] The promiscuous Mameh is eliminated from the musical, and Tateh's socialist affiliations are countered; in the stage version, he tells anarchist Emma Goldman, 'Trade unions are fine but they are not for me. [...] I was in your socialist frying pan over there; I'm not jumping into the same fire over here.'[66] In the musical, Tateh is an apolitical figure driven solely by a desire to provide for his family. His troubles are only temporary, easily smoothed over by the gentle waltz 'Gliding'. This song provides a release from his and his daughter's financial challenges; Tateh's musical imaginary of a brighter future becomes reality when the old man sells his first flipbooks of silhouettes midway through the song. 'Gliding' sweeps into a full and hopeful chorus:

> And we're
> Gliding,
> Gliding far away.
> Pirouettes,
> Figure eights,
> Silver skates
> Just down the track.
> Glide with me, little one.
> Glide with your Tateh.
> We'll never
> Look back![67]

The skating image is derived from the novel, which also emphasizes Tateh's desire to erase all traces of the past as he moves into the future.[68]

Still, the music of 'Gliding' contains its own trace of Tateh's past that cannot be so easily elided. The major key tune closes on an unexpected minor chord, and a mournful clarinet repeats the melody of 'A Shtetl is Amerike', echoing the klezmer sounds of the immigrants' earlier musical numbers. Tateh's heritage musically strains into his present, and his new American identity is legislated through the painful remembrance of his 'original status as alien, other, illegitimate'.[69] This musical phrase is not only a ghosting from a song earlier in *Ragtime* but also a musical citation of a popular Yiddish theatre song 'Lebn Zol Kolumbus' (Long Live Columbus!) with lyrics by Boris Thomashefsky, music by Arnold Perlmutter and Herman Wohl. Translated from Yiddish, it begins:

> America is a *shtetl*
> Where, I swear, life is great.
> The Divine rests on her;
> We should all get to live so.[70]

Introduced in the 1915 musical comedy *Der Grine Milyoner* (*The New Millionaire*), this song digs into the contradictions of the immigrant experience and the American dream with tongue in cheek. Although the sarcastic tone is stripped away in *Ragtime*, this musical haunting nonetheless points to the conflicted process of becoming American; the road to the American dream of fame and fortune is far from a seamless glide into the future. If 'everything in the theatre, the bodies, the materials utilized, the language, the space itself, is now and has always been haunted', as Marvin Carlson suggests, then musical theatre is a particularly haunted genre; it can multiply the ghostly presences at play through musical pastiche.[71] Specific songs and musical styles can drag personal and cultural memory into the present, troubling a homogeneous conception of time and disturbing a present that strives to ignore the past.

Haunting me, just like a melody

Music is, in fact, framed as a 'haunting' in the musical adaptation of *Ragtime*.[72] Early in the narrative, Mother finds a Black baby buried in her garden: Sarah and Coalhouse's illegitimate son. Rather than turn Sarah over to the police for attempted murder, Mother takes responsibility for the single mother and her child. As Coalhouse expresses regret for abandoning Sarah and longs to re-establish their relationship, he frames this woman – and music – as a spectral return:

> Now she is haunting me
> Just like a melody –
> The only song I seem to know.
> Sarah, my life has changed.
> Sarah, I miss you so.
> Sarah, I did you wrong.
> Sarah, where did you go?[73]

The tender rag introduced in this moment, gently vacillating between major and minor keys, echoes across the score of *Ragtime*; the melody returns at peak narrative moments and traces the shifting relationship between Coalhouse and Sarah, as well as between the African American and white communities.

When Coalhouse learns of Sarah's location in New Rochelle, he immediately hops into his new Model T to find her. 'Such was the coming of the colored man in the car to Broadview Avenue' and the emergence of the African American into the white middle class.[74] Coalhouse begins driving to New Rochelle every Sunday to woo the stubborn Sarah with his music, and Mother's Younger Brother is shocked to hear the racialized, urban sounds of ragtime – familiar from his nightlife in New York City – reverberating throughout his sister's home. In the musical adaptation of *Ragtime*, Coalhouse plays his own ragtime composition rather than Scott Joplin's acclaimed music. His reprise of Sarah's haunting melody symbolically domesticates the African American pianist, who is now ready to build a nuclear family with Sarah and his child. This 'New Music' simultaneously delineates a transformation in the white family:

> YOUNGER BROTHER:
> His fingers stroke those keys
> And every note says, 'Please,'
> And every chord says, 'Turn my way.'
> MOTHER, FATHER:
> I thought I knew
> What love was
> But these lovers play
> MOTHER, FATHER, YOUNGER BROTHER:
> New music!
> Haunting me,
> And somehow taunting me –
> My love was never half as true.
> FATHER:
> And I ask myself,
> Why can't I sing it, too.[75]

Coalhouse's new music demands attention; his piano playing not only draws Sarah back to his arms, but invokes the white family's participation in the performance, enacting a complex negotiation of ethnic identities at their parlour piano.

Although McNally, Ahrens and Flaherty aimed for an equal balance among storylines in adapting Doctorow's novel for the stage, Coalhouse's courtship of Sarah has an emotional heft that undeniably foregrounds the African Americans – particularly with the star-making performances of Brian Stokes Mitchell and Audra McDonald in the 1998 original Broadway production. In the novel, Coalhouse and his lover Sarah are the only characters to be given names rather than subject positions, which further individualizes their roles.[76] The music of the entire show also stems from African American bodies; a 2016 London production even used actor-musicians to emphasize the music's essential embodiment. 'It was a sort of dream of mine to realize *Ragtime* as an actor-musician show', director Thom Southerland says. 'The lyrics are all about how the music defined these people.'[77] In their pitch to Ahrens and Flaherty, Southerland and producer Danielle Tarento wrote that a crucial stage direction in the opening number of *Ragtime* – 'COALHOUSE WALKER, JR., *is playing for a lively crowd of dancers*' – had always been a lie, with the music emanating from a pianist in the pit rather than from the character's fingertips.[78] In their production, Coalhouse would truly play; this African American music would undeniably belong to the Black bodies onstage.

Ragtime music could be considered a turn-of-the-century 'audiotopia', holding out the promise of a vibrant, hybrid, multicultural future in the United States. In fact, popular music is one of our most valuable sites for performing racial and ethnic difference against the grain of national citizenships that aim to silence those differences.[79] Working within and against ongoing racial prejudice, ragtime produced a space for racial negotiations in the late nineteenth and early twentieth centuries; in this music, white Americans could potentially encounter, inhabit and learn from the racialized others in the nation.[80] Even the simple act of listening is a performance of negotiation, a way of confronting different worlds and interrogating identity; in their encounter with ragtime music, white middle-class Americans performed what we might call an act of rhizomatic listening: listening across genres and identities with an understanding and perhaps a new-found appreciation of racial difference.[81]

Yet it is unlikely that an African American pianist such as Coalhouse would be invited into a white middle-class home in the early 1900s. A wide array of media and new technologies at the turn of the century – from sheet music to phonograph records to piano rolls – mediated the encounter and separated a racialized musician from a white consumer. Doctorow's historical fiction nonetheless wields an imaginative truth: phantom racial negotiations were being performed through the syncopated sensation of ragtime in the white domestic sphere. In addition to the popularity of ragtime sheet music played on traditional pianos, the player piano offers a particularly complex, layered location to consider the process of 'ragging race' in the early 1900s. African American composers were often spectral performers on these popular domestic instruments, and the heavy breath of the machine points back to their labour and artistry.

The player piano

As an early twentieth-century Aeolian Company advertisement touts, 'Grand and light operas, Liszt's Rhapsodies, Sousa's marches, and the latest rag-time hits are practically "on your fingers' ends"' with this new technology.[82] From roughly 1897 to the stock market crash in 1929, the automatic player piano instigated a new musical democracy, allowing amateurs and even the musically uneducated to enjoy a wide range of musical performances in their home. Take, for instance, E.L. Doctorow's account of adventurer Admiral Peary performing on the player piano in his comfortable stateroom:

> He was a large man with a heavy torso and thick red hair turning gray. He wore a long moustache. In a previous expedition he had lost his toes. He walked with an odd gait, a kind of shuffle, pushing his feet along the floor without lifting them. He pedaled his player piano with

toeless feet. He was supplied with rolls of the best Victor Herbert and Rudolf Friml numbers as well as a medley of Bowdoin College songs and a version of *The Minute Waltz* of Chopin which he could pump out in forty-eight seconds.[83]

As Peary's collection demonstrates, piano rolls encompassed an array of styles, from classical music to contemporary operetta. Yet one of the most popular styles was undoubtedly ragtime, whose reign from 1896 to 1917 closely coincides with that of the player piano.[84] Like sheet music, these piano rolls are more than simply static products; they enlivened a series of complex and embodied performative processes.

Advertisements of early twentieth-century player pianos foreground the act of mediated, liminally embodied performance and focus on the instrument's domestic use: 'A Player Piano is the Heart of a Happy Home', according to the Standard Pneumatic Action Co.[85] These adverts present at least three overlapping understandings of the new technology:

1. Possession and control: emphasizing the piano operator's control over the machine/music;
2. Mediated presence: emphasizing the machine's human touch and even the composer's unique touch coming through the machine/music; and
3. Collaboration between the machine and the operator/player in the production of music.

To these advertising statements, I will add a fourth category engendered by frequent slippage among the machine, the music and the spectral composer/musician:

4. Collaboration between the (racialized) musician/composer and the operator/player.

Ragging race on the player piano is never reducible to a site of African American enslavement or liberatory self-presentation, but a constructive site to imagine mediated encounters and racial negotiations at the turn of the century.

Possession and control

Excitement about the new technology of the player piano prompted advertisements touting the owner's complete control over the machine and music. 'The ability to play any and every kind of music becomes yours immediately', brags one advert.[86] Years of laborious study are rendered unnecessary by this 'universally' accessible machine; a child can crawl up to the keys to play like a professional with the simple flip of a switch, as can a toeless Admiral Peary.[87] Advertisements often credit the operator/player with control over not only the selection of music but also the creative expression, or 'soul', of the music: 'The operation of the Cecilian is perfectly simple and yet its musical performance is artistic in every sense of the word. It is under your absolute control all the time.'[88] Particularly in the case of African American composers, this fetishistic control of the machine can be read as an ongoing, mediated form of slavery, erasing the problematic racialized body after extracting its productive artistic labour. The physical labour behind the music – years of studying piano, in addition to composing, rehearsing, playing and cutting the piano roll – is occluded; the resultant product is stripped of its history, replicated, commercialized and consumed in white American households across the nation.

Mediated presence

Alongside the excitement of a new mechanization was an undeniable anxiety about this reproductive technology's displacement of the artist; this tension is perhaps epitomized by Benjamin's 'Work of Art in the Age of Mechanical Reproduction', mourning the artwork's loss of unique presence and aura.[89] Industrial anxieties thus prompted another trend in advertising: insistence on the musician/composer's mediated presence at the keys.

The earliest player pianos were detachable 'push up' machines with mechanical 'hands' that performed on a free-standing piano.[90] 'The Pianola does not injure the piano in any way', one advert assures. 'Its felt-covered fingers rest upon the piano keys and strike the notes in the proper relation one to another as indicated on the music-sheet.'⁹¹ Advertisements frequently claimed that the mechanical hands would perform 'just as the fingers of the performer strike' and touch down on the piano 'as a human musician'.⁹² Later models were enclosed within the piano case, sometimes requiring an operator to pump the bellows, sometimes requiring simply the push of a button to begin the musical entertainment. By about 1907, player pianos had developed more extensive controls for tempo, phrasing, dynamics and pedal effects to replicate 'the full virtuosity of the artist – the nuances, the phrasing, and all the shadings'.⁹³

In addition to work by arrangers, piano rolls were 'recorded' by renowned composers and pianists. Early technologies notated music via pencil markings created by the depression of the keys in performance; these markings were then cut to become functional piano rolls.⁹⁴ As the notation process grew more precise, Ampico's spark chronograph technique transcribed a performer's key and pedal movements, as well as the hammer velocity of the keys, leading the company to claim their instruments' 'perfect recording *plus perfect re-enactment*'.⁹⁵ The Duo-Art similarly marketed the artist's 'individuality', 'style and identity' coming through the instrument, while the slogan, 'The Master's Fingers On Your Piano' succinctly captured the Welte-Mignon's advertising campaign that 'the artist himself is playing' the family's parlour piano.⁹⁶

Beyond the domestic sphere, the mediated presence of the musician/composer was marketed for studio and conservatory training: 'What would it be worth to the Teacher or the Conservatory of Music to have such an artist as Ornstein ready to play for the pupils at a moments [*sic*] notice?' asks a 1925 Ampico advert. The Aeolian and American Piano companies even collaborated in a series of promotional concerts in the late 1910s, featuring the Duo-Art and Ampico player pianos as 'unmanned soloists' with the Philadelphia Orchestra, New York Symphony and San Francisco Symphony orchestras. Preceding the high-fidelity phonograph and magnetic tape recorder, the reproducing piano was the most advanced technology available to document virtuoso performances. 'Those fortunate enough today to hear a restored instrument perform a recording cut by Gershwin, Rachmaninoff,

Paderewski, Debussy, Scriabin, Grieg, Busoni, or others will be shocked by the ghostly realism', assures historian Craig Roell.[97]

In fact, early twentieth-century advertisements sometimes portray the composer as a ghost, occupying a liminal space between embodiment and disembodiment, presence and absence, Benjaminian aura and mechanization. In one advert, a phantom musician poises his hands above the keys: 'The Apollo Reproducing Piano Brings to Your Home the Playing of' numerous renowned European composers (Figure 6).

Figure 6 Apollo Reproducing Piano advertisement. Courtesy of *The Literary Digest*, vol. 71, 1 October 1921, 51.

Now mentally replace this 'European genius' with 'classic' ragtime composers Scott Joplin, Jelly Roll Morton or Eubie Blake. Suddenly, a racialized spectre has entered the white middle-class American home, delighting the family with the latest ragtime tunes. In none of the advertisements that I have examined are African American musician/composers portrayed or even named, but their spectral presence is imaginable given this popular marketing technique.

Collaboration between the machine and operator/player

Echoing both Adorno and Benjamin, Roell posits mechanical reproduction in the player piano as a revolutionary – and detrimental – transition from an active musical culture to 'passive music for a consumer society'.[98] Yet early player models required – and were often advertised – as an active *collaboration* between machine/music and operator/player. 'The average person of today wants to take an active part in his pleasures – does not want too much done for him', suggests one advert. 'The Pianola Piano demands intelligent co-operation on the part of its performer. *It does not merely play itself* – the *performer* plays it; puts into the music the best expression that is in him, and takes keen personal satisfaction in the musical results that he achieves.'[99] Artis Wodehouse, a pianist and harmoniumist known for reclaiming music and instruments from the past, even 'played' her Gershwin piano rolls nearly a hundred times in rehearsal for a performance on a 1911 player piano.[100] Sitting at the piano, pumping the bellows and manipulating the expression levers creates an undeniably active engagement with the composer's pre-recorded performance; Roell acknowledges a certain art to the player piano performance, requiring intimate familiarity with the music and the instrument to achieve the desired sound.

In fact, the player piano challenges the notion of a solitary artistic genius without entirely destroying acknowledgement of or appreciation for artistry. This new technology blurs categories of composer, performer, editor/arranger and technician; where does one role end and another begin?[101] This confusion between machine and human, the pre-recorded performance on the piano roll and the live performance of the human pumping the bellows, creates a boundary-crossing series of productive artistic possibilities.[102] The collapsed lines among composer/musician, the machine and the player/operator of the piano engender an even more challenging site of negotiations in the turn-of-the-century United States when a racialized spectre haunts the machine.

Collaboration between the (racialized) musician/composer and the operator/player

By ragging race on the player piano, does the white upper-middle-class operator/player displace the African American composer's body and occlude the labour behind the music and the machine? Does the operator/player honour the Black musician's work? Or does the operator/player engage in a mediated collaboration with the spectral composer, musician and/or arranger of the ragtime roll? The phantom linkage between white middle-class musical amateurs and African American ragtime composers at the parlour player piano is a densely layered space of cultural negotiation at the turn of the twentieth century. With every pump of the bellows or flip of an expressive switch, the operator/player collaborated in the production of ragtime, both exerting control over and newly appreciating the sounds produced, both cognizant and forgetful of the music's racialized origins. The ghost in the machine is simultaneously past and present, visible and invisible, dead and yet very much alive.

The American parlour player piano can thus be considered an 'almost-place' of cultural encounter, bringing together typically incompatible sites in a musical space of utopian aspirations.[103] Fraught and palimpsestic, ragtime music encodes the convergences and contradictions of ongoing racial negotiations at the turn of the century, the hopes and dreams as well as the inherent violence: a steady bass underpinning a syncopated melody, always threatening to veer off course.

Ragging race

In E.L. Doctorow's novel, Mother's Younger Brother feels these conflicting ragtime rhythms as he balances between train cars en route to New Rochelle:

> He considered throwing himself under the wheels. He listened to their rhythm, their steady clacking, like the left hand of a rag. The screeching and pounding of metal on metal where the two cars joined was the syncopating right hand. It was a suicide rag. He held the door handles on either side of him listening to the music.[104]

Rather than simply employ music as a metaphor for harmonizing differences, the novel and musical adaptation draw continual attention to ragtime as 'a rhythmic *process* as well as a genre'. To 'rag' a tune is to syncopate a 'regular' melody, to modify time, to insert difference.[105] The music's intense participatory negotiations are rife with disturbances played out in the pianist's body, and the music actively engages tensions of rhythmic and racial difference.

Coalhouse Walker becomes newly attuned to the discrepancies in these rhythms when a group of white firemen, led by fire chief Willie Conklin, vandalizes the 'uppity' Black man's Model T Ford. What provokes the firemen is not so much Coalhouse's race as his brash disavowal of both race and class; as the African American pianist presses his way into the white middle class, 'apparently it did not occur to him to ingratiate himself'.[106] Yet Coalhouse's cries of injustice go unheeded in the white courts. His mounting awareness of social barriers escalates into an armed rebellion – a portent of the Black Nationalist movement in Doctorow's contemporary moment – that costs numerous lives. In Act II of the musical adaptation, Coalhouse is emboldened to violent retribution, particularly for the murder of his fiancée Sarah. 'Coalhouse's Soliloquy' comprises choppy musical hauntings of the pianist's unfulfilled dreams: Sarah's impassioned song 'Your Daddy's Son', Sarah and Coalhouse's hopeful anthem 'Wheels of a Dream', and the exuberant opening 'Prologue'. Over the course of the Black man's musical breakdown, this mash-up of melodies grows increasingly cynical and aggressive. 'Coalhouse's Soliloquy' can be read as a suicide rag; as the ideal life Coalhouse once dreamed comes crashing down, the clashing rhythms accumulate. But 'suicide' is a misnomer: similar to Bruce Bechdel in *Fun Home*, Coalhouse is placed in an impossibly inharmonious narrative situation, which generates the sensation of a linear 'inevitability' leading to his death.[107]

Increasingly agitated, Coalhouse and his followers ultimately occupy J.P. Morgan's library, a symbolic bastion of (white) history that contains such treasures as a Gutenberg Bible, four Shakespeare folios and a letter written by George Washington.[108] These African American anarchists threaten to destroy centuries of historical artefacts with bombs provided by Mother's Younger Brother, an explosives expert at Father's patriotic fireworks factory. If Coalhouse blows up the Morgan Library, he will die in the explosion; if he reduces his demands and surrenders, he is at the mercy of the white policemen surrounding the building. At this tragic crossroads, Sarah and her haunting melody return in 'Sarah Brown Eyes'. This musical dream sequence physicalizes the memory of Coalhouse and Sarah's first meeting: a gentle romance of ragtime and dance: a narrative respite that stops time to temporarily defer her – and his – death. But the spectral Sarah's song fades into the clang and clatter of an elevated train all too soon, snapping Coalhouse back to reality like the jerky sensation of the suicide rag. The plot charges forward to Coalhouse's demise; when his Model T Ford is restored, Coalhouse exits the library and is met with a volley of percussive shots that instantly kill him. In the 2016 London production, the shattering violence of Coalhouse's murder – and his sudden absence from stage – felt all the more present in light of Black Lives Matter, a movement launched in 2013 in response to police brutality against Black bodies.

With both Sarah and Coalhouse dead, the surviving Black baby is left to Mother and Tateh, who are newly united after Father passes away on an expedition. Raymond Knapp theorizes the 'divorce trope' as a parallel to the 'marriage trope' of conventional Golden Age musicals. While the marriage trope uses the union of a heteronormative couple as a synecdoche of broader social relations, the divorce trope uses the splintering of a relationship to facilitate a newly liberated musical world for the once disempowered female, who can now construct her own musical alternative to the 'real' (male-dominated) world.[109] In *Ragtime*, the divorce trope and the marriage trope work in tandem; several splintered relationships enable Mother to choose her life partner, and the successful immigrant film-maker completes his national assimilation by marrying into the white family. The musical's ending offers a sentimental vision of racial conflict being harmoniously resolved in a rapturous reprise of Sarah and Coalhouse's anthem, 'Wheels of a Dream'. Although Sarah and Coalhouse have passed away, their son will ride into a bright utopian tomorrow.

In the final stage image of the original Broadway production, the miscegenated nuclear family strolls into the sunset as the era of ragtime draws to a close. Yet the embodied performance of this finale incorporates the ghosts of Sarah and Coalhouse, whose presence can potentially disturb the musical's forward-looking vision. Which histories, voices and bodies have been occluded in a 'steady march' into the future? What spectral stories have been elided? Can musical memory sweep us back to the tense and haunted negotiations of race at the turn of the century, and can an anthem encode unfinished visions of social justice still in need of reprises beyond the theatre? Perhaps we should locate the utopian potential of *Ragtime* not in its sentimentally harmonized narrative conclusion, which strikes a particularly jarring and false chord today, but in its model of an imaginative historiography that always exceeds a neatly 'integrated' narrative and compels us to acknowledge and take responsibility for our cultural ghosts as they persist in our present.

4

'I Just Projected Myself Out of It': Rehearsing Identities in Youth Musical Theatre

SUE: *High school is a caste system. Kids fall into certain slots. Your jocks and your popular kids, up in the penthouse. The invisibles and the kids playing live-action druids and trolls out in the forest? Bottom floor.*

WILL: *And where do the Glee kids lie?*

SUE: *Sub-basement.*

'Pilot', *Glee*[1]

For cheerleading coach Sue Sylvester, musical performers fall even lower than dorky sci-fi/fantasy fans in the high school hierarchy. Like the subjectivity of the white gay male show queen explored in Chapter 1, the pecking order of high schoolers – from the popular football players and cheerleaders to the marginalized musical theatre fans – is a persistent stereotype of the contemporary public education system in the United States. As Sue is quick to quip, liking showtunes doesn't make you gay, 'It just makes you awful.'[2] How did the American musical, once a pinnacle of mainstream popular culture, come to be so marginalized in the early twenty-first century? And who are these strange theatre geeks and self-identified Gleeks who persist in belting from the sub-basement of the high school social strata?

The marginalization of the musical in millennial youth culture – and the attendant marginalization of its young fans – can be traced to at least two intertwined issues: a sharp divide between showtunes and contemporary popular music, and a sidelining of the arts in the US public education system. During the early decades of the twentieth century, musical theatre and popular music were coextensive. Tin Pan Alley composers churned out songs that were performed on the Broadway stage and published as sheet music that spread across the nation. Popular singers such as Ella Fitzgerald and Frank Sinatra recorded the emerging American songbook of hits by composers such as Irving Berlin, Cole Porter, and George and Ira Gershwin, which were easily extractable from the revues and musical comedies in which they were introduced. With the rise of the integrated musical in the 1940s, original cast albums tracked songs in the show order (or in an order that made narrative sense for the record) and sometimes included dialogue to provide narrative context; the record sleeves featured plot summaries and photographs that allowed the listener to imagine the Broadway show coming to life in their home. Extracting these integrated songs into popular music became more difficult as lyrics were more closely tied to character and plot.[3] Still, original cast albums and musical soundtracks topped the US LP charts throughout the 1950s and 1960s. *South Pacific* – in original cast album and film soundtrack forms – was Number 1 for over two years and stayed in the charts for over thirteen years in total, while *The Sound of Music* and *My Fair Lady* remained in the charts for almost a dozen years.[4]

Yet popular music criticism of the 1950s and 1960s rarely included Rodgers and Hammerstein, Lerner and Loewe, or Meredith Willson; the rise of rock 'n' roll began to overshadow and even elide musical theatre's ongoing popularity. From the 1960s onwards, the musical was increasingly relegated to a 'Golden Age' earlier on the timeline of music history. In other words, musical theatre was confined to the past while rock 'n' roll propelled popular music into a divergent future.[5] Nostalgic show queens exacerbate the musical's relegation to the past by hailing the death of musical theatre post-1970; the very title of Ethan Mordden's *The Happiest Corpse I've Ever Seen: The Last Twenty-Five Years of the Broadway Musical* denies the possibility that the genre might still live in the present in revivals, revisals (revised revivals) and new musicals.[6] Juggernauts *Hamilton* and *Six* aside, musical theatre today is often imagined not only as separate from contemporary popular music but as a relic of a previous generation; the genre can have a distinctly anachronistic charge.[7] Musical theatre is a strange genre out of time and out of place. So, too, are its contemporary fans.

Teenage musical theatre fans are perhaps most affected by the genre's anachronistic associations. While teens are culturally and commercially expected to follow the latest popular music trends, young musical theatre fans identify instead – or, in some cases, also – with a passé genre. While their friends keep up with the Billboard Hot 100 and the latest music videos, show queen teens add to their cast album collection of Broadway shows, old and new. They scour YouTube for bootleg videos of performances by their favourite actors; and, in the absence of fellow musical theatre friends in their (small, middle of nowhere) hometowns, they solidify their fandom with digital communities on TikTok, Twitter, Tumblr, Facebook, and message boards such as All That Chat and BroadwayWorld.com. A sprawling cross-platform creative universe called Averno (encompassing TikTok, Instagram, Spotify, YouTube and more) has become an exciting locus of new musical theatre development in 2020 – but curiously, its teenage writers are still reticent to openly embrace the genre. 'I'm not really interested in musicals', says Averno creator and musical theatre writer Morgan Smith. 'I'm interested in telling stories that use music to further an emotion. I'm not trying to write the perfect Broadway standard – I'm trying to tell the best story I can.'[8] Sounds suspiciously like a musical to me.

Mickey Rapkin, author of *Theater Geek: The Real Life Drama of a Summer at Stagedoor Manor, the Famous Performing Arts Camp*, identifies the first use of 'theater geek' in a 1995 *Washington Times* tribute to director, playwright and producer George Abbott. But the term theatre geek was in colloquial use years earlier: sometimes as a pejorative label, sometimes reclaimed as a self-empowering identification. Rapkin's book begins with his own 'coming out' as a theatre geek: crying during the opening to *Les Miserables* in 1994 as he 'imagined the raw anticipation, the all-for-one camaraderie, the happy thrill those lucky few actors must have felt to do what they loved eight times a week'.⁹ Being a theatre geek is more than just being 'a different breed of kid', as Stagedoor Manor camp director Barb Martin suggests: it marks a desire for a different way of life.¹⁰ Rapkin defines theatre geeks by a longing cultivated from a young age: a desire for theatricality and fantasy, and a community with whom to share those dreams.¹¹ In the late twentieth and early twenty-first century without significant representation in mainstream media, theatre geeks seemed to be few and far between.

In *The Geeks Shall Inherit the Earth*, Alexandra Robbins develops the notion of 'quirk theory' to describe those 'geeks, loners, punks, floaters, nerds, freaks, dorks, gamers, bandies, art kids, theater geeks, choir kids, Goths, weirdos, indies, scenes, emos, skaters, and various types of racial and other minorities' who are rejected from a school's in-crowd.¹² Although an ever-expanding set of subcultural labels is now available to describe teenage identities, the high school hierarchy still frequently collapses into a binary of popular and unpopular – and the theatre geeks usually fall on the unpopular side of the divide.¹³ Quirk theory suggests that the differences that cause a student to be scorned in school are precisely the qualities that others will value in adulthood and outside of school: artistry, creativity and innovation.¹⁴ Yet quirk theory relies on a promise of futurity; it validates students' refusal to conform to the status quo with the confidence that their lives can improve once they leave the educational system.¹⁵ Much like the It Gets Better Project, quirk theory promises a brighter future for teenage outsiders while struggling to answer the more critical question: what can be done to improve their *present*?¹⁶

However cliché, the arts can be a safe haven for these outsider identities.¹⁷ In the visual and performing arts, participants can create divergent realities, imagine different ways of being and establish affective communities. Yet the US public education system often fails to cultivate the free time and space for youth involvement in the arts. With the passing of the No Child Left Behind (NCLB) Act in 2001, high-stakes testing began to emphasize core academic subjects to the detriment of arts education.¹⁸ A 2008 survey of 349 public school districts found that 58 per cent of districts increased instructional time for reading and language arts and 45 per cent increased instructional time for mathematics since the NCLB Act was passed, while arts instructional time decreased by 16 per cent.[19] Though the law was replaced in 2015, the systemic damage remains. Standardized curriculum and testing create a high school assembly line, mechanically moving students from grade to grade while allowing little creative divergence from the regimented norm. Perhaps it is no surprise that many students perceive life 'as "a conveyor belt," making monotonous scheduled stops at high school, college, graduate school, and a series of jobs until death'.[20] Along this linear trajectory, the arts are framed as hobbies to be practiced in leisure time, but they are considered frivolous and inessential to a 'real' education, normative career or productive life. Teenagers with talents and interests in these neglected disciplines are often marginalized not only by their peers but also by the overarching educational system that structures much of their childhood existence.

This chapter explores the fictionalizations of marginalized youth musical theatre communities in the cult movie *Camp* (2003) and the hit television show *Glee* (2009–15). In these delightfully campy productions, the teenagers who identify with and participate in the arts are outsiders defined by alternative sexualities and other differences from the popular jock and cheerleader mould. As I explore in Chapter 1, musical theatre's identificatory charge for such spectators often derives from its hybrid layering of the arts: a shifting array of scene, song, dance, design and other elements. The exuberant, exhibitionist performance of a musical number can diverge from a linear, language-dominant narrative to offer a compelling site of aesthetic and temporal difference that enables marginalized and semi-marginalized subjects to imagine different ways of being in the world. In *Camp* and *Glee*, musical numbers are glimmering sites of transformative potential that punctuate the dreary, linear high school trajectory. Quirky teens can rehearse new subjectivities and forge alternative communities in the quasi-utopic time and space of the musical. Singing and dancing can make the fleeting present not only bearable, but beautiful – no matter what they say.

Camping it up at *Camp*

'Who *are* you people? What planet did you beam down from?' disillusioned musical theatre camp counsellor Bert Hanley asks in the cult favourite *Camp*.[21] When writer/director Todd Graff's indie film premiered on a grand total of three screens across the United States in 2003, teenage show queens were an alien – and accordingly alienated – group living in a parallel universe, or at least in a bygone era. 'Michael Bennett's dead. Bob Fosse is dead. Times Square is a theme park now', the one hit wonder composer tells the kids at the fictional Camp Ovation. 'The foundation that's being laid here is not going to help you in the real world. It's going to lead to waitressing jobs and bitterness and the obsessive, pointless collecting of out-of-print original cast albums.' Yet the drive to achieve fame is beside the point for most of these marginalized kids; rather than focus on the future, the kids care about how this summer theatre programme can improve their *present* by providing a respite from a relentless school year of isolation and bullying. At Camp Ovation, social outcasts – gay boys, nerdy musical theatre girls, cross-dressing divas and more – annually return to a cultural community that shares their penchant for performance and their esoteric knowledge of Sondheim shows.

Summer camps, first established in the late nineteenth century, are a rite of passage that enable kids to navigate identity beyond their family and home neighbourhoods for the first time. The intensified summer camp experience fosters the potential to experiment with identity in a protected environment. Camps exist in a charged time and space of children's leisure; whether kids are away for a single week or several, they are separated from their everyday lives long enough to perceive themselves differently upon return. Including the hours spent sleeping, the concentrated time at camp can add up to the equivalent of a school year; camp accordingly has its own strange and heightened rhythm, full of encounters with different personalities, politics, cultures and religions.[22] The monumental scale of camp events such as performances, competitions and dances can further raise the emotional pitch of each moment – almost like a musical number – and amplify the sense that the time and space of camp diverges from the mundane world.[23]

The fictional Camp Ovation of *Camp* is based on the real-life Stagedoor Manor, which director Todd Graff attended as a teenager. Graff's experience at this Catskills performing arts programme pervades the film, intertwining the fictional and the 'real'. *Camp* was shot on location at Stagedoor for twenty-three days in 2002, and the narrative structure accordingly follows the Stagedoor schedule; this intensive theatre training for kids aged ten to eighteen mounts twelve productions during each three week session. As Mickey Rapkin chronicles in *Theater Geek*, Stagedoor has provided a safe and open-minded environment for teens to explore their emerging identities since it was founded in 1975. This 'oasis' is particularly a refuge for gay teens, 'but you could replace the word *gay* with *awkward, self-conscious, green, blue* or *purple*', he writes. 'The camp provides a haven for any child with a love of the arts who, for whatever reason, feels *other than*.'[24] Todd Graff has aligned Stagedoor Manor with Oz, a sepia world turned Technicolor the minute one steps off the bus. Former camp counsellor Eric Nightengale similarly calls Stagedoor an 'island of lost toys' for kids who have no community in their high schools.[25] Whether Oz, Neverland or Hogwarts, Stagedoor Manor is a fantastical parallel universe that many marginalized children come to call 'home'.[26] Tumblr user watchagirlunfold blogs about waking up in her own room for the first time after returning from camp and hashtags it '#i miss home already', referring to her Stagedoor community.[27] shebelongstothestars even reads her personal experiences of Stagedoor Manor through the lens of *Camp* with a post entitled 'Here's where I stand, here's who I am.' While crying over this empowering ballad in Graff's movie, she blogs about being homesick for her Stagedoor friends: yet another case of '#stagedoormanorproblems'.[28]

Camp is rife with performances that similarly cross fiction and reality until the two are no longer so easily separated. Graff's film opens on an outdoor amphitheatre where a troupe of theatre geeks perform

'How Shall I See You Through My Tears' from *The Gospel at Colonus*, a relatively obscure show in Broadway-centric musical theatre fandom; the musical achieved only a short-lived Broadway run in 1988, although it was a finalist for the Pulitzer Prize following its 1983 premiere at the Brooklyn Academy of Music. Rendering Sophocles' *Oedipus at Colonus* as a parable in a Pentecostal gospel service, this critically acclaimed musical by director Lee Breuer (founding artistic director of Mabou Mines) and composer Bob Telson crosses classic and contemporary, pagan and Christian traditions, in a compelling morality play.[29] Ismene sings 'How Shall I See You Through My Tears' when she finds her long-suffering father Oedipus and her sister Antigone at Colonus. With ecstatic improvisational riffing, Ismene brings a promise of restitution for her family's pains: 'A world that casts you out forgives you, and those who blame you sing your praises now', she proclaims.

Whether or not the moviegoer knows the original narrative context for the song, this gospel ballad provides an empowering message of acceptance and inclusion that embraces the community of artistic misfits on- and offscreen. In fact, *The Gospel at Colonus*' relative obscurity within the musical theatre canon makes the song readily available for recontextualization – while marking those rare spectators who are familiar with the original musical as insiders of the theatre geek culture, close kin to the teens performing the musical number in the film. With the opening lines, 'Father, Sister, Dearest voices', the young African American soloist in *Camp* invokes her theatrical family of fellow actors as much as she invokes her character Ismene's biological family. Her chosen family at Camp Ovation supports one another through the trials and tribulations of their marginalized high school lives. The Greek chorus – a choir of gospel singers – brings sonic emphasis to community through tight, supporting harmonies on the repeated incantation, 'How shall I see you through my tears'.

Three cutaways during the song's instrumental breaks establish the main characters of the film – Vlad, Ellen and Michael – as marginalized theatre geeks in their hometowns, thereby amplifying the significance of the communitas they find at camp. Sporty, straight guy Vlad makes a speech of self-empowerment into his bedroom mirror: 'I only am who I am 'cause I was born that way. I have a gift, and I'm trying not to be selfish about it, but to use it. Okay? If you're gonna knock me for that, that's your problem. Jealousy will get you nowhere. And I'm gonna keep rockin' on.' Being 'born that way' refers not to homosexuality in this context, but to being born a theatrical personality and to being born with obsessive-compulsive disorder (OCD), a disorder that Vlad can only shut out when he inhabits a theatrical character in a focused stage performance.[30] In a second cutaway, a dorky girl named Ellen begs her brother to take her to the school dance; he taunts her and refuses, calling her a loser as he tosses pesky little objects into her shower. Camp is the one place where Ellen feels loved, supported and understood – particularly by her show queen friends like Michael.

In the third and most affecting cutaway, gay Latino Michael is rejected from his junior prom for dressing in drag: a feathered leopard print dress and a long curly wig topped with a tiara.[31] Not only does a teacher rip up his admission ticket and dismiss him from the dance, but Michael is beaten by a group of bullies as he leaves. As 'How Shall I See You Through My Tears' climaxes, Michael lies prone on the school hallway; his battered face convulses in ecstasy as he projects himself into the alternate world of Camp Ovation. The staging diverges from the theatrical narrative of *The Gospel at Colonus* as Michael imagines himself back at camp; the stripped and vulnerable boy – playing 'himself', not a character in the drama – is encircled and embraced by his fellow theatre geeks during the final chorus of the song. Michael's act of projection cannot stop the bullies from beating him or erase the scars on his face, but neither is his musical imaginary sheer escapism. Rather, Michael's musical community at Camp Ovation emboldens him to survive a tumultuous present and serves as a sonic balm to his worldly wounds.

This multilayered performance of 'How Shall I See You Through My Tears' positions *Camp* in a deep history of intertextuality and adaptation, transforming texts to the concrete needs of the present moment. Every contemporary performance of Greek tragedy is necessarily a translation and an adaptation, since the original theatrical, musical and choreographic conventions are speculative; unbound from specific historical expectations, Greek drama lends itself to experimenting with aesthetic intersections of diverse world theatre traditions and transpositions to different social, political and personal situations.[32] The outsider kids in *Camp* are well accustomed to reconfiguring a song or monologue – such as the rapturously emotional 'How Shall I See You Through My Tears' – and applying it to their own lives as a healing balm and empowering encouragement.[33] A degree of campiness arises in taking high school drama (in both senses of the word) so seriously, particularly when likening these teens' travails to Oedipus' own. Yet issues of teen identity formation are, in fact, monumentally important. For theatre geeks, performance is a mode of survival, and as the name Camp *Ovation* indicates, these teens are simply seeking recognition in a world that casts them out.

If by your pupils you are taught, then even the cynical counsellor Bert Hanley learns to let the sun shine in by the finale of *Camp*. Hanley has struggled with alcoholism and depression ever since his fictional one hit wonder *The Children's Crusade* in 1989. He never stopped composing, yet he never produced another show out of a crippling fear of failure. Hanley now lives in drunken regret for chances never taken; teaching at a kids' performing arts camp and accompanying esoteric new musicals in Brooklyn is a far cry from composing for Broadway. One night when Vlad confronts Hanley for insulting the campers' ambitions, the teen stumbles upon a treasure trove of unperformed sheet music sprawled across the songwriter's bedroom floor. 'It's like the Holy Grail of musical theatre', Ellen exclaims. Championing Hanley's rejected works, the campers redeem the composer and his music through performance; a revue of Hanley's genre-bending songs closes the summer, reviving the art form by pulling Hanley's work to life in the present and by attempting to bridge the gap between musical theatre and popular music once more. 'There's funk, gospel. There's this awesome, like, rootsy Neil Young song', Vlad explains to the utterly confused show queen Ellen. Both *Camp* and *Glee* locate the revivification of musical theatre in the hands of a youth culture that can turn iTunes to shuffle, navigating across multiple styles and eras.[34]

While Vlad idolizes Hanley's genre-bending style, it is undeniable that composer/lyricist Stephen Sondheim's musicals are the most lauded throughout *Camp*. Michael keeps a framed picture of the composer on his bedside table, and Sondheim even makes a delightfully campy cameo at the end of the summer revue, when he is attacked by a group of squealing teenage fans as if he were a pop star. It is no wonder that the theatre geeks at Camp Ovation connect to Sondheim's canon; his musicals are sympathetic to outsiders such as the perpetual bachelor Bobby in *Company* (1970), the vengeful barber *Sweeney Todd* (1979) and even a community of alienated individuals who attempt to assassinate presidents of the United States in *Assassins* (1990).[35] The pointillist artist Georges Seurat – protagonist of *Sunday in the Park with George* (1984) – is particularly akin to Sondheim's celebrity persona; Sondheim composes what has been criticized as unemotional, academic music on darker themes, stylistically subverting musical theatre's typically hummable hit songs and happy endings. Indeed, Sondheim's musicals defer the happily ever after to consider what it means to survive when dreams go unfulfilled or fall apart; he gives voice to struggle, suffering and disillusionment, with the occasional glimmer of hope in human connection and artistic fulfilment. After being critically maligned and underappreciated in his early years, Sondheim has only recently been elevated to the 'fucking king of musical theater', as fan Tumblr Fuck Yeah Stephen Sondheim so eloquently puts it.[36]

Sondheim is the most frequently produced musical theatre writer in the repertoire at Stagedoor Manor; kids clamour for the opportunity to play disenchanted fairy-tale characters, cynical married couples and ageing Follies girls. The Stagedoor ethos is to learn by doing, which sometimes means performing age-inappropriate material – and which makes for one of the campiest aspects of the movie *Camp*.[37] In an audition sequence, an array of female campers performs the showstopping 'I'm Still Here' from *Follies*. These diminutive ten to eighteen year olds sing the role of a diva several times their age with compelling conviction. Rather than channel their teenage trauma through angsty, 'age-appropriate' rock 'n' roll, these girls pronounce their endurance in a determined musical theatre number; they proclaim, 'I got through all of last year, and I'm here', with a whole year of high school marginalization supporting their right to belt out Carlotta's big number. In a production of *Company* later that summer, a little girl named Fritzi – who has long attempted to ingratiate herself to the camp's elite by serving camp favourite Jill – finally steps up to the spotlight. The unexpectedly conniving little diva poisons Jill's drink and shows up backstage at the opportune moment, ready to take her place for the showstopping 'Ladies Who Lunch'. After tugging Jill out of the spotlight, Fritzi – played by pre-fame Anna Kendrick – commands the stage as the cynical Joanne, a role made iconic by Elaine Stritch. As she belts, 'Rise! Rise! Rise!' at the number's chilling conclusion, the audience actually begins to rise to its feet, in awe of this 'scary little girl' who has finally wrangled her way into a lead role. Attention must be paid.[38]

At performing arts summer camps, a talent model reigns: a 'meritocracy' that Mickey Rapkin asserts makes sense to the kids.[39] Raymond Zilberberg, a director at Stagedoor from 2006 to 2013, agrees that the kids take putting on a show very seriously; the only children who may find themselves ostracized are those who have a questionable work ethic that their peers perceive to be negatively affecting the process. 'Finding connections and friendships is easy regardless of skill or talent. [Campers are] just happy to find other self-proclaimed "weirdos"', Zilberberg says. 'I would have had so many more friends as a kid if I'd gone to Stagedoor.'[40] Stagedoor also has an unwritten policy that children who have attended several summers must graduate from the chorus to a cameo or supporting role at some point. Dedication is paramount, and it is rewarded. Yet the drive to win a lead role can occasionally override the communitas fostered in this collaborative art form, and while the social hierarchy may serendipitously differ from the kids' everyday high school lives, a hierarchy stands nonetheless. Long-term campers and established divas can dominate younger kids, and an 'honest-to-God straight boy' such as Vlad often occupies a privileged position – a favourite with female (and a few male) campers, as well as a prized talent since he can easily 'play straight'.

At Stagedoor, kids may worry about their place in this hierarchy. The Stagedoor Manor message boards are full of notes from teens who are concerned about being unmoored from their familiar social lives, including a Newbie nicknamed 'Red':

> Honestly though, the more I see the more it seems as if everyone at Stage Door is like a soon to be professional actor or actress and I'm really not and I'm so worried that I'm going to spend three weeks as this outcast because I'm so inexperienced and that people are going to get frustrated that I'm not better or more professional or something. Am I nuts?[41]

Despite reassurances that Stagedoor Manor is a supportive and welcoming community, the stress lingers – especially when one factors in the growing reputation of the camp as an elite training ground for young talent. Stagedoor counts among its alumni *Camp*'s own director Todd Graff, as well as Natalie Portman, Robert Downey Jr. and *Glee*'s Lea Michele. When summer camp is perceived as a stepping stone to fame, the focus shifts from its value in the present to its potential value in the future, and a collaborative community can be traded for cut-throat competition.

According to the American Camp Association, the number of performing arts camps rapidly escalated in the early 2000s; camps with a focus on arts education grew from 527 in December 2001 to 811 in June 2009, marking an increase of over 40 per cent.[42] While these camps fulfil a desperate need for arts education no longer provided in US public schools and offer a haven for artistic identities, they also capitalize on a budding fantasy of fame and fortune cultivated by reality shows such as *American Idol* (2002–present) and *So You Think You Can Dance* (2005–present). Stagedoor Manor is one of the three golden standards in performing arts programming, along with French Woods and Michigan's Interlochen Center for the Arts; of these three,

Stagedoor is the only camp to focus exclusively on theatre. What's more, Stagedoor is located within easy distance of New York City, which makes it a prime location for agents and managers to scout talent. In recent years, the camp has even collaborated with MTI and Disney to workshop and cast new youth musicals.[43]

Although the increasing corporatization of this camp gives cause for concern, Stagedoor's production director Konnie Kittrell insists that community and collaboration are still the camp's first priorities: 'If your child finds something in this experience – finds an outlet they need, or finds self-confidence – how could you say it's wasted money?'[44] Yet the cost is precisely the most glaring limitation to Stagedoor Manor and other specialty camps. However utopian the vision of diverse ethnicities, sexualities, genders and talent levels in the theatrical community cultivated at camp, social class is rarely factored into the equation. Resident camp tuition can vary widely, from $630 to over $2,000 per week;[45] at $6,195 per three-week session (or $2,065 per week) in 2019, Stagedoor Manor's cost is undeniably steep.[46] Scholarships are sometimes available, but financial support from Stagedoor is most often reserved for return campers whose families have fallen on hard times; other kids seek support through Big Brother, Broadway Kids, community theatres and local organizations. Meanwhile, the Stagedoor Manor message boards are dotted with unanswered messages from teens seeking financial aid, knowing that their families could never afford the tuition.

If cultural community at Stagedoor Manor comes at an unaffordable cost, *Camp* acts as a mass-mediated balm in the meanwhile. Todd Graff's film has become a calling card for young theatre geeks worldwide; although limited in its original theatrical release, the VHS and DVD formats opened *Camp* to a cult audience of young fans at a time when the musical was at a decided low point in mainstream popularity. Theatre geeks who were unable to attend a performing arts camp such as Stagedoor Manor imagined themselves into Camp Ovation and delighted in the campy onscreen adventures of their fellow teen misfits; they belted along with the onscreen divas and danced 'Turkey Lurkey Time' while seeking out what artistic opportunities they could in their local schools and community theatres.[47]

Finding *Glee*

'By its very definition, glee is about opening yourself up to joy', reads a plaque honouring the director of William McKinley High School's show choir, Lillian Adler. Alas, the stuffy, puffy-faced Mrs Adler died in 1997, and the glory days of the glee club passed on with her; the last time this fictional high school's show choir won the national championship was 1993. The club has since sunk to the lowest rungs of the social ladder in the cultural wasteland of Lima, Ohio. In the pilot episode of *Glee*, which premiered on FOX in May 2009, the enthusiastic Spanish teacher Will Schuester takes over the student organization. Renaming the group New Directions, Mr Schue plans to rebuild glee club to its former glory, on par with Sue Sylvester's award-winning cheerleading squad. In the process, he hopes to create a time and space for the school's unpopular, invisible kids to find their voices. After all, Mr Schue recalls how musical performance gave him a feeling of self-knowledge and belonging in his tumultuous teenage years. Performing with Mrs Adler's glee club in the national championships is one of his fondest memories: 'Being a part of that, in that moment, I knew who I was in the world.'[48]

Glee creators Ryan Murphy, Ian Brennan and Brad Falchuk drew on their own strange show choir memories in conceptualizing the television series. 'It still strikes me as weird that people dress up in sequins and perform song-and-dance numbers', says Brennan, who sang in his high school show choir in Mount Prospect, Illinois. 'But, at the same time, I find it interesting that there is something in everybody, a longing for something transcendent, particularly in a place like Mt. Prospect, a place that's very suburban and normal and plain. Even in places like that, there's this desire to shine.'[49] Producer Ryan Murphy, known for his dark comedy television series such as *Nip/Tuck* and *American Horror Story*, similarly remembers the transcendent sensation of singing in his college glee club: 'You sort of feel that the world is suddenly available to you, and you have so much optimism about what you can become. [...] It doesn't even have to be about being a performer. It's about a belief in yourself.'[50] For the ephemeral moment of performance, music can seem to expand the potentialities of the present, enabling teenagers to explore and express 'selves' that diverge from the norm. This exploration of different identities is particularly valuable for the outsider kids that constitute the glee club New Directions.

Glee functions on a dual narrative structure. The overarching plot of each season follows this competitive show choir's road to nationals, while each individual episode shows the trials of adolescent identity formation, negotiated in song and dance. Not every episode directly progresses the plot; some explore hot-button high school issues like sexuality, bullying, drugs and alcohol. *Glee* typically draws on an established catalogue of showtunes and popular music rather than original songs (with the notable exception of one episode in season two, 'Original Song'). In this way, *Glee* aligns itself with the jukebox musicals, movies turned to musicals and other recycled pop culture increasingly common on the corporatized Great White Way. As in a backstage musical, the musical numbers are most often diegetic, performed as part of a rehearsal or staged performance. Yet this TV musical is strongest when its tunes serve a double function: preparing the glee club for competition and reflecting thematically on the characters, an ensemble of McKinley High's minorities and misfits. *Glee*'s aesthetic structure walks a fine line between musical numbers' integration and extractability – and at its heights, the show manages to locate a deep interiority beneath the flashy surfaces of popular culture.

In the pilot episode, McKinley High School's finest losers audition for New Directions, and their audition song choices immediately indicate the teens' marginalization and desire for social recognition. African American diva Mercedes Jones wails a demand for 'Respect' *à la* Aretha Franklin, and flamboyant, falsetto-voiced show queen Kurt Hummel identifies with Roxie Hart's invisible husband Amos in a sixteen-bar cut of 'Mr. Cellophane' from Kander and Ebb's *Chicago*. The centrepiece of the auditions is 'Jewish American Princess' Rachel Berry, who takes the stage with the confidence and professionalism of a seasoned actress. 'Hi, my name is Rachel Berry, and I'll be singing "On My Own" from the seminal Broadway classic *Les Miz*', she announces to Mr Schuester. As a diegetic audition song, 'On My Own' showcases Rachel's strong mezzo belt and clinches her role as the female lead of glee club. Yet 'On My Own' simultaneously serves as a mode of personal expression for this lonely teen.

The original context of 'On My Own' is pivotal to Rachel's song selection. In Alain Boublil and Claude-Michel Schönberg's 1987 megamusical *Les Miserables*, 'On My Own' is an 'I want' song performed by the lovelorn Eponine, who wanders the moonlit streets of Paris and dreams of a man who she knows would never return her affections. On the surface of 'On My Own', Eponine longs for romance – yet Eponine's desire for the student revolutionary Marius can also be read as a broader wish for a shift in the social order. In the genre of musical theatre, a character – most often, a woman – can 'dream herself into being' via a musical crush. The crush operates on a hierarchy that makes an actual romance with the more powerful character unlikely, but the showstopping song enables the character to momentarily assume the more powerful person's characteristics. In 'On My Own', Eponine creates an evocative dreamscape of possibilities, akin to Dr Horrible's imaginary in 'Freeze Ray' or Usher's 'Inner White Girl'.[51] Eponine knows that her visions of walking with Marius 'til morning are only in her mind, yet her pleasurable, self-generating representations temporarily reconfigure the power dynamics on stage; in one of *Les Miz*'s most memorable musical numbers, Eponine's soaring vocals hold the plot – and the audience – captive to her romantic fantasies. In fact, the self-generating visions of 'On My Own' are closely aligned with the self-generating political revolution of the collective anthem 'One Day More', the rousing Act I finale that propels the 1832 Paris Uprising. Musical performance contains transformative potential that is realized in the moment of the song – and may seep into the surrounding 'reality' to effect concrete social change.

Projecting into the theatre as if it were a packed Broadway house, Rachel begins the familiar strain: 'On my own, pretending he's beside me.' The floating piano accompaniment continues as the camera cuts to the audition sign-up sheet in the hall. 'On My Own' initiates a flashback sequence that explains Rachel's character and amplifies the significance of her song choice; the scene juxtaposes Rachel's visions of fame with the reality of her miserably unpopular high school life. Earlier that day as Rachel signs up for the show choir audition, she posts a gold star next to her name; in voiceover, she explains that this star is a 'metaphor' for her dreams of stardom. The shimmering symbol bursts into flames to reveal Rachel's beaming face – which is soon doused in a cherry slushie. 'On My Own' stops abruptly when football player Puck pummels Rachel with the icee, shattering her aspirational song. After a beat, this reminder of Rachel's low social standing propels the determined girl to action. In a flashback set to a buzzing a cappella rendition of 'Flight of the Bumblebee', Rachel connives to get glee club coach Sandy Ryerson fired so that she can assume her rightful place as queen of the club. To a peppy 'Golliwog's Cakewalk', Rachel chronicles her family history; her gay dads put their little show-off in voice and dance lessons to give her a competitive edge from an early age. The strains of 'On My Own' pick up again as present-day Rachel sets up a video camera in her bedroom and records herself singing a cappella. Rachel explains in a voiceover that her Myspace schedule – posting a video a day to develop her talents – keeps her far too busy to date any of the boys at school. Yet her heartfelt performance of the lyrics, 'Without him, the world around me changes', reveals that unwanted isolation is another motive for Rachel to project herself onto the internet. Rachel's rampant pursuit of fame is a way of coping with and combating her loneliness.

With select lyrics emphasized, 'On My Own' crosses and confuses Rachel's character (Eponine) and her 'self'. Piano accompaniment sneaks back into the sound mix as Rachel uploads her video and reads cruel comments from the high school cheerios (cheerleaders): 'If I were your parents, I would sell you back', 'I'm going to scratch out my eyes', 'Please get sterilized.' At the song's emotional peak – 'A world that's full of happiness that I have never known!' – the camera cuts from a close-up of Rachel staring at her computer screen back to Rachel at her glee club audition. As she belts and extends the word 'known', Rachel transfers her gaze; from directly addressing the audience, she shuts her eyes tightly, then looks to the sky with tears in her eyes. In this shift, Rachel takes Eponine's song into her own person. She relives the painful slushie from earlier that day in a flashback with an extended reaction shot, her awestruck face dripping with red ice. When the camera finally cuts back to her audition, Rachel calmly returns her gaze to the audience, reassumes character and sees the song through to the end. Rachel navigates the trials of her high school existence through the contours of 'On My Own', and she emerges triumphant in her performance – if not in her social life.

By selecting 'On My Own' as her audition piece, Rachel Berry could be performing her crush on popular football player Finn, who is undeniably out of reach for a glee club loser.[52] More aptly, though, Rachel's musical crush in this moment is Eponine. The megamusical ballad empowers Rachel to adopt Eponine's performative strength, to 'dream herself into being' as a star and to temporarily shift the social structures at William McKinley High.[53] For the moment of 'On My Own', Rachel doubles herself into someone new by dreaming herself into showstopping fame, or at least into a community of belonging with fellow musical performers. If only her musical imaginary of a more equitable social world could alter her peers' perspectives: 'Being a part of something special makes you special, right?'[54]

Rachel's rendition of 'On My Own' highlights a central paradox of musical performance: Rachel expresses her 'self' by assuming a theatrical character, and her self-knowledge is inextricable from her desire for acknowledgement by others. The musical body can thus exhibit a thrilling hybridity, not only crossing and confusing performer and character, but rupturing our traditional sense of character and plot by making visible a multiplicity rather than a singular, unified subject.[55] In an integrated show, a character's transition from dialogue into song and dance is often framed as delving deeper into character by performing a 'true' or 'hidden' self, yet the act of 'coming out' in song does not reveal character interiority so much as it doubles the character, revealing that the character has been – and always will be – a performer. The transition from dialogue into song is almost religious, always offering the performer a chance to create someone new and different.[56]

The potentialities of this hybridity and multiplicity in performance can threaten a high school social structure in which teens are expected to fit stable stereotypes. As Sue Sylvester sees it, 'Children like to know where they stand'; blurring the lines between the popular cheerleaders and football players, the geeky sci-fi invisibles, and the sub-basement Gleeks would only complicate the 'natural' hierarchy that assigns each student to a single, fixed position. Football coach Ken Tanaka agrees that 'the herd' will take care of reining in anyone who 'tries to rise above, be different'.[57] Yet as the first season of *Glee* progresses, football players and cheerleaders gradually join the ranks of show choir singers – and vice versa. Mr Schuester might have to blackmail straight, white, popular football player Finn Hudson into joining glee, but soon, Finn can't fight the feeling that he might actually belong to this band of misfits. Performing with the glee club taps into the instability and performativity of his own social position; although he may come across as cool and collected at the top of the social ladder, and although he undeniably comes from a more privileged position than many of the Gleeks, Finn struggles with basically 'the same thing others kids do: peer pressure, bacne'. As Finn comes to realize, everyone in high school is a loser: insecure in his identity, uncertain of where he belongs, awkwardly performing a role. At least the Gleeks embrace the performance.

At its best, *Glee* emphasizes the performed nature of all identities, riffing off the familiar high school stereotypes to complicate and destabilize them. (At its worst, *Glee* perpetuates these problematic stereotypes – although whenever the writing falters, the episodic structure can function as a corrective.) The extracurricular glee club becomes a ludic time and space for these kids to rehearse identities that defy the narrow norms of high school popularity. For Black diva Mercedes, show queen Kurt, aspiring Broadway star Rachel, football player Finn, goth Asian Tina Cohen and wheelchair user Artie Abrams, the stage offers a realm of potential in which difference and 'loserdom' is not only accepted, but celebrated in song and dance.[58] Similar to *Camp*, *Glee* centres straight characters Rachel and Finn in the pilot episode (which is the focus of this analysis) – but as the series progresses, the marginalized 'others' often become the beating heart of the show. Fans root for Kurt and Blaine (affectionately known as Klaine), swoon over Brittany and Santana's blossoming relationship, and are awed by transgender Unique's vocal prowess. These characters and relationships offered up significant milestones in LGBTQ+ representation on television for teens – and yet M. Shane Grant points out that this 'queer community' is still predominately white. The series' frequent refusal of intersectionality unfortunately undercuts the full queer potential of the glee club's community.[59]

For a television show that prides itself on difference, *Glee* also arguably employs an overabundance of mainstream popular music. Of the 132 total songs in season one, 17 are from stage musicals and 3 from movie musicals, making up only 15 per cent of the music; of the 138 songs in season two, 23 are from musical theatre and 7 from movie musicals, making up 22 per cent of the music.[60] *Glee* often circumnavigates the anxieties of self-expression in song by making the music diegetic and using pop songs instead of show tunes – in other words, by avoiding artifice and self-conscious theatricality. Musical aficionados Rachel and Kurt are the most apt to perform theatrical numbers (generally in a diegetic format, such as an audition or when performing a musical is part of the plot), while characters like macho football player Finn are more likely to perform pop songs of the past and present, which define him in opposition to the theatrical personas in the glee club.[61]

Yet *Glee* demonstrates how popular music is always and already theatrical. A pop song may in fact have a pre-existing narrative context; a slew of rock musicians from The Who to Bono have written for the stage, and an even longer list have conceptualized albums by projecting fictional characters into a narrative, such as the Beatles' *Sgt. Pepper's Lonely Hearts Club Band* (1967) and David Bowie's *The Rise and Fall of Ziggy Stardust and the Spiders from Mars* (1972). But even without this kind of theatrical projection, a dense history accrues to a song: the history of the artist, the song's shifting reception across time and space, and the song's resonance in the (re)performer's personal history. When the glee club performs popular music as a rehearsal, performance and/or soundtrack to their personal lives, they theatrically don these pop music histories much as Rachel Berry dons the role of Eponine in her performance of 'On My Own'.

Take, for instance, the triumphant finale to the pilot episode, in which the quirky members of the new glee club first unite in song: Journey's 'Don't Stop Believin''. When the single was released in 1981, 'Don't Stop Believin'' hit Number 9 on the Billboard Hot 100. The studio album on which the song appeared, *Escape*, was Journey's most successful, soaring to Number 1 on the Billboard 200. Yet the song's reputation – more aptly, the reputation of the band and the entire decade of the 1980s – had devolved into affectionate parody by the 2000s. The power ballad had become a cheesy standard of tribute bands and drunken karaoke performances. 'Don't Stop Believin'' even serves as the finale of *Rock of Ages*, an unapologetically silly jukebox musical (and 2012 feature film) of 1980s hair bands.

In the pilot episode of *Glee*, a flashback to Finn's childhood emphasizes the ridiculous, outdated taint to the power ballad – yet the campy quality of this flashback stems precisely from its earnest performance. Finn's single mother Carole had a fling with an Emerald Dreams lawn specialist in the 1990s; the teen remembers crooning Journey's first Top 20 hit, 'Lovin' Touchin' Squeezin'', while spray painting the lawn with the greasy, mullet-haired Darren. 'That was the first time I really heard music', Finn explains in voiceover. 'It set my soul on fire.' Father figure Darren encourages the boy's youthful passion and talent; he ruffles Finn's hair and urges him, 'Seriously, if I had that voice, my band would still be together. Stick with it!' In a way, a power ballad is not unlike Emerald Dreams: self-consciously kitschy, but capable of brightening a mundane day when the theatrical veneer is wholeheartedly embraced.

Alas, Darren leaves Finn's mom for a hot young blonde he meets at Pic-n-Save. 'Lovin' Touchin' Squeezin'' swells as Darren drives out of their lives; Ms Hudson, decked out in a light wash pair of mom jeans and a denim vest, chucks a carton of milk at the disappearing Emerald Dreams truck and breaks down in the middle of their desolate suburban street. Much as Rachel Berry navigates the trials of her high school career through the empowering strains of 'On My Own', Finn navigates life through the contours of the soaring 1980s power ballads he once shared with Darren; in fact, Finn selects 'Don't Stop Believin'' as the glee club's first group number after spotting Darren singing and spray painting the football field at McKinley High. Although the relationship between popular song and the Broadway musical has shifted significantly since the mid-twentieth century, the two have never wholly split, and the synth-tastic power ballads of 1980s rock are close kin to the quasi-universal anthems of epic megamusicals like *Les Miserables*.[62] With memorable major key melodies and expansive emotions, both genres of the power ballad aim to em*power* their performers, if only for the space of a fiercely belted song – and in the 2000s, both genres needed to be rescued from the cultural detritus of the 1980s. Perhaps all they needed was a little *Glee*. Even when employed ironically or parodistically, these inspirational Broadway tunes continue to 'work' for a willing audience or performer.

Raymond Knapp's concept of a Musically Enhanced Reality Mode (MERM) is particularly useful in considering how *Glee*'s musical numbers function. MERM refers to a two-pronged approach common in film musicals: setting up a number as naturally as possible (as part of a rehearsal or performance, for instance), then moving into a MERM that allows audio and visual violations of what would be possible in reality.[63] In *Glee*, MERM's aesthetic expansions often include autotuned vocals, sweetened backing tracks and music video-like dreamscapes that plunge the viewer into a fantastical world beyond the rehearsal room or performance stage. MERM also paves the way for the sensation of direct personal expression in song; it shines a 'sonic spotlight' on the singer(s), giving the moment 'a heightened sense of reality' and an 'extra charge'.[64] For the marginalized teenagers in *Glee*, MERM also activates a sensation of expanded social possibilities. In the glow of a musical number such as 'Don't Stop Believin'', the Gleeks sense the potential to transform their social landscape by bonding as an ensemble and perhaps even shifting audience members' perceptions of their social standing.

'Don't Stop Believin'' chronicles the glorious intensity of a midnight encounter between a lonely man and woman, although the song's narrative takes on a decidedly more innocent veneer when performed on the teen-friendly TV show. With minimal staging and a few flashes of theatrical lighting, wearing only basic red tees and black pants as costumes, the newly formed glee club accesses their performative potential on the stage of their high school theatre. In this first hit song (and in most early episodes of *Glee*), Rachel and Finn are positioned as the club's male and female leads: the 'small town girl' and the 'city boy' of the power ballad. Yet the ensemble always serves an essential role. In fact, 'Don't Stop Believin'' establishes a semi-democratic relationship among the glee club members – Finn chooses the song, Rachel choreographs, Artie recruits the jazz band, Mercedes designs costumes – and the song's driving piano riff is performed a cappella at the top of the number, emphasizing the collective. The ensemble of young performers must listen to one another, syncing their vocals in a pulsing foundation from which Finn and Rachel's soaring solos can emerge. Although the ensemble is staged as backup singers during the verses, the entire company belts the final chorus together. As in many a musical theatre number, the take-away message of 'Don't Stop Believin'' – set to an equally catchy take-away melody – is to embrace the present moment, together.[65] The teens reinvigorate this simultaneously mainstream and maligned pop song by performing it in earnest and by proudly donning its performative optimism. Glowing in the showstopping aura of the song, the Gleeks' Musically Enhanced Reality actively improves their present.

The reactions of the glee club's unseen audience demonstrates the transformational potential of the musical number for performers and audience members alike. On the verge of quitting his job to pursue a more profitable career and raise a family, Mr Schuester hears the strains of 'Don't Stop Believin'' floating down the hallway. The kids' performance transports him back to his high school glory days, and the talent and potential radiating from the glee club's song convinces him to stay at McKinley High. Meanwhile, a group of cheerleaders – with a stern Sue Sylvester at the helm – glares down on the glee club from the balcony, and football player Puck steps into the theatre out of curiosity. This talented ensemble of singers threatens to unmoor the high school hierarchy that elevates these sports stars above the rest.

Most importantly, the glee club performs to an unseen television viewership. Before *Glee* premiered, critics highlighted the musical flops of recent decades and shed doubt on the long-term viability of the new TV show. Although *Fame* – a television series about a high school for the performing arts – attained cult success and a five-season run in the 1980s, most experiments in musical television shows throughout the 1990s and early 2000s met with a quick and devastating demise. *Cop Rock*, a 1990 musical police drama on ABC, barely survived a season and was subsequently ranked Number 8 on *TV Guide*'s Worst TV Shows of All Time; *Hull High*, a soap opera high school musical, played only eight episodes that same year on NBC; and *Viva Laughlin*, a 2007 mystery drama, was cancelled after only two episodes on CBS. Based on these television trends, *Glee* seemed primed for a ridiculed, short-lived stint on FOX.

Yet *Glee* also premiered at the apex of a re-emerging interest in the performing arts onscreen. Television audiences auditioned in nationwide searches and voted for their favourite competitors on reality TV talent competitions such as *American Idol*. In the UK, Andrew Lloyd Webber cast leads for West End revivals of *The Sound of Music* (2006), *Joseph and the Amazing Technicolor Dreamcoat* (2007), *Oliver!* (2008), *The Wizard of Oz* (2010) and *Jesus Christ Superstar* (2012) on BBC One; in the United States, the pop musical *Legally Blonde* scouted out their next Elle Woods on MTV (2008).[66] Meanwhile, the movie musical resurfaced with Baz Luhrmann's *Moulin Rouge* (2001) and Rob Marshall's *Chicago* (2002), not to mention Disney's *High School Musical* trilogy (2006–8). Although Ryan Murphy consistently denies that *Glee* was inspired by *HSM*, this series of made-for-TV movies undeniably paved the way for *Glee* in style, substance and commercial potential. The poppy strains of 'Start of Something New' and 'We're All in This Together' heralded a *Grease* for a new generation, where the all-star basketball player boy and the nerdy new girl could unite in song and dance. *High School Musical* ignited a tweenage franchise that ultimately included a national tour, lunch boxes, karaoke games, melodic toothbrushes and more.[67]

FOX hoped to tap into a pre-established audience of aspirational music lovers by previewing the pilot episode of *Glee* immediately after the season eight finale of *American Idol* on 19 May 2009, and the tactic paid off; the *Glee* premiere ranked number seven in that week's Neilsen ratings among adult viewers ages eighteen to forty-nine and number fourteen among all viewers. The musical TV series was continually touted as an underdog success story when the show began to win widespread critical acclaim: 'The scripts are written as though the kids are underdogs and I tell the actors all the time, this show feels like an underdog', Ryan Murphy said in a 2009 interview.[68] The first season captured the 2010 Golden Globe for Best Television Series (Musical or Comedy), as well as Emmy Awards for Jane Lynch, guest star Neil Patrick Harris and Ryan Murphy's direction of the pilot episode. After its second season, *Glee* again claimed the Golden Globe for Best Television Series, as well as Best Supporting Actor and Actress awards for Chris Colfer and Jane Lynch. With an avid teenage fan base, *Glee* erupted into a lucrative franchise with merchandise ranging from T-shirts and hoodies to a 3D concert movie, from an Official William McKinley High School Yearbook to a special edition Yahtzee game with a slushie dice cup. *Glee*'s discography is undoubtedly its hottest commodity, consisting of dozens of soundtracks, compilation albums and EPs, as well as hundreds of singles released digitally. The cast of *Glee* holds the record for hit singles on the Billboard Hot 100, with 207 hits – and the pilot episode's 'Don't Stop Believin'' as their top-ranked success.[69] Peaking at Number 4 on the Billboard Hot 100, *Glee*'s version even surpassed Journey's original.

The pilot episode of *Glee* struck a promising balance of art and commerce that gradually caved to the commercial as the series continued. With the tunes increasingly tangential to narrative, this hit factory franchise feeds into Jean Baudrillard's conception of the hypermarket, a fourth-level simulacra in which the 'original' no longer retains its primacy. Where techniques of mass reproduction prevail, the art objects are less important than their 'serial, circular, spectacular arrangement'.[70] Even music education is presented as a spectacular product, rather than a process, throughout *Glee*.[71] The show rarely shows students learning music or dance steps; rather, rehearsals are fully staged production numbers that just happen to take place in a rehearsal room. With the addition of autotuning to correct pitch in the recording studio, even the cast's diverse array of voices is processed into product-driven perfection. These aesthetic choices can sometimes negate *Glee*'s narrative celebration of difference.

What's more, a spectacular disjuncture exists between the economic situation of the fictional William McKinley High and the multimillion-dollar franchise that *Glee* has become. Budget cuts to the public education system drive the plot from the pilot episode. Principal Figgins relegates the bulk of the school's limited extracurricular funding to Sue Sylvester's cheerleading squad, whose high visibility on FOX Sports Net makes them profitable for the school. Figgins even demands that Mr Schuester pay $60 a month to maintain glee club, and the organization must use costumes and props that the school already owns; New Directions will only be allocated funding once they begin to garner prestige in the community. Granted, *Glee* is a campy musical comedy that makes little pretence to dramatic realism – but the sparkling abundance of costumes, sets and special effects in the glee club's performances stand at striking odds with the economic realities on which the plot often hinges. The disjuncture is even greater when juxtaposing the blockbuster television show to struggling public schools across the United States.

Then again, perhaps such an entertaining spectacle is precisely the splashy boost that arts education needs. The politics of visibility plays a huge part in how social groups are treated in high schools; providing equal support and recognition to extracurricular activities – not just to the money-making sports teams – can help to level the high school social hierarchy.[72] *Glee*'s mainstream visibility certainly drew attention to the precipitous decline of arts education in the United States and the potential marginalization of kids who are passionate about these sidelined pursuits. According to Ralph Opacic, founder and director of the Orange County High School of the Arts in Santa Ana, students began demonstrating a greater grassroots commitment to the arts after *Glee*'s premiere. Opacic has been a determined advocate for music education through several challenging decades for the arts. When he started as a high school choral teacher at Los Alamitos High School in 1982, the programme had only thirty students, but by 1985, the programme had expanded to 300 students in five choirs – including the future Mr Schuester himself, actor Matthew Morrison. 'I had the star football players and cheerleaders, and show choir became cool', Opacic remembers. 'It broke down all of the traditional cliques, and over time it created a culture of acceptance.'[73] Opacic appreciates *Glee*'s arts advocacy and notes that more challenging choreography and an increase in popular song arrangements have followed from the TV show.

Of all the products circulating in the *Glee* franchise, one of the most exciting is undoubtedly the sheet music arrangements published by Hal Leonard. A search on Sheet Music Plus currently locates over 700 choral arrangements for sale: templates for teens' own aspirational performances of pop songs and showtunes, old and new. The sheet music collection emphasizes finding glee as a performative process, rather than a static series of spectacularly arranged products. Filled with uplifting messages of survival, acceptance and empowerment, *Glee*'s choral arrangements range from Katy Perry's 'Firework' to Bruno Mars's 'Just the Way You Are', from Madonna's 'Express Yourself' to *The Rocky Horror Picture Show*'s 'Time Warp'. Glee clubs across the world can now don the performative optimism of New Directions in their own high school – and perhaps begin to transform the social landscape in the process.

Some school arts programmes seem to have been saved and revitalized thanks to a resurging interest in glee; misfit kids who were already musical performers identified strongly with the television show's quirky outsiders, and other youth decided that trying out for their school's show choir or musical may not destroy their social life after all (Figure 7). In fact, when the National Association for Music Education polled choir directors about *Glee*'s impact in 2010, 43 per cent indicated a rise in student interest and enrolment in music programmes as a result of the show.[74] At Arizona State University, music education majors started a show choir called GLEEders for local Tempe middle and high school students; working on a small budget of undergraduate student grants and local business donations, their club featured themed weeks – just like the popular television show.[75] With the show readily available to stream on Netflix, *Glee*'s popularity persists with musical theatre geeks in 2020; my secondary school students at ArtsEd (a top-ranking London performing arts school, whose president is Andrew Lloyd Webber) still frequently request the 'Glee version' of a song for performance.

Figure 7 *Chapter 2*, an original musical written, composed and directed by Nightingale-Bamford School student Jordan Polycarpe. Photograph by Sarah Taylor Ellis, who mentored the project.

'Every time I try to destroy that clutch of scab-eating mouth breathers it only comes back stronger like some sexually ambiguous horror movie villain', Sue Sylvester complains.[76] Indeed, musical theatre is currently enjoying its greatest popularity since the pre-rock era – particularly among young people.[77] As composer Michael Friedman explains, musical theatre has begun to re-emerge in the mainstream, or 'for lack of a better term, [come] out of the closet', with recent successes such as *Glee* and *The Book of Mormon*: 'It's become fashionable, which is shocking and even a little upsetting to somebody like me who still thinks of it as a little bit shameful.'[78] Theatre historian and 54 Below programming director Jennifer Ashley Tepper asserts that we are living in a new Golden Age – nay, a Platinum Age – of musical theatre. She cites recent movie musicals (*Les Miserables* and *Into the Woods*), live broadcast musicals (*The Sound of Music Live!* and *Grease*) and television series (*Crazy Ex-Girlfriend*) as examples of how the musical is no longer relegated to a 'niche market' – and 'this is all without mention of the *Hamilton* juggernaut that earned Broadway an ever-present spot in the pop culture conversation.'[79]

So what about *Hamilton*?

Indeed, it seems no conversation about contemporary musical theatre is complete without a discussion of the *Hamilton* phenomenon. When Lin-Manuel Miranda first picked up historian Ron Chernow's dense biography of founding father Alexander Hamilton, he marvelled that no one had thought of turning it into a musical before. Following in the footsteps of *1776* and *Bloody Bloody Andrew Jackson*, Miranda's hotly anticipated sophomore project follows this 'bastard, orphan, son of a whore and a Scotsman, dropped in the middle of a forgotten spot in the Caribbean by providence, impoverished, in squalor' who '[grows] up to be a hero and a scholar'.[80] As evidenced in this opening rap, *Hamilton* effects a critical time warp on American history; a vibrant, contemporary sound animates these historical characters, who are vitally embodied by actors of colour. *Hamilton* makes visible the diverse young, scrappy and hungry immigrants who are the backbone of the United States – both then and now.

Miranda's 'groundbreaking', 'revolutionary', 'historic' hip-hop musical has penetrated the mainstream and captured the zeitgeist in a way that few musicals have since *Hair*, the 'American tribal love-rock musical', which followed a parallel trajectory of premiering off-Broadway at the Public Theater in 1967 before taking Broadway by storm in 1968. For *The New York Times* critic Ben Brantley, *Hamilton*'s off-Broadway premiere in February 2015 made the past palpably present, which is no small feat on 'the progress-challenged continuum of the American musical'. He observes that the musical's fresh mix of hip-hop, rap and R & B could just as easily be heard on a mainstream radio station as in a Broadway theatre – an exciting crossover in genres that hadn't existed for at least six decades.[81]

In fact, the most conventional musical comedy tune in *Hamilton* – 'You'll Be Back' – is firmly positioned as old-fashioned, backwards-looking entertainment within the show. In a showstopping solo, King George III – the only white character – enters the stage wearing a comically oversized royal robe, which impedes much movement and immediately sets this number in contrast to the exuberant animation of all the other songs. The king's physical restraint is matched in musical restraint: Jonathan Groff's vocals are crystalline and straight-toned, with an occasional regal flourish. Rather than a driving electronic pulse, simple piano chords begin this chipper breakup song in which the petulant monarch warns his colonies against rebelling. 'You'll Be Back' was one of the earliest songs composed for *Hamilton*, and musical director and orchestrator Alex Lacamoire employs a smart combination of harpsichord in tandem with sounds of the late 1960s British invasion, including instrumental homages to 'Getting Better', 'Penny Lane' and 'Being for the Benefit of Mr. Kite', to mark the song as 'dated'.[82]

Yet the catchy, upbeat melody just keeps coming back. In the first reprise, 'What Comes Next?', King George reflects on the challenges of America's new-found freedom; in the second reprise, 'I Know

Him', the king contemplates how John Adams could possibly run the country after the titan George Washington. Whether a monarch or a glam supervillain, musical theatre will always be back – but perhaps it can continue to return with a difference. Lin-Manuel Miranda does not dismiss musical theatre traditions, after all, but transforms them in his theatrical work. He displays an obvious affection for and in-depth knowledge of the musical genre throughout *Hamilton* – with playful sampling of Gilbert and Sullivan, Rodgers and Hammerstein, Jason Robert Brown and more embedded at key musical moments. 'My Shot' is undeniably a hip-hop twist on a traditional 'I want' song, while 'The Room Where It Happened' updates a vaudevillian Kander and Ebb-esque number for the twenty-first century. It is also worth noting that *Hamilton*'s predecessor – *In the Heights* – is one of the most well-integrated musicals in decades, both aesthetically and politically. This slice-of-life show about a Latinx community in Washington Heights traces its structural lineage to Rodgers and Hammerstein, with one critical difference: people of colour are at the centre of the story, gaining access to the musicalized American dream. While *Hamilton* as a product may not be revolutionary, then, its artistic practices – particularly its style and casting – may be.[83]

If both *Camp* and *Glee* dream the musical forward with avid fan cultures and a robust relationship between popular music and musical theatre, then we must ask: Is *Hamilton* the revolution? Are *Hamilton* fans (or Hamilfans) musical theatre fans? Or are they just *Hamilton* fans? And are *Hamilton* fans hip-hop fans, or are they just *Hamilton* fans? Has *Hamilton* actually engendered rhizomatic listening, diversifying our playlists and turning them to shuffle, or has it reached a crossover audience that is otherwise content to maintain their segregated listening habits? Does *Hamilton* herald a stylistic pivot in the American musical as a whole? Considering how long it takes to write and develop a new musical, it may be too soon to tell; in fact, this lag time may be one of the biggest barriers to musical theatre and popular music ever having a perfectly symbiotic relationship. However, this 'crossover episode' feels ripe with possibility. 'The hip-hop narrative is writing your way out of your circumstances', Miranda explains. 'All my favourite hip-hop songs are really good musical theatre "I want" songs' – songs that articulate a longing for something more, for something better than this.[84] Perhaps for musical theatre fans, *Hamilton* and indeed the entire genre is an ever-changing 'I want' song: a utopian performative desirous of difference and open-ended possibilities.

5

'Just an Illusion': Identity and Musical Form

THOUGHT 5: *So* A Strange Loop. *What's the significance of the title?*
USHER: *Well, don't fall asleep but it's a cognitive-science term that was coined by this guy named Douglas Hofstadter. And it's basically about how your sense of self is just a set of meaningless symbols in your brain pushing up or down through one level of abstraction to another but always winding up right back where they started. It's the idea that your ability to conceive of yourself as an 'I' is kind of an illusion. But the fact that you can recognize the illusion kind of proves that it exists. I don't totally get it. But it's also the name of this Liz Phair song I really love. Originally, I was gonna use a bunch of her songs in the show but then she wouldn't give me permission. Her spirit lives on in the piece in other ways though.*
Michael R. Jackson, *A Strange Loop*[1]

When Douglas Hofstadter first came to the head-spinning realization that consciousness was a mirage, his teenage self quickly jotted down his thoughts in the form of a dialogue between two characters, flippantly named Plato and Socrates. It is perhaps no surprise that Hofstadter's initial writings about the 'strange loop' of identity came in the form of a two-hander play, externalizing his 'internal' argument in two bodies.[2] Theatre – and perhaps particularly musical theatre, with its fundamentally dis-integrated form – offers an exceptional playground for exploring the complexities and illusions of selfhood. This chapter explores intersecting manipulations of time and identity in *Fun Home*,

Company and *A Strange Loop* – a musical which was in part inspired by Hofstadter's theories.³ In each of these non-linear shows, the protagonist is split into multiple selves represented by several actors coexisting on stage: Alison illustrates her life story alongside Small and Medium Alison, Bobby refracts his married friends' cynical views on relationships and Usher has an in-person conversation with his daily self-loathing. These formally inventive musicals illuminate the multifaceted, performative processes of constituting identity – and particularly identities in difference.

Performing the illusive 'I'

Psychologist Erik Erikson's work on identity development in the 1950s and 60s is a foundation for our contemporary understanding of the term 'identity', which too often goes uninterrogated. In his psychosocial framework, identity constitutes a desired 'unity of personal and cultural identity', bringing together a person's inner life (per a Freudian id-ego-superego model) with the external or social categories to which they belong, such as nationality, race, ethnicity, gender, sexuality and class.⁴ Although Erikson posits identity as something that 'comes upon you' as a recognition rather than something quested after, he also sees identity as a process and even invokes theatrical language when discussing how the modern search for identity involves many 'roles', 'appearances' and 'postures'.⁵ Interestingly, Erikson's definition of identity as 'a *subjective sense* of an *invigorating sameness and continuity*' implies both stability and movement; the self's 'sameness and continuity' is not an abiding truth, but rather a 'subjective sense' of its truth.⁶

Cognitive scientist Douglas Hofstadter elaborates on this subjective sense by positing human identity as a self-referential structure, or a 'strange loop', from which consciousness arises; this brain loop relies on the repetition of patterns to provide an illusion of continuity to the self.⁷ Crucially, this 'internal performance' of identity is not entirely self-contained. The caged-bird metaphor of one person contained in one body breaks down as humans are social beings; 'my' strange loop is housed in my brain, but it is simultaneously held in a collection of other brains to different degrees, and my brain also holds the strange loops of other humans, which can overlap in significant ways.[8] In Hofstadter's concept of identity, then, humans are not completely individual, but neither are they all one and the same: each strange loop lives partially in the other, and identity is continuously generated through the circular processing of familiar patterns.[9]

With a phenomenological focus on the body, Judith Butler reaches similar conclusions about the construction of social identities. Gender is a fiction constituted through repeated performative acts; bodily gestures, movements and other actions create a compelling illusion of stable gender and selfhood.[10] Race likewise has no biological truth, but its abiding fiction powerfully structures our world today; skin – that persistent visual marker of 'race' – is a tenuous border between the 'inside' and 'outside' that requires policing.[11] Performed patterns of gender, sexuality, race and ethnicity, and other social identities – as well as how to 'read' those patterns – are all carefully taught. As with Hofstadter's strange loops, repetition of familiar frameworks is key to the legibility and perceived stability of identity.

Still, we often cling to the myth that the 'I' is a unique, stable and integrated whole – or at least that it *should* be a unique, stable and integrated whole, and that we are on a narrative journey from fragmentation to unity, from confusion to understanding. Western culture places us on a Darwinian evolutionary trajectory bound towards integrating our biological and cultural levels of existence: 'We sense that even where harmony is lacking, there is always some way to get to it not far off', composer and theorist Tim Hodgkinson explains.[12] Or as one of my students recently articulated, 'I think once you learn about yourself and you feel comfortable in your own spirit, I think maybe that's when you're fully integrated with all the other parts of yourself.'[13]

In *Hedwig and the Angry Inch*, East Berlin rock star Hedwig recounts such a mythic integration story in 'The Origin of Love'. Inspired by Aristophanes' speech in Plato's *Symposium*, Hedwig sings of love as an attempt to repair a fundamental rift. Long ago, there were three types of human beings – male, female and androgynous – that were complete and whole, with four arms and four legs; they knew nothing of love. When these humans grew too powerful and tried to attack the gods, Zeus punished them by cutting each of them in two. Now each half forever pines for its partner – seeking wholeness, integration and completion through love. While this origin story validates a multiplicity of sexualities, sadly, this mythic wholeness is never to be found for Hedwig; with an angry inch from her botched sex-change operation, she remains forever stuck between gender identities and cannot find her 'other half'. As Knapp observes, Hedwig's 'in between' position acts as a bridge across a binary divide but also reinforces the separateness of the sides, neither of which feels like 'home'.[14]

The narrative journey to a mythic wholeness can feel particularly elusive for those on the margins, who may be more aware of the varied and sometimes conflicting roles they play navigating a white, cis male, straight, non-disabled mainstream. W.E.B. Du Bois describes this sensation as double consciousness:

> It is a peculiar sensation, this double-consciousness, this sense of always looking at one's self through the eyes of others, of measuring one's soul by the tape of a world that looks on in amused contempt and pity. One feels his two-ness, – an American, a Negro; two souls, two thoughts, two unreconciled strivings; two warring ideals in one dark body, whose dogged strength alone keeps it from being torn asunder. The history of the American Negro is the history of this strife, – this longing to attain self-conscious manhood, to merge his double self into a better and truer self.[15]

While Du Bois writes of his particular lived experience as an African American man at the turn of the twentieth century, the concept of double consciousness can resonate with other identities in difference. The journey to self-consciousness may register as a deep and purely 'internal' journey for the straight white male, seamlessly interpellated into his social role and inhabiting a heroic narrative that dubiously stands in for the 'universal' – but for a marginalized subject, the 'external' is a dominant determining factor and may bring about this strange double consciousness. A straight white man's identity is just as socially constructed, of course, but the perception of straightness, whiteness and maleness as the cultural norm can make it seem an 'authentic' or 'essential' identity, which, thus, goes uninterrogated.[16]

What's more, marginalized identities are frequently misread, neglected and even erased when they do not neatly fit into existing patterns of understanding. Anne Anlin Cheng excavates the painful negotiations of identity that must be undertaken by racialized subjects, with their always insisted on difference; this continual negotiation is particularly fraught and melancholic when one exists between or outside of a dominant binary, such as Black/white or male/female.[17] Problematic erasures also occur when treating social categories as mutually exclusive; in her seminal 1989 article, Kimberle Crenshaw introduces the critical concept of intersectionality with a telling Black women's studies book title: *All the Women Are White, All the Blacks Are Men, But Some of Us Are Brave*. A single-axis framework that ignores multidimensional experiences can further sideline and even erase those who inhabit multiple marginalized social categories. We need ever-more nuanced analytical structures to discuss the complexities of identity and solve problems of exclusion.[18]

It feels crucial that W.E.B. Du Bois's striving 'to attain self-conscious manhood, to merge his double self into a better and truer self' does not mean complete integration of his Africanness and Americanness into a unified identity.[19] He wishes neither 'self' to be lost in this process. Perhaps instead, his selves can stand alongside one another, embracing their multiplicity and difference. In this chapter, I am interested in how the multifaceted experiences of navigating marginalized identities are translated to the hybrid form of the musical; in fact, the theatrical technique of fragmenting a single character into multiple actors is used almost exclusively for roles that are female, LGBTQ+ and/or characters of colour.[20] This multiplication of 'selves' often extends beyond the stage, as the authors of the musical and/or source text often share DNA with their musical protagonists. The musical is an inherently dis-integrated form that always and already showcases disjunctures of identity, if we want to see them – and if identity is 'tenuously constituted in time', then there are vital possibilities of transformation in repeating with a difference.[21] The musicals I will discuss here not only dissect the construction of human identity, but they also rip into the 'integrated' form of the musical by playing with time and structure. These musicals break out of the strange loop on multiple levels; they make visible, audible and tangible the illusions of integration in both human identity and in the identity of the musical as a genre.

Until now gives way to then: *Fun Home*

> *Caption: My Dad and I both grew up in the same*
> *small Pennsylvania town*
> *And he was gay.*
> *And I was gay.*
> *And he killed himself.*
> *And I ... became a lesbian cartoonist.*[22]

In *Fun Home*, lesbian cartoonist Alison Bechdel's search for identity is a complex and ongoing process effected through writing and rewriting, aiming to make coherent a collection of memories. The 2015 Tony Award-winning musical with book and lyrics by Lisa Kron and music by Jeanine Tesori positions adult Alison as the show's narrator. Through a collection of non-chronological scenes and songs, Alison strives to reconcile her relationship to her father – who was closeted through his life and killed himself only a few months after Alison came out – and to her childhood and college 'selves', who are physically represented onstage by different actors. Given the subject matter of the musical, *Fun Home* may seem an oddly playful choice of title, but much like Alison's identity, the title contains multitudes. The Bechdel family runs a funeral parlour, which the kids call the 'fun home' for short – but 'fun home' also gestures towards a fun house of labyrinthine passages and distorting mirrors, in which one encounters strange reflections of one's 'self'. By physicalizing Small Alison (age nine) and Medium Alison (age nineteen) in separate bodies who coexist with Alison (age forty-three) onstage, the musical adaptation turns the self into a stranger: familiar, and yet different. The original Broadway production's costumes by David Zinn and hair and wig design by Paul Huntley emphasize both continuity and change across the three onstage Alisons: a red striped T-shirt grows more boxy and 'boyish' as Alison grows older, and a messy bob gets chopped into a comfy crew cut (Figure 8).

There is of course another spectral Alison present throughout the musical as well: the real-life Alison Bechdel, whose 2006 autobiographical graphic novel of the same name was the source text for the adaptation. Through the novel, Bechdel grapples with the complexities of subjectivity and the foibles of memory; writing becomes a process through which she attempts to make sense of her experiences. After she developed obsessive-compulsive disorder at

Figure 8 *Fun Home* – Alison Bechdel, Sydney Lucas, Emily Skeggs and Beth Malone. Photograph by David Gordon. Courtesy of David Gordon.

the age of ten, Bechdel's father gave her a wall calendar in which she began to chronicle her life as a way of organizing her thoughts. Soon becoming cognizant of the constructed nature of her diary and the gap between her experience and its archive, Bechdel had an epistemological crisis: 'How did I know that the things I was writing were absolutely, objectively true? All I could speak for was my own perceptions, and perhaps not even those.'[23] Bechdel ultimately turned to drawing, with illustrations interacting with text, in a search for a more truthful representation of her experiences; this duality has been a cornerstone of her work ever since, from her cult favourite comic strip *Dykes to Watch Out For* to her graphic novels *Fun Home* and *Are You My Mother?*[24] Agnès Muller discusses how these separate modes of expression – text and image – both stand apart from one another and blur in *Fun Home*. Interestingly, Muller suggests opera as an example of another medium in which disparate media – words and music – simultaneously compete for the audience's attention and enrich one another.[25]

Bechdel's aptly subtitled 'family tragicomic' refuses to sit comfortably in a single genre or medium, and the graphic novel's hybrid form lends itself to adaptation in the similarly hybrid genre of musical theatre, which is constantly negotiating scene, song, dance, design and other theatrical elements. Adaptation can be considered a fundamentally queer process: adapting and queering both involve transformation – turning something, making it strange and new. By always being placed in relation to an 'original' or norm, adaptation and queerness can also challenge assumptions about authenticity and value.[26] A further adaptation is undertaken when translating a musical from the page to the stage, as all productions are contingent on their historical and cultural contexts; a musical, then, is always unfinished, always in a state of becoming.[27] A queer adaptation in every sense, *Fun Home* vibrantly showcases identities in difference in their ongoing processes of becoming.

Jill Dolan calls *Fun Home* the first lesbian coming-of-age story on Broadway.[28] While musical theatre has long been a domain of gay creatives and, more recently, explicitly 'out' male characters, lesbian creators and narratives are still too often spectral.[29] A 2015 *Slate* article about *Fun Home*'s impending transfer from the Public Theater to Broadway was in fact titled: '*Fun Home*: Is America Ready for a Musical about a Butch Lesbian?'[30] In this article, Lisa Kron – known for her theatre company the Five Lesbian Brothers prior to her first outing as a musical theatre librettist – recalls seeing several contemporary musicals where the word 'lesbian' was used as a funny non sequitur: 'I'd be so on board, and then I'd be slapped in the face by it. It was just like, *This character's a joke. This is not a person.*'[31] For *Fun Home* to not only tell a lesbian coming-of-age story but to multiply the lesbian bodies onstage provides a pleasurable thrill for feminist spectators such as Dolan. 'I've spent so many years watching for lesbian subtext and trying to read queerness underneath protestations of heterosexuality', she writes after her first off-Broadway viewing of the musical. 'To see lesbian desire as the *text* felt almost startling—and more wonderful than I can even begin to describe.'[32]

As both a graphic novel and musical, *Fun Home* eschews a traditionally integrated musical's linear narrative drive; instead it uses the slippery nature of memory as its organizing structure. As Lisa Kron expresses in her forward to the libretto, the graphic memoir is so evocative as to feel like a linear story, but it is actually 'a recursive meditation, circling around and around the four months between when Alison came out to her parents and her father's suicide.'[33] The musical adaptation similarly follows an 'emotional chronology' or memory play structure instead of a temporal chronology.[34] The elusiveness of memory even applies to the stunning Broadway set design in the round by David Zinn. With the magic of mechanical lifts, Victorian furniture pieces rise and fall through holes in the ground – memories surfacing and disappearing just as quickly.[35] This shifting set enhances the 'fun home' metaphor, as Alison's father Bruce was a master of illusion: his artful restoration of their Gothic Revival home both conceals and reveals his closeted gay identity.

While early workshops of the musical featured images from Bechdel's graphic novel projected onto the set, the creative team found a more theatrical analogy to the structure of the book by placing Alison at a wheeled drawing table, from which she narrates her memories.[36] It is significant that Alison's narration is 'internal' rather than directed to the audience – and in fact, Kron prefers to call Alison a 'character, doggedly pursuing a goal' rather than a narrator.[37] Evoking Brecht, Kron emphasizes that theatre can only show behaviour, not a person's 'inner life'; thus Alison's 'internal' acts of thinking, feeling and remembering must be externalized in performance.[38] Alison relives each memory moment by moment and pieces together her truth by sketching and scrapping drawings, testing different captions ('Caption: My dad and I were exactly alike'/'Caption: My dad and I were *nothing* alike') and reshaping and refining her work as new memories arise.[39] As Alison's past comes careening into the present, the audience becomes aware of the contingency of each moment in time and the multiple ways in which each instant can be captured and framed. Kron and Tesori rip further into the fabric of time by employing looping lyrics and musical motifs that represent fragments of memory coming back.[40] Rebecca Applin Warner analyses how Tesori employs musemes (small musical units, akin to leitmotifs) that link Alison to her father, her former selves and the family as a whole.[41] From the 'He wants' museme indicating her father's homosexual desire to the 'La'/'Maybe Not Right Now' musemes through which her mother blocks out reality, Alison frequently picks up on musical motives that are first established by her parents; this shared musical material calls into question how much she has inherited their identities.[42]

Although *Fun Home* is a memory play, the musical is simultaneously forward-looking, showing an overarching developmental journey for Alison as she seeks to answer a key question about her identity in relation to her father: 'Am I just like you?'[43] In the analysis below, I employ a 'song plot' to understand Alison's character development. The song plot Jack Viertel outlines in *The Secret Life of the American Musical* is a fundamentally conservative outline used to uphold traditionally 'integrated' Golden Age musicals; as the former artistic director of New York City Center's Encores! series, Viertel is in the business of preserving the past.[44] In a traditional song plot, the protagonist's 'I want' song (often the second song of the show) initiates a chronological developmental journey, climaxing in an 11 o'clock number that indicates a significant moment of change and growth in character just before the show's denouement. Sometimes the want may deepen into an even greater desire over the course of the show, but the integrated musical's narrative remains fundamentally linear and implies an inevitability of character development: the 'want' leads to the 'change', or A to B. 'Shows begin with infinite possibility', Viertel says. 'They conclude with all possibilities removed save one.'[45] In *Fun Home*, however, character development is built with a difference – and simply because the pathway is non-normative does not mean the show is 'formless', as Viertel suggests of kindred musicals *Bloody Bloody Andrew Jackson* and *Passing Strange*.[46] Alison's emotional chronology can still be outlined through strategic placement of songs, which arise at defining developmental moments in her life, but a different actor sings each musical number, and the songs do not neatly fall in chronological order. Rather than initiate a preordained developmental arc for Alison, then, each song lifts the narrative out of the present moment and elaborates on thrilling, fleeting moments of recognition: 'I know you.'

The first moment of recognition in the musical comes not from Small Alison, but from Medium Alison (played by Alexandra Socha off-Broadway and Emily Skeggs on Broadway). In what Viertel would plot as an 'aftermath song', the exuberant 'Changing My Major' elaborates on Alison's first sexual experience with a woman.[47] This song could just as easily be 'Ten Minutes Ago' from Rodgers and Hammerstein's *Cinderella* or 'A Wonderful Guy' from *South Pacific*; the song's popular verse/chorus format normalizes the ecstasy and awkwardness of a first love, regardless of gender or sexuality. While a post-coital Joan sleeps tangled up in Alison's college dorm bedsheets, Alison aims to extend this spectacular moment of connection forever – even if it means taking out a 'dementedly huge high-interest loan' to stay in school.[48] In a quick 4/4, Alison dances around in her polo short and tighty whities while unleashing a stream of overflowing feeling – a refreshingly down-to-earth expression of 'first time' excitement and anxiety. The patter song verses contrast with the revelatory 3/4 waltz of each chorus. Evocative of 'Being Alive' in *Company*, the chorus employs an additive structure that layers and heightens the moment:

> But I must say that I'm
> Changing my major to Joan
> I'm changing my major to sex with Joan
> I'm changing my major to sex with Joan
> with a minor in kissing Joan[49]

Each phrase lyrically extends the last and melodically reaches higher, looping into something new. Alison's emotional transformation is made even clearer with each chorus taking a bold semitone step up from the verse's Ab major to a new tonal area, A major.

Importantly, this transformative moment arises by way of Medium Alison seeing her 'self' as a stranger. In a bridge full of new musical material, she sings, 'I don't know who I am / I've become someone new / Nothing I just did / is anything I would do'.[50] Shaky and scared, with the harmonic grounding shifting beneath her, Alison wonders whether she is 'falling into nothingness / or flying into something so sublime?'[51] Despite the contingency of the moment, Medium Alison emerges into a final chorus that is still a semitone higher in Bb major; she gains confidence as she reasserts her change with another fresh lyrical variation. It is through repeating the chorus of 'Changing My Major' that Medium Alison begins to constitute her new-found lesbian identity – and by employing the musical theatre trope of a jubilant 'first love' song with a woman as the object of her affection, she constitutes her sexual identity with a critical difference. A tenuous sense of self-knowledge and wholeness is achieved in this fragile, beautiful moment, so rarely accorded lesbians onstage, and her 'heart feels ... complete'.[52]

It is only following this transformative moment of identity constitution that Alison can retroactively 'make sense' of her feelings as a child and incorporate them into her new-found sexual identity.

In 'Ring of Keys', Small Alison (played by precocious Sydney Lucas in both the Public Theater and Broadway productions) struggles to pinpoint just what it is about a butch delivery woman that seems so familiar. Bechdel describes the moment of recognition in the graphic novel: 'Like a traveler in a foreign country who runs into someone from home – someone they've never spoken to, but know by sight – I recognized her with a surge of joy.'[53] While in the novel Bruce immediately forces a disavowal of Alison's identification with the bulldyke delivery woman ('Is that what you want to look like?'), the musical offers Small Alison an expansive and sustaining moment of recognition through song.[54]

'Ring of Keys' is rife with rests as Alison searches for the words to express what she feels upon seeing this stranger walk through the door. In the verses, anacruses of 'I feel –', 'I want –' and 'You're so –' all leave the downbeat of the next measure open and unsung; the sparse accompaniment is exposed in these moments, oscillating between two suspended chords. In the chorus, the linguistic rhythm picks up, but rests and syncopation continue to leave the downbeats open as Alison grasps for the right descriptors. With repetitive, reaching phrases that circle within the span of a fifth, she sings in the chorus:

> Your | [rest] swagger and your | [rest] bearing
> And the | just-right clothes you're | [rest] wearing
> Your | [rest] short hair and your | [rest] dungarees and your | lace up boots
> And your | keys, oh, your | ring of | keys[55]

As illustrated above, the lyric that finally lands firmly on each and every downbeat is the title line of the song. The anacrusis of 'And your' is a launch pad; the tonality shifts from E major to an unexpected G major on 'keys', followed by an exuberant melisma and a confident reiteration of 'your ring of keys' with measured dotted quarter notes.[56] Small Alison feels an 'internal' connection to this delivery woman purely through her 'external' actions, attire and accessories. 'Do you feel my heart saying hi?' she asks in the bridge, with a shy melisma on 'hi' echoing her earlier 'oh'. One might consider this butch a 'fun house' reflection of Alison's future self; by the end of the song, Small Alison finds herself more able to articulate her identificatory feelings with a simple and repeated, 'I know you / I know you / I know you.'[57]

In Warner's schema, both 'Changing My Major' and 'Ring of Keys' qualify as 'contrasting musemes'; as moments of personal realization, they do not significantly draw on shared musical musemes and instead establish Alison's own unique character.[58] These tunes are two of the most traditionally structured songs in the show; their form makes them stand apart in a score that is otherwise full of unconventional song structures and looping musical ideas. Yet both songs also very intentionally repeat musical theatre tropes with a difference. While musicals often contain an 'I am' song confidently asserting a character's identity (for instance, Ado Annie's 'I Cain't Say No' in *Oklahoma!*), 'Ring of Keys' comes in fits and starts, emphasizing the contingency of Alison's identity in this moment. Particularly with its non-chronological placement after 'Changing My Major', this song points to the openness of this identificatory moment; it does not inexorably determine Alison's identity. Emily Skeggs in fact points out that each actor playing Alison '[got] to make choices on our own because people change and grow. But I've had a really good time watching Beth, because that's where I'm going, and watching Sydney, because that's where I was.'[59]

A ring of keys is one of the most repeated images through the musical; it is the very first object that Alison takes from a battered cardboard box, arranges on her drawing table and begins sketching at the start of the show, bringing Small Alison to life. The ring of keys returns in 'Telephone Wire', as father and daughter go for a drive together – a drive that turns out to be their last. Shortly after coming out to her family, Medium Alison returns home from college with her girlfriend Joan; her mother Helen has just recently told Alison of her father's affairs with men, and so the visit is tense and weighted with spoken and unspoken truths. Up until this point in the musical, adult Alison has refused to become too involved in her memories, repeating to herself, 'It's only writing, it's only drawing, I'm remembering something, that's all.'[60] But timelines finally collapse in 'Telephone Wire'; Bruce's attention shifts firmly from Medium Alison to adult Alison (played by Beth Malone) as he asks: 'You ready to go for that drive? Kiddo?'[61] The moment is theatrically arresting; this act of surrogation, in which adult Alison must fully step into her past and re-embody her final moments with her father, places her back in the body of her awkward teenage self, grasping for the right words, wishing to prolong the moment together and push through to a different version of this story in which her father does not kill himself.[62]

Like 'Ring of Keys', 'Telephone Wire' makes vital use of silence, with a critical gap between what is said and unsaid, and between text and subtext. This moment is the only one in which father and daughter fleetingly discuss their homosexual experiences, but they still struggle to connect over this similarity. The double-page scene in the original novel uses un-captioned images to slow the sequence's rhythm and generate uncomfortable 'rests' in the conversation, while the musical version employs a churning internal monologue for Alison that registers as an awkward silence on the drive.[63] 'Telephone Wire' begins with an anticipatory vamp outlining a fifth: an eighth note followed by a dotted quarter that seems to extend a moment too long, building anticipation for someone to say something – anything. Yet when Alison begins to sing, she does not address her father; rather, she details what she sees outside the window in a detached internal monologue that Bruce cannot 'hear'. Nouns and simple descriptors soon give way to memories attached to the places they pass; the verse begins in a low, conversational register and musically builds to a pressure point. 'Say something, talk to him', Alison belts – but her syncopated line always falls behind the beat, always too late to have the conversation she so desperately wishes she could have with her father.[64]

Musicalizing their inability to connect, Tesori's composition vacillates between two different tonal and temporal areas; while Alison exists in a propulsive 4/4 in A major, Bruce sits in a nostalgic 3/4 metre in G major.[65] Each time Alison seems ready to break out from her churning internal monologue and begin conversation in earnest, Bruce interrupts with his B section and pulls back to a reflective colla voce waltz, reminiscing on some of his first homosexual experiences without explicitly identifying himself as gay. Alison's initial command to herself, 'Say something, talk to him', transforms to a plea to her father in her final A section: 'Say something, talk to me.'[66] But she is too late: her plea to be seen, and her desire to likewise see and acknowledge her father, goes unspoken. The crucial question of *Fun Home* – 'Am I just like you?' – comes to a head in this moment. Is Bruce a 'fun house' mirror of his daughter Alison? Would saying something in this contingent moment have changed anything? Will she share his fate? Adult Alison even undertakes this journey into the past at age forty-three, the same age as her father when he took his own life.

Fun Home's song plot reinforces a duality in the musical's dramatic structure: Alison's non-linear character arc runs parallel to Bruce's journey, which follows a more conventional and linear musical theatre pathway. After all, it is Bruce and not Alison who receives both the traditional 'I want' song and 11 o'clock number in *Fun Home*. In a twist on the typical solo 'I want' song, 'Welcome to Our House on Maple Avenue' is performed by the entire Bechdel family; wife Helen and the children polish and shine Bruce's pristinely restored home to create a perfect image for an important guest from the Allegheny Historical Society. As in 'Ring of Keys', however, the chorus comes in insistent fits and starts, with heavily accented instrumental stabs in the rests of an off-kilter, syncopated line: '[rest] He wants – / [rest] He wants – / [rest] He wants – '.[67] It is telling that Bruce as a desiring subject is largely absent from his own 'I want' song; he only joins the singing family towards the end of the tune and, in fact, he spends the first half of the song primping offstage.

Beneath Bruce's surface desire to organize and beautify his heteronormative household lies a different 'want' that goes unspoken in this number, although it becomes apparent in the staging: the guest snaps a photograph at the end of the family's highly orchestrated performance, and the frozen moment inadvertently captures Bruce staring at a handsome young man who has just entered the room. 'He wants more', Alison realizes as she looks back on this moment in time.[68]

At key moments through *Fun Home*, the 'He wants' museme returns with Bruce periodically taking ownership of his underlying homosexual desire: 'I want, I want, I want', he sings, seducing their young yard worker Roy while his wife plays piano in the next room.[69] As Bruce continues to live a double life and navigate the heteronormative matrix, he stumbles into trouble with young boys that nearly destroys his family. At the end of his chilling 11 o'clock number, comprising disjointed fragments of his past, Bruce ultimately kills himself by stepping in front of a truck.[70]

A traditional musical theatre arc from an 'I want' song to an 11 o'clock number sets up a sensation of inevitability: A can only ever lead to B, Bruce's homosexual desire could only lead to his death. This trope is all too familiar, and yet it establishes a false causality; this path was not the only possibility for Bruce. Kron has emphasized that any attempt to link scenes of the show in a linear order to imply cause-and-effect relationships should be resisted, particularly when it comes to Bruce's death.[71] 'There's a different version of this visit, Dad, where it's alright, where everything turns out alright', Alison narrates before their final drive.[72] Despite her knowledge of the future, Alison sees each moment as contingent and does not resign Bruce to a predetermined 'fate' – even as she worries that his 'destiny' will be her own as well.

Bruce and Alison have strikingly different character journeys through *Fun Home*, yet they also share a core 'want' identified in the opening number. In a rare moment, father and daughter harmonize on a shared lyric: 'I want to know what's true, dig deep into who and what and why and when, until now gives way to then.'[73] For both characters, truth can come only from digging, uncovering, polishing, refining and vitally bringing the past into the present – whether refinishing a Victorian home or writing a graphic memoir. As Alison comes to learn through the process of writing through her memories, 'truth' is not necessarily something that is objectively true.[74] The house that her father refurbished is a place of death and life, both a funeral home and a home. Her graphic novel is both image and text, comedy and tragedy, fiction and reality. The past is both past and present. Bruce is both a gay man and also her father – and Alison both is and is not Bruce. All of these truths can coexist. It is perhaps no surprise, then, that Alison's journey ultimately loops her back to her past selves, who both are and are not 'past', who both are and are not 'Alison'. The finale traces Alison's fleeting moments of connection to her father across all three timelines.

A beloved trope of Jeanine Tesori musicals are time collapses, when two or three actors – all representing the same character at different ages – share the stage; in some instances, they may even be able to 'see' one another across the years and interact. In *Shrek*, three Fionas (Fiona, Teen Fiona and Young Fiona) dream of the day their prince will come in 'I Know It's Today'; while they lyrically look towards a heteronormative future, their soaring female trio delights in the 'meanwhile' of the waiting.[75] In *Violet*, the title character's life as a twenty-something runs parallel to and sometimes overlaps with her past as an insecure teenager, grappling with her hyper-visible facial scar from an accident with an axe blade. And in *Fun Home*, both Alison and Bruce's journeys are reconciled in a spellbinding finale harmonizing Small, Medium and adult Alison.

'Flying Away' can be analysed in three loose sections: a combination song collapsing fragments of the past into the present, a fresh moment of recognition between Alison and her father, and a push into the future. The finale begins by musically and lyrically returning to the opening of the show, with Small Alison demanding her Daddy's attention: she wants to play aeroplane. This moment of play was deferred in the opening scene; rather than launch his daughter into the air, Bruce roped his daughter into polishing a bunch of old junk for the fun home. In the finale, Small Alison finally prevails upon him to put his feet on her belly, take her hands and push her up. As adult Alison begins sketching this vivid memory, she captions the image with slow and measured construction: 'Daddy (comma) hey Daddy / come here okay (question mark) I need // you.' Small Alison bursts onto the scene and overlays the constructed caption with the full velocity of 'real time' dialogue: 'Daddy, hey, Daddy, come here, okay, I need you.'[76] Medium Alison soon appears and layers in, echoing 'Telephone Wire' as she pushes herself to say something to her father on their final drive.

Rather than simply reiterate familiar musical material that now lives in both Alison's and the audience's memory, Tesori actively regenerates the musemes in the finale; in the first section, the musemes are made new through their combination, and in the second section, the music begins to move beyond previously established motifs to generate a fresh path forward for Alison. As Small Alison calmly and assuredly instructs her father how to play aeroplane, adult Alison flips through her pages of drawings and sees her father as if for the first time: 'There you are, Dad.'[77] In the third section of the finale, the layering and looping of the past ultimately enables Alison to 'fly away' into a different future.[78] As Bruce launches Small Alison into the air, precariously balanced on 'the pivot point between his feet and my stomach', all three Alisons ecstatically release into soaring new terrain.[79] As Warner points out, Tesori never gives the Alisons a moment of unison or even a homophonic sung texture in the finale: their one shared lyric is a shimmering, melismatic 'fly away'.[80] Each Alison exists in her own timeline, reliving fleeting moments of connection in the present tense: the moment her father succumbs to a rare instance of physical contact in a game of aeroplane, the moment Alison and her father share their likeness on their final drive – and the moment adult Alison pieces together a vital, impressionistic 'picture of my father […] made of little marks'.[81]

Alison's selves, then, are never wholly united in this culminating moment: they still stand apart as strangers, the same and yet different, interweaving with one another in stunning polyphony. Bruce's body is absent from the stage in the finale – and yet the audience 'sees' him through the ecstatic build of the music, the exuberant performances of the three Alisons and the final projection of the aeroplane illustration from the graphic novel. Bechdel considers this projection a 'perfect' moment that sums everything up: 'Alison gets launched by her father, and because of that, she is able to go on and do something he wasn't able to do.'[82] Although aeroplane is a fictional game, Alison's launch is both metaphorical and real. In this 'rare moment of perfect balance' as she soars above her father, Alison has a bird's-eye view on her life; she can fleetingly, fabulously harmonize her selves and 'see all of Pennsylvania'.[83]

Sometimes that theatrical experience enables the audience to see all of Pennsylvania too – and thus Alison extends into a new body. After seeing the Public Theater's Public Lab workshop on 28 October 2012, I – or rather, Medium Sarah – blogged:

> I know that [it] is a fundamental impossibility – to be wholly understood, even to myself – but there are moments in literature and moments in music and moments in theater when I feel a mythical coherence. When I understand the art and the art understands me. When a hand reaches out and takes my own. I felt that at *Fun Home* on Sunday afternoon.[84]

The curious case of Bobby/Bobbie

From Greek choruses to temporal collapses, from ghosting to episodic frameworks, Stephen Sondheim's musicals delight in experimenting with temporality and form.[85] In fact, *Fun Home* shares both musical and temporal DNA with Sondheim's *Sunday in the Park with George* about pointillist painter Georges Seurat; working through memory via art enables both George and Alison to bring together the past and present to 'move on'. Sondheim's work even inches towards deconstructing the mythically integrated straight white male, whose fictional 'wholeness' is often upheld by the genre. For instance, *Follies* (1971), with book by James Goldman and originally directed by Hal Prince, fragments all four of its lead characters – Sally, Phyllis, Ben and Buddy – into their older and spectral younger selves. On the evening before a crumbling Broadway theatre is set to be demolished, the former Weismann's Follies performers reunite for a final party. As they reminisce and reperform their old acts, the aged actors find themselves haunted by the follies of their past and the possible roads they could have taken. The musical amplifies the contingency of each moment in time – how different one's life may have been if an alternative path were taken. Everyone is filled with heteronormative regret for choosing the wrong partner. After all, it is a Sondheim musical.

The show I am most interested in discussing here is *Company*, which circles around a similar theme and serves as an essential intertextual reference for the other musicals analysed in this chapter. With an organizing theme rather than a linear plot, *Company* is considered one of the first 'concept musicals' – a form that tentatively began to disrupt the 'integrated' musical's dominance in the 1970s. The show originated as eleven one-act plays about flawed partnerships seen from the angle of single outsiders; in adapting them for the musical stage, George Furth amalgamated the singletons into a central protagonist: Bobby, a New York City bachelor.[86] Bobby observes his married friends while grappling with his own commitment issues in non-linear scenes and songs linked by his thirty-fifth birthday party, which opens and closes each act and can be considered to be either a single celebration or a succession of birthdays. 'I am certain they were one', Hal Prince says. 'I wouldn't be surprised if George Furth believes there were four. It doesn't matter.'[87] *Company* has been raising questions about temporality and identity since the musical debuted, as critics and audiences often seek to (mis)read Bobby as an 'integrated' character with a deep interiority. An ongoing attempt to layer unity and integration onto the concept musical draws attention to the complications of a singular framework for understanding both identity and the musical as a genre.

One of the most common critiques of *Company* from 1970 to the present is that Bobby feels like an empty theatrical vessel – 'a cipher and even a bit of a bore' who simply mirrors back his friends' views on the challenges and virtues of relationships.[88] While the show circles around 'Bobby bubi', the character is notably absent in his own life as an active, desiring subject – a striking contrast to the 'want'-driven protagonist of the integrated musical. 'You were always outside, looking in the window while everybody was inside dancing at the party', Joanne criticizes him.[89] His girlfriends Kathy, Marta and April even liken Bobby to an undead zombie: 'Knock knock, is anybody there?'[90] Bobby's friends also lack a sense of interiority; rather than emotionally expand character, their songs operate as Brechtian commentary and counterpoint on the complications of contemporary relationships.[91] Joanne's 'The

Little Things You Do Together' offers a pointed commentary on the daily dysfunctions that make up 'perfect' relationships, while Marta's 'Another Hundred People' highlights the loneliness of the contemporary city, evoking T.S. Eliot's *The Waste Land* with dystopian imagery of Manhattan's 'crowded streets and the guarded parks [...] the rusty fountains and the dusty trees with the battered barks'.[92] This song's structure is even further fragmented by being interspersed with scenes in which Robert repeatedly fails to connect to potential partners.

Yet Bobby's interactions with his sorry/grateful married friends are intended to 'contribute to an overall arch' for the character; Bobby learns from his episodic observations and progresses to a personal breakthrough about the necessity of relationships.[93] While the song plot has varied through the years, three solos now hoist the musical's dramatic structure while also providing insight into Bobby's 'internal' life: 'Someone Is Waiting', 'Marry Me a Little' and 'Being Alive'.[94] The score can be analysed through the interval of a second – two notes which are so close as to be nearly in unison, yet just different enough to create tension. Over the course of these solos, Bobby learns to lean into dissonance and to find beauty in the expanded harmonic possibilities; after all, that tension is what defines the human experience of 'being alive'. As a way of activating this passive protagonist and further emphasizing his arc, several productions of *Company* have been directed as an 'internal' journey of self-discovery for Bobby; the 1996 Sam Mendes production, for instance, implies that most of the show takes place in Bobby's memory or imagination as he decides whether or not to attend his thirty-fifth birthday party.[95] Tantalizingly, Furth's original playlets were written at the suggestion of his therapist, and Sondheim has posited that the action may take place on a psychiatrist's couch.[96]

Still, is Bobby's character arc believable? Does the audience leave the theatre convinced that Bobby has finally realized the necessity of relationships, despite their challenges? Sondheim calls the ending a cop-out, considering it 'too small a moment', while Hal Prince observes that because the ending is not structurally 'eased' into, the audience may not be convinced of the change.⁹⁷ 'Being Alive' offers a compelling transformative moment as a stand-alone song, but it is arguably an unsatisfying deus ex machina within the context of the show: Bobby's earlier solos are deeply ambivalent about his 'want', and the musical as a whole does not set up a steady linear developmental journey that gives 'the sense of inevitable progression and growth that would suggest the gradual enlightenment of a hero'.⁹⁸ Like Alison's trajectory to understanding her 'self' in *Fun Home*, then, Bobby's character arc is built with a difference.

Since the original production, speculation has run rampant about Bobby's 'difference': Is Bobby actually gay? 'So many winks does Bobby share together with us that if we don't take this character for a gay cryptogram, it is only because there seems nothing cryptic about him', D.A. Miller asserts.⁹⁹ From his penchant for decorating his own apartment to his affinity for ladies who lunch, this perpetual bachelor is clearly coded. John Clum posits that, perhaps at the end of the musical when he disappears from his circle of married friends, Bobby is finally cutting off his straight ties and escaping to a new queer life.¹⁰⁰ And yet in interview after interview, the creators repudiate Bobby's homosexuality. The 1996 Sam Mendes and 2006 John Doyle productions even reintegrate a cut scene that seems designed to end these suppositions; when his recently divorced friend Peter makes a pass at him, Bobby blows off his proposition as a joke. However, the dialogue actively opens up conversation about Bobby's sexuality and is too ambiguous to completely foreclose the possibility that he may be gay.¹⁰¹ Furth and Sondheim's initial insistence on Bobby's heterosexuality may have stemmed from anxiety about critics' homophobia; a slew of bad reviews in 1970 (only one year post-Stonewall) could have condemned the new musical, which has retrospectively been considered Sondheim's first outing as composer/lyricist in a show that would come to define his unique style.¹⁰² What's more, both writers may have desired to deflect any speculations about their own sexuality and thwart attempts to read their personal lives into the musical.¹⁰³

In some instances, an incredibly charismatic actor can 'fill out' this cipher of a role and 'get the juice of' this elusive character. Adam Feldman observes that the most successful performances of Bobby have been by gay men, who can perhaps more easily tap into the subtext of the part:

> The straight Dean Jones originated the role in 1970, and was never comfortable in it; he was released from his contract soon after the show opened, and replaced with the gay Larry Kert (who became the only replacement actor to ever [to] be nominated for a Tony). History nearly repeated itself in 1995, when the Roundabout revival of *Company* – starring the straight, lukewarmly received Boyd Gaines – failed to transfer to a longer run because the producer of the proposed production wanted to replace Gaines with gay actor Michael Rupert. In the 1998 biography *Stephen Sondheim: A Life*, the composer said that he only time he had ever believed his own *Company* finale, 'Being Alive', was when he heard it sung by the late, gay David Carroll. And another gay actor, John Barrowman, earned widespread raves for his 2002 Bobby at the Kennedy Center.[104]

Feldman penned this article in response to Raul Esparza's coming-out interview in *The New York Times*, published while Esparza was portraying Bobby in the 2006 John Doyle actor/musician revival. But an explicitly gay Bobby has yet to be presented on stage, with several attempts having been shut down by Furth's estate and Sondheim's lawyer. News emerged in 2013 of a Sondheim-approved developmental reading helmed by John Tiffany that would feature Daniel Evans as Bobby, Alan Cumming as Joanne, and Bobby Steggert and Michael Urie among Bobby's 'revolving door of boyfriends'. When asked about this U-turn in casting, Sondheim explained, 'Marriage is seen as something very different in 2013 than it was in 1970' – but the concept never made it beyond the reading.[105] As a result, Bobby bubi remains a perpetual tease, resisting unity of character and endlessly provoking us with the possibilities.

While an explicitly 'out' Bobby has yet to be seen, Marianne Elliott's gender-swapped revisal premiered in London's West End in 2018, starring Rosalie Craig as Bobbie. The initial impetus for this female-led production actually came from Elliott's (male) business partner Chris Harper, who was listening to the *Company* cast album on repeat as he visited the hospital where his premature twins had recently been born: 'It was because of the twins that I thought of doing Company', he says.[106] A successful week-long workshop, which Elliott asked Sondheim to evaluate with a group of young people and women, convinced the composer of the concept's merit, and the revisal proceeded to production.

'At last, "Company" has a human pulse and a proper dramatic core. And for that to happen, it took a woman', begins Matt Wolf's rave review in *The New York Times*.[107] Emphasizing the 'internal', critics note how this revisal finds 'hidden depths' in the classic,[108] how Elliott 'frees the musical's feelings',[109] and how the show's 'heart' finally caught up with its head.[110] Brantley particularly praises the 'emotional coherence' that Rosalie Craig's performance brings to the show: 'Bobbie wears her feelings on her face – and in her long-limbed question mark of a body, and in her tender, yearning voice – in a way that the audience can always read, even if her friends and lovers can't.'[111] The reviews' word choices are notable since both Bobby the character and Sondheim the composer have historically been accused of cold, masculine intellectualism. Although the production sticks closely to the original script and score, critics consider the simple gender swap transformative; by filling out this cipher of a part with a 'feeling' female, they suggest, the musical suddenly develops a new sense of depth.

For Matt Wolf, the root of that new-found interiority is the timeline imposed by the biological clock: 'We know that, because she's a woman, her body clock is surely ticking', he writes. 'And if she wants to have children, she'll need to settle on a man to do it with.'[112] Temporal pressure is exerted on Bobbie from the outset of the revisal. In Bunny Christie's Alice in Wonderland-like set, Bobbie's impending age – thirty-five – haunts her on front doors, clothing and increasingly gigantic party balloons that crowd her studio apartment. Her married friends bombard her with questions as to when she is going to settle down. And in a nightmare 'Tick-Tock' sequence, Bobbie splinters into multiple selves, attempting to navigate a horrifying flurry of future roles with her possible partners and children. In the original production, 'Tick-Tock' is an orgasmic number of sexual encounter; Kathy – played by then-little known Donna McKechnie – explodes into a sensual solo choreographed by Michael Bennett. In this dance sequence, the ticking clock represents Bobby's distraction and fear of intimacy; even as he is in bed with April, Kathy is dancing in his head.[113] In many other revivals, this number has simply been cut; on a practical level, there may be too few Donna McKechnies in the world to carry the four-minute dance routine.[114] But in Marianne Elliott's revisal, the 'tick tock' returns as an incessant biological clock – and for a female Bobbie, a moment of sexual encounter must linearly lead to reproduction.

While many critics note the 'external' or societally imposed pressures on Bobbie to marry, they often pinpoint this new ticking clock as something internal – a biological pressure from 'within'.[115] But the biological clock is a cultural myth that only entered our lexicon in recent decades. After its first mention in a *Washington Post* article in 1978 and the publication of a 1979 book entitled *Up Against the Clock: Career Women Speak on the Choice to Have Children*, the concept of the biological clock took root in the 1980s as a new regulatory mechanism for constituting the gendered body. In a fresh form of Foucauldian biopolitics, the biological clock intertwines the contingency and specificity of culture with 'what are perceived to be objective biological facts' to temporally manage 'female' bodies.[116] While reproductive abilities do end at a certain age, the cultural construct of this ticking clock exerts heteronormative pressure and imposes on the female body a masculine, goal-oriented temporal pattern geared towards a particular type of (re)productivity. The biological clock represents a desire to 'turn back the clock', employing a 'pseudo-biological determinism' to perpetuate traditional gender roles and a narrow definition of family; it shifts and actively forecloses a woman's other possible futures.[117]

Unfortunately, then, the 'finely crafted unity' that the gender swap newly brought to *Company* was nothing but a masculine, linear developmental narrative imposed on Bobbie's journey.[118] In one of the few critical pieces of criticism about this revisal – and one of the few pieces written by a woman – Lauren Sheehan-Clark elaborates:

> On one hand, [Bobbie] gets her time in the limelight as a strong female protagonist who learns how to *want* something. On the other hand, that 'something' turns out to be marriage. It's almost as if women haven't been hearing for centuries that marriage should be their end goal in life, especially when they get to an age as 'old' as Bobbie's 35 years.[119]

Despite the production being directed by a woman, the alternately frustrating and exhilarating sense of openness to the concept musical's protagonist is foreclosed by the ticking pseudo-biological clock of the revisal. While 'Being Alive' could always have been read as a capitulation to societal expectation, it feels particularly depressing as Rosalie Craig kicks about on the stage instead of standing firm and self-possessed. Transposing this song into a higher register also diminishes its vocal power, weakening the song's 'believability' even as a stand-alone number. A gay couple may be 'Not Getting Married Today' in this revisal, but the production's gender swaps are highly selective so as to as ensure Bobbie's prospective partners are all male; even the 'Ladies Who Lunch' scene has been altered so that Joanne no longer propositions Bobbie, but offers Bobbie her husband instead. The heteronormative imperative prevails, and the pressure to mate and reproduce is intensified by the gender swap.

Perhaps this production was designed to be the most Brechtian revival of *Company* yet, exposing the machinations of gender – but the exuberant critical response, which emphasized a compelling 'internal' transformation of the protagonist and new-found unity of dramatic form, complicates any critical stance intended by the revisal. I would rather watch a cipher, refracting a world of open possibilities.

I am *A Strange Loop*

We begin in 'Blackness'. Suddenly, intermission chimes begin. Lights up on a Broadway usher with his back towards us, ringing the chimes again and again. Audience members begin to pester our leading man: 'Usher-usher! Usher! Usher!' they call.[120] Repetition makes a familiar word begin to sound strange; through different rhythms and melodies, the word loses its meaning as it spirals into thrilling polyphony. This strange loop begins *A Strange Loop*, the 2020 Pulitzer Prize-winning musical by Michael R. Jackson.

'Usher' is both our protagonist's job and his name; he is being interpellated, called into being in this contingent moment in time, by these pesky audience members. And yet, an usher is not all Usher is; it is simply how he makes his money. In a daydream during his day job, Usher's own musical *A Strange Loop* unfolds – a show 'about a Black gay man writing a musical about a Black gay man who's writing a musical about a Black gay man who's writing a musical about a Black gay man, etc.'[121] As with Alison in *Fun Home*, the looping, revisionary process of making art is a way for Usher to make sense of his multifaceted, intersectional identity. Rather than write a graphic novel hybridizing text and image, Usher writes a musical featuring scenes, song, dance and other spectacular elements whose juxtaposition generates a more 'truthful' representation of his experiences as a queer Black man.

'Usher, usher!' is undeniably evocative of the opening of *Company*, in which the perpetual bachelor's good and crazy married friends incessantly call him: 'Bobby … Bobby … Bobby baby … Bobby bubi … '[122] *A Strange Loop* is a kindred concept musical: episodic, non-linear and 'stuck' in time. Much like Bobby's recurring birthday parties that frame *Company*, the leitmotif of intermission chimes frame this (intermission-less) musical, which unfolds entirely between the first and second act of *The Lion King* – while simultaneously unfolding in the theatre in Usher's mind and, of course, the theatre where the audience is presently watching the show; the musical premiered off-Broadway at Playwrights Horizons in 2019 and had a 'pre-Broadway run' at DC's Woolly Mammoth in autumn 2021. Usher's 'big, Black and queer-ass American Broadway show' comes into being in the gap between the 'action', the time in which 'nothing happens', the liminal space in which audience members get a drink and check their phones and use the toilets.[123] Intermission is not a glamorous space of emergence, but there certainly isn't much space being made for such a big Black gay musical on Broadway.[124]

Musical theatre rarely centres marginalized, let alone intersectional, identities and experiences. The genre exists precisely because of Black performance practices from jazz music to tap dance, and yet a 'Cool White Guy' narrative often whitewashes and erases this foundational labour to 'legitimize' and elevate the musical as an art form.[125] Michael R. Jackson notes that the musical theatre industry is even more predominately white than 'straight' theatre; no matter how colour-conscious white writers aim to be, a lack of representation behind the scenes still means 'you never have that other consciousness delivering the stories and bodies that will disrupt the default assumptions'.[126] Despite a history of gay creators of musical theatre, explicitly queer stories have also only recently been foregrounded in the genre – and gay characters are still frequently flattened into stereotypes of the 'drag queen', the 'drama queen' and the 'dancing queen'.[127] How strange and thrilling, then, to see a new musical that centres the multifaceted complexity of a Black gay musical theatre writer. Usher describes himself in the opening number, 'Intermission Song', with an almost comedically long list of identifiers:

> a young overweight-to-obese homosexual and/or gay and/or queer, cisgender male, able-bodied university-and-graduate-school educated, musical-theater-writing, Disney-ushering, broke-ass middle-class far-Left-leaning Black-identified-and-classified American descendant of slaves full of self-conscious femme energy and who thinks he's probably a vers bottom but not totally certain of that obsessing over the latest draft of his self-referential musical *A Strange Loop*![128]

Full of options and in-betweens, Usher's self-description is poetic, fluid and impossible to contain; the show's episodic structure further suggests that Usher's journey to understanding the full complexity of his identity is open, unfinished and far from linear.

Not only is Usher Black and queer, an usher and a musical theatre writer, but he is further multiplied by being 'surrounded by his *extremely* obnoxious Thoughts!'[129] Whereas in *Fun Home* Alison is fragmented into her 'selves' at different ages, in *A Strange Loop*, Usher simultaneously exists in the body of 'Usher' – powerhouse Larry Owens in the off-Broadway premiere – and six 'Thoughts', played by six queer performers of colour: Antwayn Hopper, James Jackson Jr., L. Morgan Lee, John-Michael Lyles, John-Andrew Morrison and Jason Veasey. These swirling Thoughts inhabit the 'strange loop' in Usher's mind much like a Greek chorus; they both comment on the action and take part in it as *Lion King* patrons, imaginary love interests, Usher's daily self-loathing and his parents. All of these characters are facets of Usher but simultaneously queer people of colour themselves, fully embodied on stage and showing diversity within this marginalized group. Jackson has emphasized that the show's structure is not one of a 'star and ensemble'; as in *A Chorus Line*, all of the characters are stars who bring their own unique energies, vocal qualities and acting types to the story of this man called Usher.[130] Femme and butch and neither, 'treble clef and also bass', these seven actors demonstrate that the 'Black gay experience' is a vibrant multiplicity.[131]

A Strange Loop manipulates time to show how intersectional identities emerge through a critical reworking of mainstream cultural texts in which they are frequently reduced to stereotypes, if they are represented at all. José Muñoz's theories of disidentification provide important grounds for understanding these processes of identification, which can activate a mythic selfhood for queer people of colour. While identification implies a seamless interpellation into ideology and counteridentification implies a complete ideological rejection, the process of disidentification rewrites a mainstream text to expose the text's exclusions and to empower minority identities and identifications.[132]

As a survival strategy, disidentification offers a space of social agency within hegemonic systems of power. Finding himself locked out of the halls of representation in both the (white) gay community and the (straight) Black community, Usher reworks texts from *The Lion King* to Liz Phair to express his multifaceted selves. In writing and performing these episodic disidentifications, Usher discovers that he is his own biggest, best creation – a mash-up of fictions freed from a mythic desire to integrate his diverse parts into a unified 'whole'.[133]

Throughout *A Strange Loop*, Usher draws glaring attention to stereotypical representations of Black identity in popular culture. As a starting place, recall that the entire musical unfolds during the intermission of *The Lion King*, Disney's African animal pageantry by white creators. 'There will be performers running down the aisles and wearing pantaloons and gaudy flowing robes that I think are meant to indicate the wholesome beauty of "Mother Africa!" There will be swinging birds on fishing poles and a Black Ken doll with a crossover dialect in a lion costume!' Usher exclaims as he attempts to usher patrons back to their seats in the opening number.[134] Character names from *The Lion King* pop up in outrageously clichéd situations throughout the script, such as when Usher's mother Sarabi calls to gossip about the family's 'babymamadrama'. Sarabi speaks in an exaggerated Black dialect and eats Popeyes chicken while gabbing about how Scar may have raped Rafficki; she urges Usher to turn it all into a reality show – a fiction profitably sold as 'reality'.[135]

These stereotypes uncomfortably overlap with the world created by Black creative Tyler Perry, perhaps best known for his alter-ego, gun-toting and Bible-wielding sassy grandma Madea. Even with a Black writer/director/producer behind the scenes, Perry's movies, television series and gospel plays trade in stereotypes that Michael R. Jackson considers kin to a minstrel show.[136] And yet Usher's family and Ancestors proclaim that Tyler Perry writes 'real life'; moreover, Perry's products sell – and employ Black people in the process.[137] Usher's mother and agent urge the starving artist to write a Tyler Perry gospel play to make some money and serve the Black community – but as in *Fun Home*, 'real life' sets up a tragic narrative inevitability. The exaggerated Tyler Perry scene that Usher ultimately writes culminates in an ironic gospel funeral for a gay man who died of AIDS. 'AIDS is God's punishment' is harmonized and elaborated by a choir as gospel truth; the refrain repeats again and again in unnervingly lush and powerful variations. This shockingly infectious number pits text against music to hold the audience accountable for their entertainment: Which identities are these stories celebrating, and which are they excluding? Will the audience clap along?

The dark twist to the Tyler Perry gospel play draws attention to how frequently trauma is the focus of Black narratives in mainstream entertainment.[138] While Usher's identity is undeniably legislated through this grief (and indeed, Michael R. Jackson lost his musical collaborator Darius Marcel Smith to HIV-related complications in 2019), Michael R. Jackson aims not to centre trauma in *A Strange Loop*. 'There are difficulties that one can go through in that body that are not necessarily about their destruction', Michael R. Jackson says.[139] Usher's reworkings of Black characters and narratives show not a complete disavowal of mainstream representations, but a desire for more complexity and multiplicity to the representations available.[140]

Disidentification paints desire into psychoanalytic schemes of identification, and thus Usher's identity is most vibrantly unleashed by his 'Inner White Girl', who comes out to play on days when his Blackness feels like a burden. With 'authentic' singer-songwriter vibes, Usher puts on a performative mantle of strength, power and self-expression in a guitar-driven song *à la* Liz Phair, Tori Amos or Alanis Morissette.[141] In fact, an early version of *A Strange Loop* circled around Usher's relationship to Liz Phair's emotionally raw, sexually explicit music; through the narrative, Usher doggedly pursued Phair to write mash-ups of her songs, which would culminate in her song 'Strange Loop'. 'Because we live in an imperialist, white supremacist, capitalist patriarchy, there's constant policing of your self-expression and your thinking and of what you want for yourself and your life', Jackson explains – but white rocker women boldly express themselves without consequence.¹⁴² Throughout 'Inner White Girl', Usher's Thoughts continually remind him of his Blackness, cooing 'Who, who is you?' in background vocals evocative of *The Little Mermaid*'s faux-Calypso ballad 'Kiss the Girl'.¹⁴³ Although Usher is frustrated by the contrast between all that white girls can do and the strict limits placed on Black boys, the performative power of this song momentarily empowers the writer to break himself out of his strange loop of self-loathing and tap into the ability to self-express in his own way.

Usher's own way happens to be through the genre of musical theatre, although he is not seamlessly interpellated into that form either; after all, since when has musical theatre been the bastion of queer people of colour in all their complexity? Usher observes that most 'Black musicals' relegate performers of colour to 'sha-la-la-ing in the background with bouffant wigs on or being blackfaced white characters', and of course, both *The Lion King* and Tyler Perry's gospel plays are themselves types of musicals (a Disney film/stage musical and a play with music) that flatten Black identity into stereotypes.¹⁴⁴ During the intermission of *The Lion King*, a well-meaning tourist from Florida – portrayed by Thought 1 – strikes up a conversation with Usher and imparts some words of wisdom to help him break through his writer's block. Her musical theatre-style advice song shares wisdom similar to that of a self-possessed white girl rocker: 'Live your life and tell your story in exactly the same way: Truthfully and without fear! Despite those who wish you would disappear.'¹⁴⁵ Yet her light and breezy tune overflows with inane platitudes, which ring flat and meaningless in the end; the advice not to overcomplicate his life or his writing does not resonate with Usher, as it is precisely for his complexity that he most wants to be seen.¹⁴⁶ As he writes *A Strange Loop*, then, Usher must rework the form of the musical to embrace his complexity and difference.

It is here that we must add another twist to the strange loop: that Michael R. Jackson is a 'real life' counterpart to Usher. A strange slippage between the real and fictional Black gay musical theatre writers naturally occurs while analysing this show. *A Strange Loop* began with a thinly veiled autobiographical monologue Jackson wrote shortly after graduating from NYU's Dramatic Writing BFA programme; 'Why I Can't Get Work' described a young Black gay man attempting to understand his alienation in the theatre industry. Jackson was in a negative feedback loop at the time: 'It was like I was on the outside of my body looking in and on the inside of my body scratching to get out', he recalls.[147] As he began studying at NYU's Graduate Musical Theatre Writing programme and penning thematically related material, this monologue slowly began spinning into a full-length ensemble piece refracting his experience as a Black gay man.[148]

While *A Strange Loop* riffs on personal experience, Jackson prefers the term self-referential to autobiographical.[149] This choice of terminology refers to Douglas Hofstadter's theories of identity: as elaborated in the introduction to this chapter, Jackson's musical explores identity as a self-referential structure, or a 'strange loop', from which consciousness arises. Notably, the theory followed the art: only midway through the process, after writing the draft that would have culminated in Liz Phair's 'Strange Loop', did Jackson google the term 'strange loop' and stumble upon Hofstadter's ideas.

> When I read that it was all about self-reference, I screamed because the piece itself was about self-reference though that's not what I was thinking of it as formally. So it was this weird thing where Liz Phair, who I was using to help write about self-reference led me to Douglas Hofstadter who had a whole theory about self-reference, which gave me a container for a piece that was inherently about self-reference. So it was like a 'strange loop' in and of itself.[150]

In addition to being a Black gay creative in a majority white field, Jackson is notable for penning all three elements of the musical: book, music and lyrics. While the industry now expects musical theatre performers to be triple threats (or even quadruple threats who sing, dance, act and play a musical instrument), musical theatre writing is still often split among collaborators: sometimes a trio, but often a duo with one collaborator writing music and another words (as in Rodgers and Hammerstein's collaboration) or with one writing songs and another writing script (as in Sondheim's collaborations with various bookwriters). Critics often express suspicion of creatives who perform such radical hybridity; for Jackson, the anxiety of not being a 'real' composer was also self-imposed, as he used to feel his self-taught musicianship was inferior to his university-trained book and lyric writing. Jackson has only recently come to fully accept the mantle of 'composer' instead of simply 'songwriter'; he still sometimes moonlights as a performer as well.[151] And yet the fact that *A Strange Loop*'s book, music and lyrics come from the same artistic mind does not ensure their complete integration; rather, Jackson boldly juxtaposes these theatrical elements. Jackson discerns a critical convergence between the intersectionality of the musical as a genre and the intersectionality of identity: 'Writing for theatre is fucking *hard*', he says. 'When you add music to the mix, it gets even more complicated because of the pluralistic ways music can function in storytelling. And when you add people of color to *that*, talk about intersectionality!'[152]

If the musical as a genre is its own self-referential strange loop, then for decades, an 'integrated' identity has been repeated, often marginalizing and even erasing the genre's inherent multiplicity and complexity in the process. *A Strange Loop* turns the musical into a stranger: familiar, yet different. In fact, we may 'see' the genre as if for the first time through this new musical. Michael R. Jackson's musical repeats familiar patterns with a critical difference: a radical acceptance of theatrical elements' hybridity and an embrace of the possibilities of their juxtaposition, which is particularly suited to represent our world in all its intersectionality and complexity.

A Strange Loop contains a familiar song plot, but this tenuous arc cannot be so easily reduced to a linear drive of inexorable character development; Usher's 'want' and his non-linear, episodic disidentifications lead to a highly unexpected conclusion. Usher's 'I want' song, 'Today', establishes his daily desire to 'change my whole life forever', which is tied to the process of editing his musical to correct every imperfection – but he is stuck in a loop of self-hatred. The verses of 'Today' circle around the tight range of a third, and any time the chorus ambitiously reaches into new melodic territory, the change is interrupted by Usher's Thoughts. Manifesting as 'backtalk' show host Wendy Williams, Usher's daily self-loathing interjects to remind him how worthless he is; his financial faggotry updates him on how much he owes in student loans; and his supervisor of sexual ambivalence shuts down his sex-deprived body and mind. While the accompaniment grows more tense and dissonant with each verse, Usher tries to drown out the cycle of self-loathing and make a change, even invoking his Inner White Girl for support – but the song's looping verse/chorus structure never modulates to a transformative new key, nor does it end with a high belt and determined button. Usher and his Thoughts continually throttle his own ambitions and cut off his song mid-phrase: 'Oh, girl, *whatever!*'[153]

Usher's desire to change himself returns as a leitmotif at key moments throughout the show, but he is continually impeded from 'moving on'. In a traditionally integrated musical, Usher's 11 o'clock number would finally drive him to the transformative change he so badly wants; the 11 o'clock number is often a propulsive and outwardly focused song of self-realization, a spotlit solo directed to the audience.[154] But in *A Strange Loop*, Usher retreats to an introspective mode after the darkly ironic Tyler Perry gospel play in which he attempted to make visible 'real life'.[155] By this point in the show, Sarah Whitfield observes, any semblance of a traditional structure has collapsed, and something different is emerging.[156] The verses of 'Memory Song' are made up of gapped melodic mirrors – not a perfect inversion, but an evocative reflection of one another. Underpinned by a glassy and minimalistic piano vamp, Usher calls and responds with himself, with the call in a higher and more youthful register, and the response lower and more grounded:

CALL: Five foot four / high school gym / sneaking a cupcake
RESPONSE: These are my memories / These are my memories
CALL: Shooting hoops / off the rim / slow on the uptake
RESPONSE: These are my memories / These are my memories[157]

An extended mid-range phrase gives a momentary release to the call/response structure, then bridges seamlessly into the refrain: 'These are my memories of one lone Black gay boy I knew who chose to turn his back on the Lord'.[158] The relentlessly repeated note and stalwart rhythm of 'one lone Black gay boy I know who chose to turn his back on the Lord' emphasizes Usher's 'stuck' and lonely position.

Michael R. Jackson recalls church as a double-edged sword: while jamming on gospel songs was his greatest pleasure, the music was always tied to a sex-negative, homophobic religious tradition. 'I think that was always in me, that duality', Jackson explains – and that duality becomes a formal conceit throughout *A Strange Loop*.[159] As Usher works through his increasingly 'sweet sour' memories in his 11 o'clock number, he dreams that he is flying – not soaring as in *Fun Home*'s finale, but rather struggling for survival, 'flapping both my wings so hard to keep me from dying / with a crown of godforsaken thorns on my head'.[160] In the final iterations of the refrain, the accompaniment rhythmically intensifies and the Thoughts begin to echo and support Usher. His gentle melisma on 'Lord' soon begins to loop beyond the interval of a third, the interval in which Usher has continually found himself stuck since his 'I want' song. As the melismatic phrase spirals higher and higher, Usher leaps up an octave to belt the refrain – and suddenly, in a stunning reversal, this 'lone Black gay boy' realizes that turning his back on the Lord is both what condemned him and what ensured his survival. Both/and. His memories and music calm and return to the glassy vamp of the song's beginning.

And so Usher turns his back to the audience, as in the beginning of the show, and he rings his chimes. That's it. That's really how the show ends. But of course, 'The audience can't go home ... Until [Usher] faces himself' – or rather, faces his selves, in the bodies of his Thoughts. Usher's 'self' is also now coextensive with the audience, as Jackson makes clear in a thrilling stage direction: 'Usher turns to the audience and faces himself.'[161] With the audience as his mirror, Usher begins singing the finale, which sounds strangely familiar. The exact melody of Usher's 'I want' song returns, this time rhythmically expanded with space for reflection between each line and new harmonic possibilities underpinning it. He lyrically reflects on the many conflicting parts that make up his illusion of identity, but the chorus that previously pushed for change never arrives. Instead, the verse keeps looping in fresh new variations: slight rhythmic tweaks, the layering in of new instruments, the addition of Usher's Thoughts. Rather than interrupt Usher, they now echo and support him in his luminous, expansive moment of self-reflection. The conclusion is bold in both content and form. Rather than change himself, Usher accepts his many divergent selves; in so doing, he asks the audience to contemplate the strangeness of selfhood and the complex particularities of life in a Black queer body.

Jackson's critical act of disidentification with the genre of musical theatre does not mean a wholesale rewrite of the form. It merely requires seeing things from a different angle: eschewing the musical's drive towards integration and high art, and instead making visible the multiplicity that has always been in the self and in the form. The deep interiority of the musical, as it turns out, is its multifaceted surface. A Neil Gaiman quotation used as an epigraph in an earlier version of the script likens this hybridity to facets in a jewel; the way the light catches a facet, we can see one aspect of the gem at a time, but never the whole. *A Strange Loop* thrills because the content and form are not at all 'integrated', but they mirror, refract and complicate one another; they urge us to hold multiple facets in our strange loop of a brain at once without attempting to smooth them out or unify them. *A Strange Loop* celebrates multiplicity, hybridity and intersectionality in the way that only a musical really can: through song and dance, colour and light. It is important not to read *A Strange Loop* as an 11 o'clock number heralding an exciting generic change in a linear narrative history of the musical. Rather, it is a fresh moment of recognition: I know you.

We begin in 'Blackness'. Suddenly, intermission chimes begin. Lights up on a Broadway usher with his back towards us, ringing the chimes again and again. Audience members begin to pester our leading man: 'Usher-usher! Usher! Usher!' they call. Repetition makes a familiar word begin to sound strange; through different rhythms and melodies, the musical spirals into thrilling polyphony. So many possibilities.

Conclusion: 'Everything You're Feeling Is Appropriate'

> *It's going to go on a lot longer than you're going to want it to.*
>
> Taylor Mac, *A 24-Decade History of Popular Music*,
> St. Ann's Warehouse, 8 October 2016[1]

> *We're going through this history together, we've got the onslaught of history, all this weight on our shoulders, and what are we going to do with it?*
>
> Taylor Mac, *The Guardian*[2]

It is 31 December 2020. It has been nine months since the World Health Organization declared the novel coronavirus outbreak (Covid-19) a global pandemic, and there is nothing like a pandemic to make one intimately, viscerally aware of the construction of time.[3] Time moves too quickly. Where did the summer go? Christmas happened already? Time is packed – working from home, homeschooling, caring for family, caring for self, caring for the world. Zoom fatigue is real, and the 24-hour news cycle is relentless. Time simultaneously moves too slowly. What day of the week is it again? Days melt into one another without a schedule, without events, without the dopamine rush of change, novelty, excitement.[4] Time empties out – social plans dissolve, jobs vanish. How do you measure a day, a month, a year when unmoored from routine? Another Netflix binge? More sourdough bread making? With no clearly defined end to the pandemic in sight, time drags.

The time of capital shifts, revealing our norms as they are actively reconfigured by the crisis.[5] We shop less for clothing and electronics; we hoard toilet paper and pasta sauce. Entertainment venues shutter; jigsaw puzzle sales boom.[6] 'Mom and pop' high street shops collapse in the quiet of another lockdown while online groceries run out of delivery slots and Amazon Prime's shipping guarantee can no longer be guaranteed due to demand. Cafes and restaurants hesitantly reopen – perilous for cooks in close proximity and for waiters and delivery workers with hundreds of contacts on any given day. Not everyone's job can be performed from home. Time is biased, and there is nothing like a pandemic to expose inequality.[7] While some are furloughed and some are fired, others are on the frontline, overworked and underpaid; time takes its toll on these labouring bodies.[8] Black and minority ethnic groups are disproportionately exposed to the virus and devalued in the healthcare system. Women bear the brunt of childcare; many leave the workforce entirely. The greatest protection against Covid-19, it turns out, is privilege.

There is no respite from the pandemic and no time for collective grief and mourning. The numbers keep rising – at least in Western countries such as the United Kingdom and the United States, where staunch beliefs in exceptionalism and individualism lead to a prioritization of private freedoms over the health of the community, the time of the economy over the time of a human life. The successes of East Asian countries are sidelined, and lessons from their swift and precautionary approaches are ignored; though this is a global pandemic, widely varying national responses and border controls dictate whether 'normal time' can safely resume in any given location. But perhaps the problem is that 'normal time' never entirely stopped. Whether working in a hospital or from a home office, whether employed or unemployed, we are expected to press ahead, to be productive, to make something of this strange moment. The impulse to output is driving, unyielding, exhausting. And so theatre artists fumble with film. Lecturers learn how to use breakout rooms. Families juggle business calls alongside multiplication tables.

All the while, the standstill of a pandemic urges us to pause, take stock and take care of one another.

'Maybe we've caught the virus of prophecy. Be still. Toil no more', Prior suggests in *Angels in America*.⁹ Parallels between HIV/AIDS and Covid-19 are not exact, of course, but an undeniable resonance exists across these timelines. 'It's a different kind of pandemic', Tony Kushner says, elaborating that Covid-19 has 'shut down so much of civilization'. 'But we have yet again a combination of a biological disaster and right-wing Republican chicanery colliding catastrophically. And their antisocial, anti-democratic psychotic individualism again manifesting at exactly the moment when it's imperative that people remember how interconnected we all are.'¹⁰ A resonance also exists in how time has been made strange by both epidemics. Queer temporality emerged most spectacularly in the wake of the HIV/AIDS epidemic at the end of the twentieth century, when gay communities' horizons of possibility were severely diminished by the health crisis.¹¹ And in the past nine months of Covid-19, time's normative construction – and the extreme biases of and limits to this empty, homogenous time – have been made visible on a staggering scale. As we imagine new futurities, time can and indeed *must* be built with a difference.

Flashback to 2016: A musical number

Lately, my thoughts return to Taylor Mac's *A 24-Decade History of Popular Music*, a freewheeling 24-hour history of the United States of America from 1776 to 2016 told through the vehicle of queered popular music. The 24-hour-long concert from 8 to 9 October 2016 featured singing, dancing, eating and even napping with 600 strangers and friends at St. Ann's Warehouse in Brooklyn. In the midst of a pandemic that requires social distancing and limiting time spent together, the memory of Mac's intimate durational experience feels especially strange and wonderful – a jolt of ecstatic time. While Mac's

24-Decade History is far from a conventional musical, the work can be read as one expansive time-warping musical number; it represents an extreme example of how musical performance can bend and even break normative narratives. Vitally memorializing lives lost to the HIV/AIDS epidemic, the performance imagines new ways of building community that lean into intersectionality, imperfection, contingency and risk. These new horizons can only be revealed by implicating spectators as performers, actively involved in warping dominant ideologies together.

Taylor Mac, a drag performance artist who goes by the gender pronoun 'judy' when discussing stagework and *he/him/his* in daily life, pinpoints an AIDS action he attended as a 'suburban queer kid' in 1987 as the catalyst for the Pulitzer Prize-shortlisted *24-Decade History*.[12] The first time Mac ever saw an 'out' homosexual, he saw thousands at once. 'What has stuck with me from that day was experiencing a community coming together – in the face of such tragedy and injustice – and expressing their rage (and joy at being together) via music, dancing, chanting and agency', Mac says. 'Not only was the community using itself to destroy an epidemic but the activists were also using a disease, their deterioration, and human imperfection as a way to aid their community.'[13] Judy's career has been about reiterating this communal experience to explore how imperfection can foster new forms of affiliation.

Crediting Sondheim, Taylor Mac wanted content to dictate form; thus popular music, with its egalitarian reach to 'the people', became the predominant mode of building Mac's community in difference.[14] The arts are often marginalized in the narrative construction of history, and even within the structures of music history, popular music is often sidelined in favour of traditionally notated Western classical traditions; judy revaluates the past to emphasize the creative, the popular and the generic. Similar to Alison Bechdel parsing through her personal history, Taylor Mac digs through the pop culture detritus of US American history and manifests this 24-hour concert as a patchwork of pop songs that makes no pretence to being definitive; the concert is titled *a* 24-decade history and not *the* 24-decade history, after all.

Recognizable hits are scattered throughout the show, but also fantastic flops and long-forgotten tunes. The very act of assembling history through such a delightful, subjective hodgepodge is an act of queering it. The motley collection of songs, from 'Amazing Grace' to 'People Have the Power', draws attention to the selectivity of our narratives, their seams and gaps, and the creative act of their (re)construction; the concert revaluates the objects included as vital to the national story. Jerry Lieblich calls Taylor Mac's epic an emotional, psychological and poetic history, making meaning through an assembly of broken contexts *à la* Walter Benjamin. 'The fact that this radical act is couched in what appears to be "mere entertainment" is a pointed choice', he writes. 'Judy is saying that singing a bunch of songs can be a revolutionary act. And I'm inclined to agree.'[15]

While Mac reclaims these popular songs, judy also imaginatively recontextualizes them to centre the voices and experiences of outsiders and to unearth queer agency throughout US national history.[16] Every decade explores a different community that is building itself as a result of being torn apart, from Native Americans to early feminists to the queer communities impacted by the AIDS crisis.[17] In the monumental first hour, Mac embraces the literal dandyism of 'Yankee Doodle Dandy'; judy reclaims the queer figure as central to American culture and immediately upends any possibility of a 'straight' historical narrative.[18] The decade of 1876 to 1886 is dedicated to a radical dinner theatre revisal of *The Mikado*; fantastically resetting the operetta on Mars with glow-in-the-dark costumes and impishly autotuned vocals, *The Marskado* critiques colonialism by showing just how 'alien' Japan was to Gilbert and Sullivan. In 1906 to 1916, Mac reframes wartime morale-booster 'Keep the Home Fires Burning' as a lesbian love song for two women who embrace their attraction to each other while their husbands are at war. Some songs are cut short, others are pleasurably prolonged; some are queered from within with the slightest shift in lyrical emphasis, others have a new narrative overlaid. Mac considers himself not a teacher, but a diviner, reminding people of things that have been forgotten or buried – and encouraging them to dig deeper: 'I've got my little divining stick called my drag and it starts to vibrate and I say to the audience, "the water is right there, go digging. Go dig for the profundity."'[19]

The overarching structure of the 24-hour concert is also fundamentally shaped by queer histories. At the birth of the United States of America in 1776, twenty-four musicians take the stage; one leaves each hour until Taylor Mac is left alone for the final decade. As the lush orchestrations by Mac's musical director Matt Ray diminish hour by hour, this musical memorial to those lost to HIV/AIDS makes the audience visibly and sonically aware of the artists' vital presence and subsequent absence; loss marks the turn of each decade, and each musician is celebrated and honoured as they exit the stage.

While popular music is an organizing concept for *A 24-Decade History*, calling the show simply 'a concert' is to ignore so many aspects of this kaleidoscopic, multidisciplinary fantasia – a mix of concert, cabaret, burlesque, drag show, performance art, musical theatre, operetta, radical faerie realness ritual sacrifice and more. 'You could describe it in 20 different ways without capturing all of its dimensions', Sasha Weiss writes in *The New York Times*.[20] Taylor Mac's wildly heterogeneous aesthetic is not only a style, but a system of ethics informed by a desire to make space for all rather than to homogenize – and a desire to understand how such radical inclusivity can impact our relationships to history, facts, fantasy and performance.[21] Mac's maximalism is also informed by the heightened stakes of political activism; judy identifies the recent trend of theatrical subtlety as a privilege only afforded to those who didn't have to shout in the streets and participate in direct-action protests to stay alive while the US government ignored the AIDS epidemic.[22]

While the decades move chronologically from 1776 to 2016, the lived experience of *A 24-Decade History* is far from linear. Cultural and historical detritus mounts with each decade, evocative of Benjamin's Angel of History who 'sees one single catastrophe which keeps piling wreckage upon wreckage and hurls it in front of his feet'.[23] This densely layered queer time explodes into queer space as the theatre fills with glitter, balloons, mattresses, ping-pong balls, apple cores, carnations, feminist tracts and a giant inflatable penis festooned with the American flag. 'History's profusion of sensory stimuli and its duration offered readerly problems: where to look? what to focus on? what happened while I was in the bathroom?' Brian Teare recalls of the Philadelphia twelve-hour 'mini' marathons.[24] Indeed, it is impossible to absorb the entire theatrical experience of *A 24-Decade History* – no matter how many repeat attendees (myself included) may try.[25]

One of the performance's least subtle elements is the parade of extravagant costumes by Machine Dazzle. Much as Mac digs through popular music history, Machine Dazzle transforms diverse cultural images and ideologies into ornate, symbolic fashion statements for each decade: a shocking murder ballad headdress of two turkeys for the Trail of Tears, a white picket fence skirt tidily encapsulating the conservative bent of the 1950s, a glorious golden womb dress that descends from the ceiling to envelop Mac and foster the birth of a new world order in the final hour of the performance. The drag appropriation is brazen and messy; Lieblich questions what to make of the garishly large Star of David necklace, leopard print shtreimel and sequined yarmulke Mac wears during the 1900s, featuring songs of the Lower East Side tenements.[26] The startling juxtaposition of these images, fabrics, tunes and times fantastically discloses the tensions, conflicts and contradictions of US history, refusing to settle into a tidy solution and raising more questions than answers. Costume pieces are visibly upcycled and thrillingly prone to fray, unravel and shed glitter as Mac moves – 'Glitter rhymes to litter', Machine Dazzle says.[27] Mac often changes on stage with Machine Dazzle's help, continually drawing attention to the costumes' fabulous construction.

Taylor Mac does not consider his stage presence a 'persona' or 'character', but an exposure of what judy looks like on the inside. While jeans and a T-shirt enable Mac to hide, drag *reveals* – and Mac and Machine Dazzle are intent on revealing not judy's personal interiority so much as the complex 'interiority' of US American culture, writ large through the flashy surfaces of these multifaceted costumes and this multidisciplinary performance.[28] Especially when donning such lavish regalia, Taylor Mac is the undeniable centrepiece of *A 24-Decade History*, but judy is not centred in the storytelling; rather, judy's performance is always deeply collaborative and outwardly focused, refracting a multitude of marginalized voices. With an intersectional politics that never denies Mac's own position of relative privilege as a white queer person in a liberal New York City, Mac is more of a ringleader than a diva throughout *A 24-Decade History*. Recognizing the limits to his own lived experience, Taylor Mac even periodically welcomes guest artists to lead: Anaïs Mitchell and the show's female musicians rock a riot grrrl song, and a different local artist or ensemble brings their own theatrical vision of a road to freedom in 'The Underground Railroad' section of each performance. Meanwhile, knitters dot the stage in the early decades (because America was founded on making things), and a troupe of dandy minions from the local community serve food, manage props – and, of course, facilitate audience participation.[29]

Gareth White opens *Audience Participation in Theatre: Aesthetics of the Invitation* with a profoundly relatable statement: 'There are few things in the theatre that are more despised than audience participation.'[30] Participatory moments make people anxious, fearful and embarrassed, not only for themselves but also for the theatremakers. Even the most 'cultured' theatregoer may shy away from audience participation, which is 'still often seen as one of the most misconceived, unproductive and excruciating of the avant-garde's blind alleys, or otherwise as evidence of the childish crassness of popular performance.'[31] But Taylor Mac embraces the awkwardness of audience participation with aplomb. Some roles are relatively undemanding, such as my own onstage appearance as 'Gloria' of the 1982 pop song (Figure 9). I am instructed to stare meaningfully into the distance as Mac growl-whispers and then belts 'Gloria' in my ear; my heart pounds, and I struggle to keep a straight face while I am internally beaming that I have been 'chosen'. Other roles are more taxing; one poor soul is stuck repeating 'Tit-Willow' for minutes on end in *The Marskado*.

Conclusion 195

Figure 9 My unexpected appearance as 'Gloria' in the 24-hour *24-Decade History of Popular Music*. Photograph by Suzy Evans. Courtesy of Suzy Evans.

Some moments of audience participation are arbitrarily based on one's location in the theatre at any given moment, but other moments specifically call out the audience's identity: All men under the age of forty must serve as soldiers in the First World War. All white people must flee to the suburbs (the outer edges of the theatre) in the 1950s, leaving the people of colour ample space to sprawl in the 'city' centre – which happen to be better 'seats' for the final hours of the performance.[32] Actor James Franco was repeatedly targeted in an unforgettable New York Live Arts performance in 2015; Franco was called upon to simulate shower sex with Mac and to play the lark disturbing Laurey's slumber in a subversive gay Nazi concentration camp cabaret performance of 'The Surrey with the Fringe on Top'. Although the participatory tasks are unevenly weighted, Mac makes audacious demands of everyone in the crowd at various moments; judy's call to action is forthright, confrontational and intentional. From bandaging wounded soldiers to dancing with a same-sex partner to Ted Nugent's 'Snakeskin Cowboys' at a queer prom, Taylor Mac urges audience interaction as a mode of investigating our own identity and positionality.[33] 'Every single audience I've gotten to do it – except one', judy says of the queer middle school prom – and the question raised by the invitation to dance is more important than the answer for Taylor Mac: 'The earnest dream is that they will consider what it means to slow dance with someone of their same gender. But more importantly, it's that they consider whether or not they were able to.'[34]

For Mac, such an invitation to audience participation is a critical moment of consideration – an active, pulsating pause in the performance.[35] It may bring up contradictory feelings: excitement and anxiety, discomfort and liberation, all mixed with the memory of being an awkward age thirteen. 'Everything you're feeling is appropriate', Mac repeatedly intones. Taylor Mac continually employs audience participation – a risky and unpredictable proposition in any live theatre scenario – because it makes the contingency of each moment in time profoundly palpable. Mac urges the audience to lean into the discomfort and uncertainty of the present, and to sense each moment as a heterogeneous mixture of feelings and possibilities – full of more questions than answers.[36] By repeatedly engaging us in these complex quandaries, Mac conditions the audience to become more deeply aware of and more comfortable with the quagmire of the present.[37] The densely layered complexity of each instant can open up new possibilities for ways of being in the world and new forms of affiliation for those who are willing to engage.

And indeed, most Taylor Mac attendees are willing. Mac creates a space of tacit consent with the audience, and mess and imperfection are key to this accord; Mac exposes everyone as vulnerable and human, including himself. 'One core value of the piece is that I'm falling apart', Taylor Mac says. 'It's supposed to be imperfect, and we're supposed to expose the deterioration. So if I sound as good at the end of the show as I did at the beginning of the show, something didn't work.'[38] This deliberate physical breakdown is largely due to the warping of time engendered by extreme marathon theatre.

Sheer duration is certainly one of the most maximalist elements of *A 24-Decade History of Popular Music*. In *Great Lengths: Seven Works of Marathon Theater*, Jonathan Kalb defines 'marathon theatre' as any production lasting longer than 'four hours or so', noting that typical Western theatre productions have been two to three hours long for several centuries.[39] Taylor Mac's epic compresses 240 years of queered history into a colossal twenty-four hours; time is packed even as it sprawls over a full day. Temporal norms are exposed as we perform nonstop from noon on Saturday to noon on Sunday. The very choice of a weekend for the 24-hour marathon event reveals normative patterns of work and leisure: 'If I sleep all Sunday afternoon and evening, I can still teach on Monday morning', I rationalize.[40]

The first decades of the 24-hour concert are hyper-energized with the full ensemble of twenty-four musicians blaring on stage and a committed crowd founding the United States of America anew. Energy levels begin to diverge as bedtimes are reached; a few nap on mattresses and sleeping bags made available in the tenements at midnight (1896–1906), but other audience members are just gearing up and raring to go at this hour. After twelve hours of performance, Taylor Mac forgets a line and asks musical director Matt Ray for a prompt. But a vitamin B shot given onstage in the Roaring Twenties revives judy, whose stamina – all the way through to the final solo hour – is galvanizing. The black box theatre may insulate us from seeing the normative passage of time outside, but every body begins to feel the impact of the all-nighter as morning dawns; though every participant experiences time differently, we are only human, after all, and the duration takes a toll. Exhaustion coexists with exhilaration, often in the same body; delirium, dizziness, confusion and wonder swirl about, a heterotopia of strange temporalities. The performance is an endurance test – not only to stay awake and to stay alert, but to stay active. Rarely are we granted a moment to rest in *A 24-Decade History*; Taylor Mac keeps the audience on their toes and never allows them to settle.

'I'm going to be falling apart and the audience is going to be falling apart', Mac hypothesized about the 24-hour event. 'But as a result, we're going to be able to create bonds and build connection.'[41] Indeed, audience participation and this collective warping of time blur the boundaries across creators, performers and audience members as the hours spin forwards; a community is forged through mess, imperfection and vulnerability. Weiss writes of awkwardness yielding to grace, exhaustion to focus, and strangers to intimacy as the collective durational experience progresses; the participatory performance breaks down its audience and builds them back up 'by essentially asking them to co-create the show'.[42] Hugh Ryan similarly notes that the borders between noun and verb, artist and art, creator and creation fade through the durational endeavour: 'We were simultaneously acting in the show, watching the show, and being forged into something new by the show.'[43] Much as judy 'marathon trained' for this extreme durational performance, judy now seems to be marathon training *us* for work that will require both great endurance and an intersectional solidarity.[44]

Hans-Thies Lehmann theorizes that the durational aesthetic of postmodern theatre can prolong time, turning it into a 'Continuous Present' in the words of Gertrude Stein; this 'time sculpture' counters the tendency of Aristotelian theatre to erase our experience of the radical temporal heterogeneity of our existence.[45] Durational works can offer 'rare and precious experiences of sustained meditation', a live and in-person tonic against a distracted media era filled with compulsive multitasking, snappy sitcoms and 'pop-ups within pop-ups'.[46] These performances can even take on a religious valence, particularly when so many audience members make long theatrical pilgrimages to commune in time-bound and site-specific locations; marathon theatre can gather people together in ambitious and potentially transformative ways that confirm their common humanity.[47]

Taylor Mac's *A 24-Decade History of Popular Music* can thus be read as a time-warping pause – a luminous musical number – in the midst of normative, productive, linear time. Such an expansive musical number (and drag performance and marionette show and ritual sacrifice) showcases time in all its radical heterogeneity. Crucially, Taylor Mac's time-warping venture is not bound by the time of the performance; Mac calls the 24-hour concert the 'exclamation point' on the project, but the project encompasses a multi-year process of gathering songs, deconstructing them, reframing them and performing them across the globe in decade cabarets, themed concerts and 'shorter' durational performances (such as a ten-hour, single-century concert).[48] Many acolytes followed Mac's work from Joe's Pub to St. Ann's, from the Curran to the Berliner Festspiele; friendships were solidified, creative collaborations begun, and new relationships forged in and through this expansive world-building endeavour.[49] The sustained time of Taylor Mac's performance sustains us, not only by providing such a jolt of such multifaceted ecstatic time but also by providing a creative and critical model for dreaming the culture forward – as well as companions for that journey. Acknowledging our shared history, investigating our own positionality and deeply engaging with the quagmire of the present can open up a new timespace for collective action towards strange new futurities.

Or as Michael Friedman might say, the song makes a space.[50]

Flashforward to 2021: Back to book time

It is 12 January 2021. Physically coming together, whether for a marathon theatre performance or a dinner party with friends, is not permitted. We sit two metres apart. We wear masks. We succumb to the sad reality that singing, whether in a church choir, karaoke bar or musical theatre production, can lead to dangerous superspreading events. We are forced to find new ways of working, new ways of making, new ways of building community. We often fail. We are so tired. This moment, in the midst of the Covid-19 epidemic, is not a lush and showstopping musical number. It is a standstill. A deeply uncomfortable one. A very long one – a test of stamina and endurance. How much longer until a return to normalcy, or even the semblance of normalcy, we ask? But when so many inequalities have been laid bare, how can we advocate a 'return' to 'normal time'? What even is 'normal time', and whose 'normal' is it? The quagmire of the present exposes messy, critical questions.

Covid-19 is not the first moment to have unmoored us in recent decades; school shootings, climate catastrophe, Occupy Wall Street, Black Lives Matter and #MeToo are all what psychoanalyst Jill Gentile calls socio-psychoanalytic interventions exposing critical gaps in our experiences and discourses.[51] These moments of pause turn confusion and discomfort into a potential space for dismantling received knowledge – and yet the pause is often too brief, and the discomfort is reintegrated into our norms. 'As soon as we incline to arrest change by imposing certainty – to turn back time, to indulge in nostalgia and familiarity, to live in a bygone world – we are shirking our duty to *face the strange*', writes Gentile.[52] Could Covid-19 mark a tipping point, a critical time warp in which each of these rifts has widened so as to become unavoidable? Psychoanalyst Philippe Gendrault posits that this crisis has forced us into the Real time of collective history, which is no longer simply an 'emergence' of the contradictions of reality, but the 'emergency' of it.[53] We can no longer live in denial of the 'strange' as it suffuses every day of our lives so thoroughly: we can no longer integrate, incorporate or homogenize these differences and contradictions. Could this complex moment hold the potential to reroute the narrative drive?

This densely layered present has multidirectional potentiality, which we sense in collective actions across the globe. Some actions are desperate attempts to reinstate an increasingly shaky 'norm', to turn back the clock, to erase difference and divergence. Boris Johnson and his cronies have exploited this precarious moment to undermine the National Health Service and 'take back control' of their borders with Brexit; Trump supporters have mobbed the United States Capitol in a coup attempt to consolidate white power and 'Make America Great Again'. But simultaneously, the strange temporalities of the pandemic have urged pause and consideration on a monumental and potentially transformative scale. They have led to a rise in protests against racism as well as self-education about the complex histories of colonialism and the construction of race and ethnicity. They have promoted urgent action towards universal health care and more encompassing social welfare programmes, even in the most capitalist countries. They have heightened awareness of our interdependence as human beings, as well as our dependence on our planet.

Giorgio Agamben suggests that 'the original task of a genuine revolution [...] is never merely to "change the world", but also – and above all – to "change time".[54] In the past nine months, time's normative construction – and the extreme biases of and limits to this empty, homogenous time – have been made palpable on a staggering scale. It is from these limits that we can begin imagining new horizons of possibility. As we imagine these new futurities, time can and indeed must be built with a difference; we can never go back to before. And as we *act* towards these new futurities, pause and consideration are vital; the great work begins by engaging the quagmire of the present. Strange, new, more heterogeneous and inclusive futurities are just on the horizon. Can we sustain the reach and begin to actualize these possibilities in this precarious present? It's going to go on a lot longer than you're going to want it to, and everything you're feeling is appropriate.

Notes

Introduction

1. Richard Dyer, *Only Entertainment* (London: Routledge, 1992), 19–20.
2. For an elaborated definition of the marriage trope, see Raymond Knapp, *The American Musical and the Formation of National Identity* (Princeton, NJ: Princeton University Press, 2005), 9.
3. See ibid., 5, and Dyer, *Only Entertainment*, 20.
4. Andrea Most, *Making Americans: Jews and the Broadway Musical* (Cambridge, MA: Harvard University Press, 2004).
5. Sean Griffin, 'The Gang's All Here: Generic versus Racial Integration in the 1940s Musical', *Cinema Journal* 42, no. 1 (2002): 21–45. Several musicals in the 1940s did attempt to treat race seriously, including *Cabin in the Sky* and *Lost in the Stars*.
6. For an exploration of the connection between African Americans and musical performers, particularly in the segregated all-Black-cast musicals of the early twenty-first century, see Arthur Knight, *Disintegrating the Musical: Black Performance and American Musical Film* (Durham, NC: Duke University Press, 2002). See also Richard Dyer, 'The Colour of Entertainment', in *Only Entertainment*, 36–45; Todd R. Decker, *Music Makes Me: Fred Astaire and Jazz* (Berkeley: University of California Press, 2011); and Sarah Whitfield, ed., *Reframing the Musical: Race, Culture and Identity* (London: Red Globe Press, 2019).
7. See D.A. Miller, *Place for Us: Essay on the Broadway Musical* (Cambridge, MA: Harvard University Press, 1998) and John M. Clum, *Something for the Boys: Musical Theater and Gay Culture* (New York: St. Martin's Press, 1999).
8. See Stacy Ellen Wolf, *A Problem Like Maria: Gender and Sexuality in the American Musical* (Ann Arbor: University of Michigan Press, 2002), which considers Mary Martin, Ethel Merman, Julie Andrews and Barbra Streisand as diverse images of women for mid-twentieth-century audiences. By analysing Martin's 'tomboy', Merman's 'butch Jewish mother', Andrews' 'femme' and Streisand's 'queer Jewess', Wolf elaborates

how theatre, film and television tended to cast women as wives, mothers, ingénues or temptresses, while musicals offered a different and more empowered view of womanhood – particularly in song and dance.

9 See Geoffrey Block, 'The Broadway Canon from *Show Boat* to *West Side Story* and the European Operatic Ideal', *Journal of Musicology* 11, no. 4 (1993): 525–44. Block likens pre-Rodgers and Hammerstein musicals to Baroque operas, in which composers and librettists 'serve larger-than-life stars who arrest the action with their show-stopping arias'. He identifies *Oklahoma* as the shifting point, after which musicals aspire to Joseph Kerman's European operatic ideal 'of a musical drama in which the various parts – song, story and movement – form an interdependent and homogeneous whole' and 'use music to define character, generate action, and establish atmosphere' (526).

10 Many scholars have questioned the paradigm of integration. See, for instance, Wolf, *A Problem Like Maria*, 32: 'In spite of the received history of musical theater, the form is hardly "integrated" at all. Although composers, lyricists, and librettists are said to have successfully "integrated" the book and the numbers, musicals are figured around what might be called Brechtian pauses, gaps, absences, interruptions, and "Alienation-effects."' In *Making Americans*, Andrea Most similarly notes a disjuncture between book and song, contrasting the 'psychological realism' of the dialogue to the 'celebratory energy' of the musical numbers (78–79).

11 Bliss Cua Lim, *Translating Time: Cinema, the Fantastic, and Temporal Critique* (Durham, NC: Duke University Press, 2009), 11.

12 Alison Kafer, *Feminist, Queer, Crip* (Bloomington and Indianapolis: Indiana University Press, 2013), 35.

13 Jack Halberstam, *In a Queer Time and Place: Transgender Bodies, Subcultural Lives* (New York: New York University Press, 2005), 1.

14 Ibid., 1. See also Elizabeth Freeman, *Time Binds: Queer Temporalities, Queer Histories* (Durham, NC: Duke University Press, 2010).

15 Ibid., 2.

16 José Esteban Muñoz, *Cruising Utopia: The Then and There of Queer Futurity* (New York and London: New York University Press, 2009), 1.

17 Ibid., 32.

18 See, for instance, Kafer, *Feminist, Queer, Crip*. Crip theory will unfortunately not be discussed further in this book, but I hope the strange temporalities discussed in this text will open up future analyses.

19 Lim, *Translating Time*, 13.
20 Tavia Nyong'o, *Afro-Fabulations: The Queer Drama of Black Life* (New York: New York University Press, 2019), 23. See also Kara Keeling, 'Looking for M – Queer Temporality, Black Political Possibility, and Poetry from the Future', *GLQ: A Journal of Lesbian and Gay Studies* 15, no. 4 (2009): 565–582.
21 Tina M. Campt, 'Quiet Soundings: The Grammar of Black Futurity', in *Listening to Images* (Durham, NC and London: Duke University Press, 2017), 17.
22 Scott McMillin, *The Musical as Drama: A Study of the Principles and Conventions Behind Musical Shows from Kern to Sondheim* (Princeton, NJ: Princeton University Press, 2006), 9.
23 Knapp, *National Identity*, 12.
24 Zachary Dorsey, 'Big Possibility: Moscow, and Musical Theatre's Subjunctive Dramaturgy', *Studies in Musical Theatre* 10 (2016): 197.
25 For a table of ways in which musicals play with chronology and time structures, see Sarah Whitfield, 'Disrupting Heteronormative Temporality through Queer Dramaturgies: *Fun Home*, *Hadestown* and *A Strange Loop*', *Arts* 9, no. 2 (2020): 69. Whitfield's categories include biographical musicals (covering long time periods), short flashback(s) used, single or double time jumps, multiple time jumps, no clear chronology or non-linear, time travel or time loops, multiple time periods occurring at the same time, in parallel timelines and compressed time.
26 McMillin, *The Musical as Drama*, 21.
27 Brecht was astounded by the innovations of the musical theatre stage in the 1940s, which he praised for a radical separation of theatrical elements. On a 1946 visit to NYC, Brecht saw several musicals – including *Oklahoma!* – and later wrote that the Broadway musical 'has been evolved to the true expression of everything that is American. Stage designers and choreographers use V-effects ["alienating effects"] to a great degree.' In fact, *Oklahoma!* 'doubled' Laurey and Curly by using professional ballet dancers for the dream ballet. See Carl Weber, 'Brecht's Concept of Gestus and the American Performance Tradition', in *Brecht Sourcebook*, ed. Carol Martin and Henry Bial (London: Routledge, 2000), 45. For more on fragmenting characters into multiple actors on the musical stage, see also Chapter 5.

28 Bertolt Brecht, *Brecht on Theatre: The Development of an Aesthetic*, trans. John Willett (New York: Hill and Wang, 1964), 71.
29 Elin Diamond, 'Brechtian Theory/Feminist Theory: Toward a Gestic Feminist Criticism', *TDR* 32, no. 1 (Spring 1988): 86.
30 McMillin, *The Musical as Drama*, 2.
31 Knapp, *National Identity*, 283.
32 Judith Butler, 'Performative Acts and Gender Constitution: An Essay in Phenomenology and Feminist Theory', in *Writing on the Body: Female Embodiment and Feminist Theory*, ed. Katie Conboy, Nadia Medina and Sarah Stanbury (New York: Columbia University Press, 1997), 401–18.
33 Raymond Knapp, *The American Musical and the Performance of Personal Identity* (Princeton, NJ: Princeton University Press, 2006), 167. See also Jill Dolan, *Utopia in Performance: Finding Hope at the Theater* (Ann Arbor: University of Michigan Press, 2005), 7.
34 Dolan, *Utopia in Performance*, 5.
35 Ibid., 13.
36 Dyer, *Only Entertainment*, 20.
37 Dolan, *Utopia in Performance*, 11.

Chapter 1

1 Philip Dawkins, *The Homosexuals* (New York: Playscripts, 2014), 11. The character Peter is of course not the first of his kind; Buzz in Terrence McNally's *Love! Valour! Compassion!* is an iconic predecessor.
2 Dawkins, *The Homosexuals*, 6.
3 Wolf, *A Problem Like Maria*, 31.
4 Miller, *Place for Us*, 3.
5 Dawkins, *The Homosexuals*, 72.
6 Halberstam, *In a Queer Time and Place*, 2.
7 For the operatic forerunner of the integrated musical, championed by Rodgers and Hammerstein in the 1940s and 1950s, see Richard Wagner, *Opera and Drama* (Lincoln: University of Nebraska Press, 1995). In his autobiography, Richard Rodgers explains, 'I have long held a theory about musicals. When a show works perfectly, it's because all the individual parts complement each other and fit together. No single

element overshadows any other. In a great musical, the orchestrations sound the way the costumes look. That's what made Oklahoma! work. All the components dovetailed. There was nothing extraneous or foreign, nothing that pushed itself into the spotlight yelling "look at me!" It was a work created by many that gave the impression of having been created by one.' See Richard Rodgers, *Musical Stages: An Autobiography* (New York: Random House, 1975), 249.

8 D.A. Miller notably makes this claim in *Place for Us* (16).
9 See Chapter 5's analysis of *A Strange Loop* for more on disidentification with the musical as a genre.
10 Stephen Banfield, *Sondheim's Broadway Musicals* (Ann Arbor: University of Michigan Press, 1993), 91.
11 Stephen Sondheim, *Finishing the Hat: Collected Lyrics (1954–1981) with Attendant Comments, Principles, Heresies, Grudges, Whines and Anecdotes* (New York: Knopf, 2010), 80.
12 Mark Steyn, *Broadway Babies Say Goodnight: Musicals Then and Now* (New York: Routledge, 1999), 313.
13 Aaron Frankel, *Writing the Broadway Musical* (New York: Drama Book Specialists, 1977), 111.
14 'Purpose of Songs', Larry Gelbart Papers (Collection PASC 22), Library Special Collections, Charles E. Young Research Library, UCLA.
15 McMillin, *The Musical as Drama*, 1. *HMS Pinafore* in 1878 and *Show Boat* in 1927 are popular rival contenders for the title of the first integrated musical.
16 Larry James Evans, 'Rodgers and Hammerstein's Oklahoma!: The Development of the "Integrated" Musical', PhD diss., University of California, Los Angeles, 1990, 154.
17 For more about the 'Cool White Guy' narrative, which whitewashes and erases the Black performances practices at the heart of the musical to 'legitimize' the genre, see Sarah Whitfield, 'Introduction', in *Reframing the Musical: Race, Culture and Identity*, ed. Sarah Whitfield (London: Red Globe Press, 2019), xv.
18 Most, *Making Americans*, 102.
19 Wolf, *A Problem Like Maria*, 17.
20 Bruce Kirle, *Unfinished Show Business: Broadway Musicals as Works-in-Process* (Carbondale: Southern Illinois University Press, 2005), 2.

21 See, for instance, Walter Benjamin, *Illuminations*, ed. Hannah Arendt (New York: Schocken Books, 2007), 260.
22 Sondheim, *Finishing the Hat*, 100.
23 Burt Shevelove, Larry Gelbart and Stephen Sondheim, *A Funny Thing Happened on the Way to the Forum* (New York: Applause Theater Book Publishers, 1991), 57.
24 Ibid., 58.
25 Banfield, *Sondheim's Broadway Musicals*, 97.
26 Busby Berkeley's choreography for musical films of the 1930s used inventive camera angles and abstracted the female body into kaleidoscopic patterns.
27 *A Funny Thing Happened on the Way to the Forum*, dir. Richard Lester (United States: United Artists, 1966), DVD.
28 'Purpose of Songs', Larry Gelbart Papers.
29 Margaret M. Knapp, 'Integration of Elements as a Viable Standard for Judging Musical Theater', *Journal of American Culture* 1, no. 1 (1978): 118.
30 McMillin, *The Musical as Drama*, 2.
31 Ibid., 208.
32 Ibid., 8.
33 Theodor W. Adorno, *Aesthetic Theory*, trans. Robert Hullot-Kentor (Minneapolis, MN: University of Minnesota Press, 1997), 1.
34 Yi-Fu Tuan, *Space and Place: The Perspective of Experience* (Minneapolis: University of Minnesota Press, 1977), 128–9.
35 Sometimes shifting a song's position can enhance the plot advancement or simply change the perspective without detracting from its narrative function; yet in musical comedies, a song's movability can further emphasize its loose relationship to the plot.
36 Shevelove, Gelbart and Sondheim, *Forum*, 45.
37 Knapp, *National Identity*, 12.
38 Carl Dahlhaus, *Nineteenth-Century Music* (Berkeley: University of California Press, 1989), 404.
39 See Brecht, *Brecht on Theatre*.
40 Wayne Koestenbaum, *The Queen's Throat: Opera, Homosexuality, and the Mystery of Desire* (New York: Poseidon Press, 1993), 38.
41 Shevelove, Gelbart and Sondheim, *Forum*, 116.

42 Shallow self-absorption and focus on surfaces is a strong trope for gay males, and Philia is already a decidedly gay version of an ingénue.
43 For a discussion of Musical Mondays, see Samuel Baltimore, 'Do It Again: Repetition, Reception and Identity on Musical Comedy's Margins', PhD diss., University of California, Los Angeles, 2013. For the poetics and politics of reperformance, see Miller, *Place for Us*.
44 Sondheim, *Finishing the Hat*, 107, my emphasis.
45 Knapp, *Personal Identity*, 9, emphasis in the original.
46 Of course, several explicitly gay characters were written into musicals in the 1980s and early 1990s, prior to *Rent* – for instance in *Falsettos* and in *Elegies for Angels, Punks and Raging Queens*. Sondheim himself wrote an openly gay character in *Road Show*. But it is worth noting that 'show queens' such as D.A. Miller and John Clum often find openly gay musicals to be less satisfying than their closeted predecessors; explicitly gay characters too often flatten into stereotypes, while a queer narrative diminishes the pleasures of diverging from an intended straight reading.
47 Steve Swayne, *How Sondheim Found His Sound* (Ann Arbor: University of Michigan Press, 2005), 149.
48 Cameron Mackintosh was the first to suggest to Sondheim that the composer's career had been spent trying to fix specifically the second act of *Allegro*. See Ethan Mordden, *On Sondheim: An Opinionated Guide* (New York: Oxford University Press, 2016), 22.
49 See Chapter 5 for more on the curious case of Bobby/Bobbie in *Company*. Sondheim's work is a refrain throughout this book; the composer and his collaborators' explorations of time, contingency and choice merit a book of their own.
50 Knapp, *Personal Identity*, 50.
51 Stephen Sondheim, 'Stephen Sondheim in Conversation', interview by Michael Kerker, Segerstrom Center for the Arts, 13 July 2012.
52 Ben Gove, 'Introduction: Passing Pleasures: Gay Men and Promiscuity', in *Cruising Culture: Promiscuity, Desire and American Gay Literature* (Edinburgh: Edinburgh University Press, 2000), 1–40.
53 For a theorization of the function of the 11 o'clock number as an outlier to integration, see Raymond Knapp, 'Getting off the Trolley: Musicals Contra Cinematic Reality', in *From Stage to Screen: Musical Films in*

Europe and United States (1927–1961), ed. Massimiliano Sala (Turnhout: Brepols, 2012).

54 Raymond Knapp was reminded of a former TA's observation that rock 'n' roll substituted duple metre for the waltz's triple metre because 'You can't fuck to 3/4.' The 2/4 section of this song is specifically coital.

55 Stephen Citron, *Songwriting: A Complete Guide to the Craft* (New York: W. Morrow, 1998), 72.

56 Brian Castles-Onion, *Losing the Plot in Opera: Myths and Secrets of the World's Great Operas* (Auckland: Exisle, 2008), 89.

57 David Craig, 'On Performing Sondheim: A Little Night Music Revisited', in *Stephen Sondheim: A Casebook*, ed. Joanne Lesley Gordon (New York: Garland Publishing, 1997), 99.

58 Gove, *Cruising Culture*, 4.

59 Citron, *Songwriting*, 52.

60 Thomas P. Adler, 'The Sung and the Said: Literary Value in the Musical Dramas of Stephen Sondheim', in *Reading Stephen Sondheim: A Collection of Critical Essays*, ed. Sandor Goodhart (New York: Garland Publishing, 2000), 523–4, emphasis in the original. See Chapter 5 for a discussion of how a linear trajectory to marriage is also layered onto the female Bobbie in *Company* – a similar critical attempt to rein in excess.

61 Citron, *Songwriting*, 72.

62 Judith Sebesta, 'Of Fire, Death, and Desire: Transgression and Carnival in Jonathan Larson's Rent', *Contemporary Theater Review* 16, no. 4 (2006): 428.

63 Halberstam, *In a Queer Time and Place*, 10.

64 David Savran, 'Choices Made and Unmade', *Theater* 31, no. 2 (2001): 93–4.

65 Clum, *Something for the Boys*, 272–4.

66 Helen Lewis, 'Renting a Queer Space: The Commodification of Queerness in Jonathan Larson's "Rent"', MA diss., Tufts University, 2007.

67 Of course, New York Theatre Workshop is a well-established off-Broadway venue whose 'fringe' status is questionable.

68 Lewis, 'Renting a Queer Space', 2.

69 David Román, *Acts of Intervention: Performance, Gay Culture, and AIDS* (Bloomington: Indiana University Press, 1998), 282.

70 David Román, *Performance in America: Contemporary U.S. Culture and the Performing Arts* (Durham, NC: Duke University Press, 2005).

71 For the most publicized controversy over the *Rent: School Edition*, see Kenneth Jones, 'The Show Won't Go On: Rent Canceled at Texas High School', *Playbill.com*, 11 December 2008, available online: https://www.playbill.com/article/the-show-wont-go-on-rent-canceled-at-texas-high-school-com-156018 (accessed 11 June 2021). The debacle has inspired a musical of its own: *Small Town Story* by Sammy Buck and Brandon James Gwinn.

72 Michael Riedel, 'Every Day a "Rent" Party: Hardcore Fans of the Hit Musical Form a Squatters Camp at the Box Office', *New York Daily News*, 3 March 1997, available online: http://articles.nydailynews.com/1997-03-03/entertainment/18034670_1_rent-heads-show-mccarthy (accessed 27 September 2012).

73 Halberstam, *In a Queer Time and Place*, 2.

74 See Dolan, *Utopia in Performance*, 11. Dolan follows anthropologist Victor Turner in her theatrical definition of *communitas*: 'the moments in a theatre event or a ritual in which audiences or participants feel themselves become part of the whole in an organic, nearly spiritual way; spectators' individuality becomes finely attuned to those around them, and a cohesive if fleeting feeling of belonging to the group bathes the audience'.

75 Jonathan Larson, *Rent: The Complete Book and Lyrics of the Broadway Musical* (New York: Applause Theater and Cinema Books, 2008), x.

76 Ibid., 2.

77 Ibid., xi.

78 Halberstam, *In a Queer Time and Place*, 2.

79 Larson, *Rent*, 43.

80 Ibid., 44.

81 Ibid., 45.

82 Knapp, *National Identity*, 12.

83 Anthony Rapp, *Without You: A Memoir of Love, Loss, and the Musical Rent* (New York: Simon & Schuster, 2006), 21.

84 Larson, *Rent*, 87.

85 Ibid., 88.

86 Benjamin, *Illuminations*, 257–258.

87 See Chapter 3 for more on spectral temporality in musical theatre and how ghosts of our past can ruffle the present.
88 Larson, *Rent*, 116.
89 See Joseph R. Roach, *Cities of the Dead: Circum-Atlantic Performance* (New York: Columbia University Press, 1996).
90 Larson, *Rent*, 38.
91 Riedel, 'Every Day a "Rent" Party'.
92 Ibid.
93 See Dolan, *Utopia in Performance*.
94 Dyer, *Only Entertainment*, 20.
95 Ibid., 26.
96 Ibid., 27, my emphasis.
97 Ibid., 35. See also McMillin, *The Musical as Drama*.
98 Ernst Bloch, *The Utopian Function of Art and Literature: Selected Essays*, trans. Jack Zipes and Frank Mecklenburg (Cambridge, MA: MIT Press, 1988), xxiii.
99 See Chapter 4 for a discussion of teen musical theatre fandom in the early twenty-first century.

Chapter 2

1 The Rocky Horror Picture Show: The Official Fan Site, 'Participation: How to Do the Time Warp', available online: http://www.rockyhorror.com/participation/timewarp.php (accessed 3 September 2020).
2 Lim, *Translating Time*, 28.
3 Tzvetan Todorov and Richard M. Berrong, 'The Origin of Genres', *New Literary History* 8, no. 1 (Autumn 1976): 159, http://www.jstor.org/stable/468619.
4 Ibid., 162–3.
5 Michael Chabon, *Maps and Legends: Reading and Writing Along the Borderlands* (San Francisco, CA: McSweeney's Books, 2008), 8.
6 Tim Dirks, 'Academy Awards Best Pictures – Genre Biases', Film Site, available online: http://www.filmsite.org/bestpics2.html (accessed 3 September 2020). Dirks identifies 'serious dramas or social-problem films with weighty themes, biopics (inspired by real-life individuals

or events), or films with literary pretensions' as the most likely to be nominated and win for Best Picture, as well as 'glossy, large-scale epic historical productions with big budgets (of various genres)'. Musical films occasionally fall into this latter category, and *The Lord of the Rings: The Return of the King* – the last in the epic *Lord of the Rings* trilogy – became the first fantasy film to win the Oscar in 2003. Dirks also provides a detailed list of the least likely genres for Best Picture: 'Action-adventures, family-oriented animation, popular "popcorn" movies, suspense-thrillers, science-fiction, "superhero" films, horror, comedies (including teen comedies), Westerns, foreign-language films, and spy thrillers are mostly overlooked, as are independent productions and children's films (although there have been a few exceptions).'

7 Charles McNulty, 'No Applause', *Los Angeles Times*, 13 April 2010, available online: http://articles.latimes.com/2010/apr/13/entertainment/la-et-pulitzer-mcnulty-20100413 (accessed 12 June 2021).
8 Dyer, *Only Entertainment*, 6.
9 David Savran, 'Toward a Historiography of the Popular', *Theatre Survey* 45, no. 2 (November 2004): 211–12.
10 Rick Altman, *The American Film Musical* (Bloomington: Indiana University Press, 1987), 2.
11 John Frow, '"Reproducibles, Rubrics, and Everything You Need": Genre Theory Today', *PMLA* 122, no. 5 (October 2007): 1633, https://doi.org/10.1632/pmla.2007.122.5.1626.
12 Savran, 'Toward a Historiography of the Popular', 213.
13 See Butler, 'Performative Acts and Gender Constitution'.
14 Knapp, *Personal Identity*, 242.
15 Michael Billington and Maddy Costa, 'The Royal Court Upstairs Marks 40 Years of Scaling New Heights', *The Guardian*, 21 July 2009, available online: http://www.guardian.co.uk/stage/2009/jul/21/royal-court-upstairs-40-years (accessed 12 June 2021).
16 Amittai F. Aviram, 'Postmodern Gay Dionysus: Dr. Frank N. Furter', *Journal of Popular Culture* 26, no. 3 (1992): 187.
17 For a discussion of off- and off-off-Broadway adult musicals that ruffled moral feathers, but ultimately made their way into the mainstream, see Elizabeth L. Wollman, *Hard Times: The Adult Musical in 1970s New York City* (New York: Oxford University Press, 2013). While partaking in the

same vision of sexual liberation, *The Rocky Horror Show* romped through campy genre films, which aesthetically set this musical apart.

18 William Glover, 'Horror As In Vile Is Key To Show', *Sarasota Journal*, 12 March 1975, available online: http://news.google.com/newspapers?nid=1798&dat=19750312&id=ZgwfAAAAIBAJ&sjid=TY0EAAAAIBAJ&pg=4664,2407510 (accessed 12 June 2021).
19 Edwin Wilson, 'Taking a Camping Trip on Broadway', *Wall Street Journal*, 14 March 1975.
20 Lynn Van Matre, '"Rocky Show" Bumps to a Different Beat', review, *Chicago Tribune*, 18 August 1976.
21 Jack Halberstam, *The Queer Art of Failure* (Durham, NC: Duke University Press, 2011).
22 The Film Makers Cooperative, 'History', available online: http://film-makerscoop.com/about/history (accessed 3 September 2020).
23 David E. James, *To Free the Cinema: Jonas Mekas and the New York Underground* (Princeton, NJ: Princeton University Press, 1992), 10.
24 *Midnight Movies: From the Margin to the Mainstream*, dir. Stuart Samuels (Stuart Samuels Productions, 2005), DVD.
25 Ibid.
26 Gertrude Stein, 'Plays', in *Gertrude Stein: Writings 1932–1946*, Vol. 2 (New York: Library of America, 1998), 251.
27 Ibid., 251.
28 Ibid., 269.
29 Knapp, *Personal Identity*, 250.
30 The Rocky Horror Picture Show: The Official Fan Site, 'Sins O' the Flesh: Los Angeles, CA', available online: http://www.rockyhorror.com/profiles/cast_2007_08.php (accessed 3 September 2020).
31 See Sarah Taylor Ellis, 'Establishing (and Re-establishing) a Sense of Place: Musical Orientation in *The Sound of Music*', *Studies in Musical Theatre* 3, no. 3 (2009): 277–283.
32 See Baltimore, 'Inventing "Tradition": Queer Musical Comedy Sings Along', in 'Do It Again'.
33 Rocky Horror Wiki, 'Liz Stockton', last modified 27 November 2019, available online: http://www.rockyhorrorwiki.org/wiki2/index.php?title=Liz_Stockton (accessed 24 August 2020). Rocky Horror

Legends have achieved fame across the RHPS fandom, beyond their home shadowcasts.

34 Minnelli Creations, 'Home', available online: https://ninaminnelli.wixsite.com/minnellicreations (accessed 24 August 2020).

35 Shawn Anthony, 'Custom Rocky Horror Costumes', available online: http://shawnanthony.com/rocky.html/ (accessed 3 September 2020).

36 The Fantasie Factory Players, 'Participation: Transylvanian University', *The Rocky Horror Picture Show: The Official Fan Site*, available online: http://www.rockyhorror.com/participation/transuniv.php (accessed 3 September 2020).

37 Stein, 'Plays', 244.

38 Ibid., 249.

39 Elin Diamond, *Unmaking Mimesis: Essays on Feminism and Theater* (London: Routledge, 1997), 104.

40 Sal Piro, 'It Was Great When It All Began', in *Creatures of the Night: The Rocky Horror Experience* (Redford, MI: Stabur Press, 1990), available online: http://www.rockyhorror.com/history/howapbegan.php (accessed 3 September 2020).

41 Lim, *Translating Time*, 28.

42 *American Scary*, dir. John E. Hudgens (POOB Productions, Z-Team Productions, 2006), DVD.

43 'Welcome to the Home of Zacherley: The Cool Ghoul', available online: http://zacherley.com/ (accessed 3 September 2020).

44 *American Scary*, dir. Hudgens, DVD.

45 Knapp, *Personal Identity*, 245.

46 Matt Hills, *Fan Cultures* (London: Routledge, 2002), 19.

47 *The Rocky Horror Picture Show: The Official Fan Site*, 'History: Rocky Horror Timeline', available online: http://www.rockyhorror.com/history/timeline.php (accessed 3 September 2020).

48 It is notable, however, that these summer blockbusters are often sci-fi, fantasy, comic book and other genre films with an established fan base, and the time of their release positions them as box office fodder, not 'serious' and 'important' works of art.

49 Roger Ebert, 'The Rocky Horror Picture Show', review, *Chicago Sun-Times*, 18 August 1976, available online: https://www.rogerebert.com/reviews/the-rocky-horror-picture-show-1976 (accessed 12 June 2021).

50 In 2017, I mentored a student-led shadowcast of *The Rocky Horror Picture Show* at the Nightingale-Bamford School, a 'girls" school in NYC. Over half of the participating students had first encountered RHPS on *Glee*; others knew the musical from the book and film *Perks of Being a Wallflower*. 'I know this sounds sad, but I'm basically living my life waiting for the next Rocky Horror rehearsal right now', one cast member shared. The rehearsal process led to more important identity work than I could have ever imagined.

51 Joss Whedon, *Dr. Horrible's Sing-Along Blog*, available online: http://drhorrible.com/ (accessed 3 September 2020).

52 Stacy Ellen Wolf, *Changed for Good: A Feminist History of the Broadway Musical* (New York: Oxford University Press, 2010). See in particular chapters 6 ('"Changed for the Better": Queer Conventions in *Wicked* (2003)') and 7 ('"It's All About Popular": *Wicked* Divas and Internet Girl Fans') for a discussion of the green-skinned outsider Elphaba and *Wicked*'s fangirl culture.

53 Mary Hart, 'Satyrs in L.A.', *Didaskalia* 8, no. 6 (2011), available online: http://www.didaskalia.net/issues/8/6/ (accessed 11 June 2021).

54 For an analysis of how this musical's refusal to cadence mirrors its most ardent fans, who present gender identities and expressions that similarly refuse closure, conclusion or definition, see Sam Baltimore, '"With my freeze ray, I will stop-": Carnival Incompleteness in Dr. Horrible's Sing-Along Blog and "Once More, With Feeling"', *Music and the Moving Image* 7. 1 (Spring 2014): 24–39.

55 Anouk Lang, '"The Status Is Not Quo!": Pursuing Resolution in Web-Disseminated Serial Narrative', *Narrative* 18, no. 3 (2010): 367–81.

56 'Filmmaker's Commentary', *Dr. Horrible's Sing-Along Blog*, dir. Joss Whedon, perf. Nathan Fillion, Felicia Day and Neil Patrick Harris (Timescience Bloodclub, New Video Group, 2008), DVD.

57 Joss Whedon and Jane Watkins, *Dr. Horrible's Sing-Along Blog: The Book* (London: Titan Books, 2011), 20.

58 People Staff, 'EXCLUSIVE: Neil Patrick Harris Tells PEOPLE He Is Gay', *PEOPLE.com*, 3 November 2006, available online: http://www.people.com/people/article/0,,1554852,00.html (accessed 12 June 2021).

59 '"Prop 8 - The Musical" starring Jack Black, John C. Reilly, and many more... ' *Funny or Die*, 2 December 2008, available online: http://www.

funnyordie.com/videos/c0cf508ff8/prop-8-the-musical-starring-jack-black-john-c-reilly-and-many-more-from-fod-team-jack-black-craig-robinson-john-c-reilly-and-rashida-jones (accessed 12 June 2021).

60 See Chapter 5 for more on the curious case of Bobby's sexuality in *Company*.
61 Whedon and Watkins, *Dr. Horrible's Sing-Along Blog*, 9.
62 In the DVD, Dr. Horrible says, 'Freeze Ray. Tell your friends.' The published script reads, 'Freeze Ray. Heard it here first.' Ibid., 16.
63 Ibid., 16.
64 See Chapter 5 for a discussion of similar character multiplicity in *Fun Home* and *A Strange Loop*.
65 Whedon and Watkins, *Dr. Horrible's Sing-Along Blog*, 18.
66 Ibid., 18.
67 Ibid., 18–19.
68 Ibid., 16.
69 Ibid., 13, emphasis in the original.
70 Lang, 'The Status is not Quo!', 370. While some were shocked and saddened by the ending, many avid Whedon fans were disappointed and angry because Whedon's oeuvre – such as *Serenity*, *Angel* and *Buffy* – frequently resorts to these unhappy endings.
71 Whedon and Watkins, *Dr. Horrible's Sing-Along Blog*, 19.
72 Ibid., 83.
73 Brian Stelter, 'Strike News: Writers Gain P.R. Advantage', *NYTimes: Media Decoder* [Blog], 19 November 2007, available online: http://mediadecoder.blogs.nytimes.com/2007/11/19/strike-news-writers-gain-pr-advantage/ (accessed 12 June 2021).
74 The Nielsen Company, *Television in Transition: The Initial Impact of the Writers' Strike*, report (April 2008), 11–12, available online: http://www.broadcastingcable.com/file/2329-click_here.pdf (accessed 14 October 2012).
75 David Carr, 'Who Won the Writers Strike?', *The New York Times*, 12 February 2008, available online: http://www.nytimes.com/2008/02/12/arts/television/12strike.html (accessed 12 June 2021).
76 Ash Kalb, 'Wait, Aren't The Emmys Supposed To Be For TV Shows?', *Mediaite*, 20 September 2009, available online: http://www.mediaite.com/tv/wait-arent-the-emmys-supposed-to-be-for-tv-shows/ (accessed 12 June 2021).

77   Whedon and Watkins, *Dr. Horrible's Sing-Along Blog*, 84.
78   Ibid., 85.
79   Ibid., 86.
80   Wagner James Au, 'NewTeeVee Pick: The Guild', GigaOm, 31 October 2007, available online: https://gigaom.com/2007/10/31/the-guild/ (accessed 12 June 2021).
81   Whedon and Watkins, *Dr. Horrible's Sing-Along Blog*, 10.
82   *The Guild*, available online: http://www.watchtheguild.com/ (accessed 3 September 2020).
83   Rick Marshall, 'What Does Felicia Day Want to See in the "Dr. Horrible" Sequel?', MTV News, 31 March 2010, available online: http://www.mtv.com/news/2596378/felicia-day-dr-horrible-sequel/ (accessed 12 June 2021).
84   Whedon and Watkins, *Dr. Horrible's Sing-Along Blog*, 80.
85   Felicia Day, available online: http://feliciaday.com/ (accessed 3 September 2020).
86   Gordon Cox, "'Ratatouille' Musical Raised $1.9 Million: Here's Where the Money Will Go", *Variety*, 11 January 2021, available online: https://variety.com/2021/legit/news/ratatouille-musical-actors-fund-1234881445/ (accessed 12 June 2021). The musical continues to collect donations for the Actors Fund; for the most up-to-date figures, see Ratatouille: The TikTok Musical, 'Home', available online: https://ratatousical.com/ (accessed 12 June 2021).
87   Whedon and Watkins, *Dr. Horrible's Sing-Along Blog*, 56.
88   Ibid., 76.
89   Kirle, *Unfinished Show Business*.
90   Kai Cole, 'Joss Whedon Is a "Hypocrite Preaching Feminist Ideals," Ex-Wife Kai Cole Says (Guest Blog)', *The Wrap*, updated 22 November 2017, available online: https://www.thewrap.com/joss-whedon-feminist-hypocrite-infidelity-affairs-ex-wife-kai-cole-says/ (accessed 12 June 2021).
91   Tasneem Nashrulla, 'Actor Charisma Carpenter Accused Joss Whedon of Being Abusive to Her on the Sets of "Buffy The Vampire Slayer" And "Angel"', *BuzzFeed*, 10 February 2021, available online: https://www.buzzfeednews.com/article/tasneemnashrulla/buffy-charisma-carpenter-

joss-whedon-abusive (accessed 12 June 2021). The cast of *Dr. Horrible* has remained remarkably silent regarding these allegations to date.

Chapter 3

1. E.L. Doctorow, 'E. L. Doctorow, The Art of Fiction No. 94', interview by George Plimpton, *The Paris Review*, no. 101 (Winter 1986), available online: http://www.theparisreview.org/interviews/2718/the-art-of-fiction-no-94-e-l-doctorow (accessed 11 June 2021).
2. E.L. Doctorow, *Ragtime* (New York: Random House, 1975), 270.
3. Scott Joplin, 'School of Ragtime', in *Complete Piano Rags*, ed. David A. Jansen (New York: Dover Publications, 1988), xii.
4. Syncopation also derives from the grammatical term syncope, the omission of unstressed sounds or letters within a word. While syncopated music emphatically emphasizes the off beats, the linguistic syncope points to erasures and elisions, the structurally essential yet unvocalized components of a word.
5. Joplin, 'School of Ragtime', xii.
6. Lim, *Translating Time*, 8.
7. David Savran, *Highbrow/Lowdown: Theater, Jazz, and the Making of the New Middle Class* (Ann Arbor: University of Michigan Press, 2009), 10.
8. Hayden V. White, *The Content of the Form: Narrative Discourse and Historical Representation* (Baltimore: Johns Hopkins University Press, 1987), 57.
9. For an analysis of how the nation is conceived of as a monolithic community 'moving steadily down (or up) history' as if on a neatly plotted timeline, see, for example, Benedict Anderson, *Imagined Communities* (New York: Verso, 1991), 26.
10. Anne Anlin Cheng, *The Melancholy of Race: Psychoanalysis, Assimilation, and Hidden Grief* (New York: Oxford University Press, 2001), 10.
11. Knapp, *National Identity*, 5.
12. Cheng, *The Melancholy of Race*, 12.
13. Susan McClary, *Conventional Wisdom: The Content of Musical Form* (Berkeley: University of California Press, 2000), xi.

14 Diana Taylor, *The Archive and the Repertoire: Performing Cultural Memory in the Americas* (Durham, NC: Duke University Press, 2003), 83.
15 Suzan-Lori Parks, *The America Play, and Other Works* (New York: Theatre Communications Group, 1995), 4.
16 Ibid., 4–5, emphasis in the original.
17 Ibid., 9.
18 Howard Reich, 'Ragtime Revisited', *Chicago Tribune*, 1 November 1998, available online: https://www.chicagotribune.com/news/ct-xpm-1998-11-01-9811010113-story.html (accessed 12 June 2021).
19 Edward A. Berlin, *Ragtime: A Musical and Cultural History* (Berkeley: University of California Press, 1980), 51.
20 Craig H. Roell, *The Piano in America, 1890–1940* (Chapel Hill: University of North Carolina Press, 1989), 33.
21 Berlin, *Ragtime*, 32.
22 For a discussion of how Tin Pan Alley pushed jazz into mainstream popularity, see Raymond Knapp and Mitchell Morris, 'Tin Pan Alley Songs on Stage and Screen before World War II', in *The Oxford Handbook of the American Musical*, ed. Raymond Knapp, Mitchell Morris and Stacy Ellen Wolf (New York: Oxford University Press, 2011), 81–95. See also Charles Hamm, 'The Music of Tin Pan Alley', in *Music in the New World* (New York: Norton, 1983), 339–72.
23 Berlin, *Ragtime*, 6, my emphasis.
24 Doctorow, *Ragtime*, 3.
25 Lisa W. Foderaro, 'Doctorow's House, His "Ragtime" Inspiration, Is for Sale', *The New York Times*, 2 December 1999, available online: http://www.nytimes.com/1999/12/02/nyregion/doctorow-s-house-his-ragtime-inspiration-is-for-sale.html (accessed 12 June 2021).
26 Bruce Weber, 'The Myth Maker', *The New York Times*, 20 October 1985, available online: https://www.nytimes.com/1985/10/20/magazine/the-myth-maker.html (accessed 12 June 2021).
27 Foderaro, 'Doctorow's House'.
28 Stephanie Dunson, 'The Minstrel in the Parlor: Nineteenth-Century Sheet Music and the Domestication of Blackface Minstrelsy', *ATQ: The American Transcendental Quarterly* 16 (1 December 2002): 245. For a discussion of the sacred aura of domesticity that accrued to Victorian representations of girls at the keyboard, see also Ruth A. Solie, '"Girling

at the Parlor Piano', in *Music in Other Words: Victorian Conversations* (Berkeley: University of California Press, 2004), 85–117.
29 Roell, *The Piano in America*, 1.
30 Dunson, 'The Minstrel in the Parlor', 243.
31 Roell, *The Piano in America*, xii. This trope functions particularly well in *Meet Me in St. Louis*, both in the early title song sequence and when Mary Astor uses the piano to reconcile the family by singing 'You and I'.
32 In Taylor Mac's *A 24-Decade History of Popular Music*, Stephen Foster and Walt Whitman are pitted against one another for the title 'Father of American Song'. See the Conclusion for more on Mac's time-warping, queered history lesson.
33 Dunson, 'The Minstrel in the Parlor', 249–50.
34 Berlin, *Ragtime*, 33.
35 T.D. Rice, *Jim Crow, American: Selected Songs and Plays*, ed. W.T. Lhamon Jr. (Cambridge, MA: Belknap Press of Harvard University Press, 2009), viii.
36 As an example, see the analysis of 'Under the Bamboo Tree', based on 'Nobody Knows the Trouble I've Seen', in Knapp, *Personal Identity*, 394.
37 Berlin, *Ragtime*, 74.
38 Ibid., 36, 123, 196.
39 Doctorow, *Ragtime*, 132.
40 Christopher Lehmann-Haupt, 'Book Review: "Ragtime"', *The New York Times*, 8 July 1975, available online: https://archive.nytimes.com/www.nytimes.com/specials/ragtime/rev-ragtime.html (accessed 12 June 2021).
41 E.L. Doctorow, 'False Documents', in *Jack London, Hemingway, and the Constitution: Selected Essays, 1977–1992* (New York: Random House, 1993), 153.
42 The recent rise of 'fake news' complicates the lines between fact and fiction in quite a different way, by questioning the veracity of established truths when they do not align with a desired narrative. Rather than ascribing truth value to fiction, 'fake news' operates by undermining fact.
43 Doctorow, 'False Documents', 159.
44 Ibid., 154.
45 Eleanor Randolph, 'America, the Musical', *Los Angeles Times*, 30 March 1997, available online: http://articles.latimes.com/1997-03-30/entertainment/ca-43409_1_musical-theater (accessed 12 June 2021).

46 Rick Lyman, 'Learning to Hear What Music Has to Say', *The New York Times*, 11 December 1997, available online: http://www.nytimes.com/books/00/03/05/specials/doctorow-musical.html (accessed 12 June 2021).
47 Randolph, 'America, the Musical'.
48 Ibid.
49 Knapp, *National Identity*, 8.
50 *Ragtime*. Book by Terrence McNally, music by Stephen Flaherty and lyrics by Lynn Ahrens (Music Theatre International [MTI], 1998), 1.
51 Ibid., 1.
52 Ibid., 3.
53 Ibid., 3–4.
54 Ibid., 6.
55 Rick Simas, 'Ragtime (review)', *Theatre Journal* 50, no. 4 (December 1998): 540, https://doi.org/10.1353/tj.1998.0124.
56 Ibid., 542.
57 Larry Rohter, 'Finding New Meaning in a Pageant of Dreams', *The New York Times*, 4 November 2009, available online: http://theater.nytimes.com/2009/11/08/theater/08roht.html (accessed 12 June 2021).
58 Most, *Making Americans*, 1–2.
59 Ibid., 25.
60 Tateh's faux aristocratic transformation is also reminiscent of Austrian-American film-makers Erich von Stroheim and Josef von Sternberg.
61 Doctorow, *Ragtime*, 218.
62 Ibid., 218.
63 Simas, 'Ragtime (review)', 540.
64 Ben Brantley, '"Ragtime" Beckons to Nostalgia of Another Century's Turn', review, *The New York Times*, 19 January 1998, available online: http://www.nytimes.com/specials/ragtime/rag-show.html (accessed 12 June 2021).
65 Jessica Hillman, 'From Rags to Riches: Ragtime and the Jewish-American Dream', *Proceedings of Association for Theatre in Higher Education*, Denver, CO (2008), 1.
66 *Ragtime*, 28–9.
67 Ibid., 57–8.
68 Doctorow, *Ragtime*, 99.
69 Cheng, *The Melancholy of Race*, 44.

70. Milken Archive, 'Lebn Zol Kolumbus', available online: http://www.milkenarchive.org/works/lyrics/568 (accessed 3 September 2020).
71. Marvin A. Carlson, *The Haunted Stage: The Theatre as Memory Machine* (Ann Arbor: University of Michigan Press, 2001), 15.
72. For a discussion of *Lady in the Dark* and the trope of a haunting melody, see Knapp, *Personal Identity*, 266–73.
73. *Ragtime*, 33.
74. Ibid., 44.
75. Ibid., 48.
76. In the musical, The Little Boy also has a name – Edgar (*à la* Edgar Lawrence Doctorow). The entire story emerges through his youthful eyes, which are open to social and political transformation.
77. Danielle Tarento, 'Ragtime Vox', *YouTube* video, 2:14, 21 October 2016, available online: https://www.youtube.com/watch?v=Srf0fWniYow (accessed 12 June 2021).
78. *Ragtime*, 2.
79. Josh Kun, *Audiotopia: Music, Race, and America* (Berkeley: University of California Press, 2005), 12.
80. Ibid., 2.
81. Ibid., 13.
82. The Player Piano Page, 'Original Player Piano Advertising', available online: http://pianola.com/ppadvert.htm (accessed 3 September 2020).
83. Doctorow, *Ragtime*, 61.
84. Berndt Ostendorf, 'The Musical World of Doctorow's Ragtime', *American Quarterly* 43, no. 4 (December 1991): 579, https://www.jstor.org/stable/2713082.
85. Roell, *The Piano in America*, 42.
86. The Player Piano Page, 'Original Player Piano Advertising'.
87. Roell, *The Piano in America*, 41.
88. The Player Piano Page, 'Original Player Piano Advertising'.
89. See Benjamin, 'The Work of Art in the Age of Mechanical Reproduction', in *Illuminations*, 217–51.
90. Andrew Durkin, 'The Self-Playing Piano as a Site for Textual Criticism', *Text* 12 (1999): 171, https://www.jstor.org/stable/30228031.
91. The Player Piano Page, 'Original Player Piano Advertising'.
92. Ibid.

93 Roell, *The Piano in America*, 42.
94 Durkin, 'The Self-Playing Piano', 176.
95 Roell, *The Piano in America*, 43, my emphasis.
96 Ibid., 44.
97 Ibid., 44.
98 Ibid., 45.
99 The Player Piano Page, 'Original Player Piano Advertising', emphasis in the original.
100 Durkin, 'The Self-Playing Piano', 185.
101 Ibid., 168.
102 Ibid., 186.
103 Kun, *Audiotopia*, 23. This idea is inspired by Foucault's concept of a heterotopia.
104 Doctorow, *Ragtime*, 143–4.
105 Berlin, *Ragtime*, 12, my emphasis.
106 Doctorow, *Ragtime*, 147.
107 See Chapter 5 for a discussion of how *Fun Home* resists a linear trajectory to Bruce Bechdel's death.
108 Doctorow, *Ragtime*, 230.
109 Knapp, 'Getting off the Trolley'.

Chapter 4

1   *Glee: The Complete First Season*, 'Pilot', prod. Ryan Murphy, Ian Brennan and Brad Falchuk, perf. Matthew Morrison, Lea Michele, Jane Lynch, Cory Monteith and Chris Colfer (Twentieth Century Fox, 2010), DVD.
2   *Glee: The Complete First Season*, 'Laryngitis'.
3   Many songs, no matter how well 'integrated', can work beyond stage and screen with altered lyrics. However, popular styles arguably moved too quickly away from Tin Pan Alley for shows to keep up.
4   Dave Harker, 'Still Crazy after All These Years: What Was Popular Music in the 1960s?', in *Cultural Revolution? The Challenge of the Arts in the 1960s*, ed. Bart Moore-Gilbert and John Seed (London and New York: Routledge, 1992), 190. See also George Reddick, 'The Evolution of the Original Cast Album', in *The Oxford Handbook of the American Musical*,

ed. Raymond Knapp, Mitchell Morris and Stacy Ellen Wolf (New York: Oxford University Press, 2011), 179–95.

5   See Elijah Wald, *How the Beatles Destroyed Rock 'n' Roll: An Alternative History of American Popular Music* (Oxford: Oxford University Press, 2009). Wald points out that music histories are often strictly divided by genre (popular, classical, jazz, etc.), and the canon within each musical style tends to encompass the original and unique, rather than the generic. His alternative history explores continuities across genres while paying particular attention to artists whose work was popular and commercial, rather than groundbreaking. His exploration accounts for the ongoing popularity of styles such as musical theatre in the 1960s, even as the fresh sounds of rock 'n' roll dominate most music histories of the era.

6   Ethan Mordden, *The Happiest Corpse I've Ever Seen: The Last Twenty-Five Years of the Broadway Musical* (New York: Palgrave Macmillan, 2004). The 1970s also saw a rise in show music that looked back to the American songbook style with greater musical sophistication and a dash of irony; this style is exemplified by Stephen Sondheim and William Finn. British show music of the 1980s often looks even farther back to opera and operetta, à la Andrew Lloyd Webber's *Phantom of the Opera*.

7   See Keith Caulfield, '"Hamilton"'s Historic Chart Debut: By the Numbers', *Billboard*, 7 October 2015, available online: http://www.billboard.com/articles/columns/chart-beat/6722015/hamilton-cast-album-billboard-200 (accessed 12 June 2021). *Hamilton* debuted at a historic high on the Billboard 200 Chart (Number 12), while also securing Number 1 on Cast Albums, Number 3 on Rap Albums, Number 5 on Digital Albums and Number 9 on Top Album Sales. *Hamilton* was only the sixth cast album to reach the Top 20 in the last fifty years. While some see *Hamilton* as heralding a new age of the musical, *Hamilton* fans and musical theatre fans are not always coextensive; more on this subject below.

8   Averno is an explicitly queer and inclusive community, and many creators use they/them pronouns. It is notable that Averno truly took flight during the standstill of the Covid-19 pandemic; the strange temporalities of the coronavirus pandemic are discussed in the Conclusion. Elisabeth Vincentelli, 'A "Marvel Universe" for Musicals? Meet the Makers of Averno', *The New York Times*, 15 January 2021, available online: https://www.nytimes.com/2021/01/15/theater/averno-musicals-over-and-out.html (accessed 12 June 2021).

9 Mickey Rapkin, *Theater Geek: The Real Life Drama of a Summer at Stagedoor Manor, the Famous Performing Arts Camp* (New York: Free Press, 2010), 1.
10 *Stagedoor*, dir. Alexandra Shiva (Blumhouse Productions, Gidalya Pictures, 2006), DVD.
11 Rapkin, *Theater Geek*, 1.
12 Alexandra Robbins, *The Geeks Shall Inherit the Earth: Popularity, Quirk Theory, and Why Outsiders Thrive After High School* (New York: Hyperion, 2011), 6.
13 Ibid., 42. To be sure, the high school hierarchy is specific to each school. Theatre geeks, musicians and other artists may reign at high schools with lauded and well-supported arts programmes. With increasing budget cuts and emphasis on high-stakes testing in core academic subjects, though, the arts – and artistic individuals – fall to the fringe in many public schools.
14 Ibid., 8.
15 Ibid., 46.
16 It Gets Better, 'It Gets Better Project | Give Hope to LGBT Youth', available online: http://www.itgetsbetter.org/ (accessed 24 January 2013).
17 See Robin Bernstein, ed., *Cast Out: Queer Lives in Theater* (Ann Arbor: University of Michigan Press, 2006), in which queer theatre practitioners share their personal histories in all their contradictions and complexities.
18 Nick Rabkin and E.C. Hedberg, *Arts Education in America: What the Declines Mean for Arts Participation*, report, 24 February 2011, 21, available online: https://www.arts.gov/sites/default/files/2008-SPPA-ArtsLearning.pdf (accessed 11 June 2021).
19 Jennifer McMurrer, 'Instructional Time in Elementary Schools: A Closer Look at Changes for Specific Subjects', *Arts Education Policy Review* 109, no. 6 (2008): 23–8.
20 Robbins, *The Geeks Shall Inherit the Earth*, 7.
21 *Camp*, dir. Todd Graff (IFC Productions, 2003), DVD, emphasis in the original.
22 Leslie Paris, *Children's Nature: The Rise of the American Summer Camp* (New York: New York University Press, 2008), 130.
23 Ibid., 120.
24 Rapkin, *Theater Geek*, 3, emphases in the original.

25 Ibid., 130.
26 Ibid., 65. See Chapter 2 for more on the intersections of sci-fi/fantasy and musical theatre fan cultures.
27 Watchagirlunfold, 'I Just Woke up at Home, in My Own Room', Tumblr, 2011, available online: http://watchagirlunfold.tumblr.com/post/8470676056/i-just-woke-up-at-home-in-my-own-room (accessed 17 October 2012).
28 Shebelongstothestars, 'HERE'S WHERE I STAND, HERE'S WHO I AM', Tumblr, 2011, available online: http://shebelongstothestars.tumblr.com/post/10630987576/heres-where-i-stand-heres-who-i-am (accessed 17 October 2012).
29 PBS documented the show as part of their *Great Performances* series. See *Great Performances: The Gospel at Colonus*, dir. Kirk Browning, perf. The Blind Boys of Alabama, Morgan Freeman and Jevetta Steele (WNET Thirteen, 1985), DVD.
30 Lady Gaga's pop single 'Born This Way', released in February 2011, quickly topped the charts and became an empowering gay anthem. When 'Born This Way' was performed in a Gaga tribute on *Glee*, the musical number extended its reach to the wide array of theatrical misfits, whom Gaga calls her Little Monsters. Gaga has mythologized herself as a high school theatre geek who has since turned her youthful pain into wildly popular performance art. The Madonna of her time, Gaga often aims to empower marginalized groups through theatricality.
31 While Michael is an incredibly affecting character and wonderfully performed by Robin de Jesus, the effete gay Latino is a problematic stereotype. de Jesus is often cast in these flamboyant roles, from Emory in *The Boys in the Band* to Jacob in *La Cage aux Folles*; his humanity always peeks through the campy stereotype.
32 Helene P. Foley, 'Modern Performance and Adaptation of Greek Tragedy', *Transactions of the American Philological Association* 129 (1999): 4, http://www.jstor.org/stable/284422.
33 See Chapter 5 for a discussion of Usher's empowering relationship with his 'Inner White Girl' rocker in *A Strange Loop*.
34 Whether teenagers' playlists actually contain such a diverse collection of music and whether this eclecticism levels hierarchies of genre are questionable. In a notable scene on the rooftop with Ellen, Vlad pits his

'regular' R & B music against her mixtape of musical theatre ballads: 'Sometimes it's nice to listen to what everyone else listens to, just to be normal for once.' Even as he aims to cross genres, he maintains popular music as the norm and musical theatre as a strange and separate entity.

35 For a discussion of the problematics of elevating a single author – most often the composer – in such a collaborative art form as musical theatre, see Jim Lovensheimer, 'Texts and Authors', in *The Oxford Handbook of the American Musical*, ed. Raymond Knapp, Mitchell Morris and Stacy Ellen Wolf (New York: Oxford University Press, 2011), 20–32. To be clear, Sondheim does not sympathize with the assassins in his 1990 musical, but he does sympathize with their sense of alienation in a country that guarantees everyone the right to be happy.
36 David Levy, 'Fuck Yeah Stephen Sondheim', Fuck Yeah Stephen Sondheim, available online: https://fuckyeahstephensondheim.tumblr.com/ (accessed 3 September 2020).
37 Rapkin, *Theater Geek*, 16.
38 Raymond Zilberberg directed *Company* in his first summer at Stagedoor Manor (2006) and vividly remembers his Joanne actually breaking her wine glass during a toast, just like Anna Kendrick's character in *Camp*. This moment is also an obvious homage to *All About Eve*.
39 Rapkin, *Theater Geek*, 87.
40 Raymond Zilberberg, email to author, 10 August 2020.
41 Red, 'A Little Scared …', Message board, 22 March 2010, Stagedoor Manor Message Board, available online: http://stagedoormanor.invisionzone.com (accessed 17 October 2012).
42 Rapkin, *Theater Geek*, 9.
43 Ibid., 11.
44 Ibid., 16.
45 American Camp Association, 'Camp Trends: Tuition', updated 26 July 2018, available online: https://www.acacamps.org/press-room/camp-trends/tuition (accessed 22 August 2020).
46 'Stagedoor Manor 2019 Application', *Stagedoor Manor*, available online: http://www.stagedoormanor.com/Letter-to-Families-2019 (accessed 6 August 2020).
47 On 4 October 2013, 54 Below hosted a tenth anniversary *Camp* reunion and screening for those kids – now adults, and many of them part of the

NYC theatre community – who had grown up projecting themselves into this movie musical.

48 *Glee: The Complete First Season*, 'Pilot'.
49 Colleen Mastony, '"Glee Club" TV Series Creator Uses Mt. Prospect High School for Inspiration', *Chicago Tribune*, 8 September 2009, available online: http://articles.chicagotribune.com/2009-09-08/entertainment/0909070170_1_show-choir-glee-ryan-murphy (accessed 12 June 2021).
50 Edward Wyatt, 'Not That High School Musical', *The New York Times*, 15 May 2009, available online: http://www.nytimes.com/2009/05/17/arts/television/17wyat.html?pagewanted=all (accessed 12 June 2021).
51 Chris Castiglia, 'The Genealogy of a Democratic Crush', in *Materializing Democracy: Toward a Revitalized Cultural Politics*, ed. Russ Castronovo and Dana D. Nelson (Durham, NC: Duke University Press, 2002), 198. See also Chapter 2 for a discussion of *Dr. Horrible's Sing-Along Blog* and Chapter 5 for a discussion of *A Strange Loop*.
52 Throughout *Les Miserables*, female characters are problematically defined by their relationships to men.
53 Castiglia, 'The Genealogy of a Democratic Crush', 198.
54 *Glee: The Complete First Season*, 'Pilot'.
55 McMillin, *The Musical as Drama*, 21. See Chapter 5 for more on the multiplicity of the musical body.
56 Most, *Making Americans*, 10.
57 In 'Stick to the Status Quo' from Disney's *High School Musical*, teenagers are inspired to share alternate identities after basketball star Troy Bolton gets a callback for the high school musical. A jock confesses his passion for baking, a brainy girl reveals her secret hip-hop skills and a skater boy whips out his cello – all to the notable disdain of their cliques. The chorus attempts to rein these hybrid identities back into stable stereotypes: 'No, no, no, no, no / Stick to the stuff you know / If you wanna be cool / Follow one simple rule / Don't mess with the flow, no no / Stick to the status quo'. Yet in the course of this musical number, all the characters bridge into a different performance mode of song and dance that inherently doubles their identities and enlivens the space with an exhilarating diversity.

58 In fact, the loser hand gesture – an L formed by extending the thumb and index fingers of the right hand – has become an iconic image for *Glee*, often taking the place of the L in the logo. The glee kids at McKinley High, as well as their avid fans, reappropriate this gesture by proudly applying it to their own foreheads to signify their unabashed difference from the norm.

59 M. Shane Grant, '"We're all freaks together": White Privilege and Mitigation of Queer Community', in *Queer in the Choir Room: Essays on Gender and Sexuality in Glee*, ed. Michelle Parke (Jefferson, NC: McFarland & Company, 2014), 69.

60 Barrie Gelles, 'Glee and the "Ghosting" of the Musical Theatre Canon', *Popular Entertainment Studies* 2, no. 2 (2011): 92, available online: https://novaojs.newcastle.edu.au/ojs/index.php/pes/article/view/66 (accessed 11 June 2021).

61 Jessica Sternfeld, '"Everything's Coming Up Kurt": The Broadway Song in the Pop World of Glee', *Proceedings of SAM/IASPM National Conference*, Cincinnati (2011), 4. In *Camp*, as well, straight guy Vlad is more likely to perform songs that verge on folk, rock, R & B and other popular genres.

62 See Jessica Sternfeld, *The Megamusical* (Bloomington: Indiana University Press, 2006).

63 Knapp, *Personal Identity*, 67.

64 Ibid., 68.

65 See the discussion of *Rent* and its 'No day but today' message in Chapter 1.

66 *Glee* introduced its own companion casting series – *The Glee Project* – on Oxygen in 2011.

67 Dave Itzkoff, 'Move Over Mickey: A New Franchise at Disney', *The New York Times*, 20 August 2007, available online: http://www.nytimes.com/2007/08/20/business/media/20disney.html (accessed 13 June 2021).

68 Maria Elena Fernandez, 'Cool for school', *Los Angeles Times*, 26 April 2009, available online: http://articles.latimes.com/2009/apr/26/entertainment/ca-glee26 (accessed 13 June 2021).

69 Gary Trust, 'Most Billboard Hot 100 Hits by Artist', *Billboard.com*, 12 November 2015, available online: http://www.billboard.com/articles/events/greatest-of-all-time/6760667/glee-most-billboard-hot-100-hits-by-artist (accessed 13 June 2021).

70 Jean Baudrillard, *Simulacra and Simulation* (Ann Arbor: University of Michigan Press, 1994), 77.
71 Brent C. Talbot and Margaux B. Millman, 'Discourses Surrounding Marginalized Groups, LGBTQ Issues, and Music Learning and Teaching Practices in Season 1 of Glee', in *Proceedings of Establishing Identity: LGBT Studies and Music Education*, University of Illinois School of Music, Champaign, IL (2011), 16, available online: https://bcrme.press.uillinois.edu/proceedings/Establishing_Identity/14_Talbot_Millman.pdf (accessed 27 October 2011).
72 Robbins, *The Geeks Shall Inherit the Earth*, 387.
73 Schuyler Velasco, 'How "Glee" Is Changing High School Choir', *Salon.com*, 21 September 2010, available online: http://www.salon.com/2010/09/21/glee_changing_show_choir/ (accessed 13 June 2021).
74 Christopher Loudon, 'The Glee Effect', *Jazz Times*, 16 September 2010, available online: http://jazztimes.com/articles/26514-the-glee-effect (accessed 13 June 2021).
75 Mary Shinn, 'ASU Glee-inspired Show Choir Returns', *The State Press*, 9 February 2011, available online: https://www.statepress.com/article/2011/02/asu-glee-inspired-show-choir-returns (accessed 13 June 2021).
76 *Glee: The Complete First Season*, 'Vitamin D'.
77 David Kamp, 'The Glee Generation', *The New York Times*, 11 June 2010, available online: http://www.nytimes.com/2010/06/13/fashion/13Cultural.html (accessed 13 June 2021).
78 Rebecca Panovka, 'On the Phone With Composer J. Michael Friedman '97', *The Harvard Crimson*, 8 November 2012, available online: http://www.thecrimson.com/article/2012/11/8/on-the-phone-friedman/ (accessed 13 June 2021).
79 Jennifer Ashley Tepper, 'Are We Living in a New Golden Age of Musical Theatre?', *Playbill.com*, 23 February 2016, available online: https://www.playbill.com/article/are-we-living-in-a-new-golden-age-of-musical-theatre (accessed 13 June 2021).
80 Lin-Manuel Miranda and Jeremy McCarter, *Hamilton: The Revolution* (London: Little, Brown Book Group, 2016), 16.
81 Ben Brantley, 'Review: In "Hamilton," Lin-Manuel Miranda Forges Democracy Through Rap', *The New York Times*, 17 February 2015,

available online: https://www.nytimes.com/2015/02/18/theater/review-In-hamilton-lin-manuel-miranda-forges-democracy-through-rap.html (accessed 13 June 2021).
82 Miranda and McCarter, *Hamilton: The Revolution*, 55.
83 Ariel Nereson, '*Hamilton*'s America: An Unfinished Symphony with a Stutter (Beat)', *American Quarterly* 68, no. 4 (December 2016): 1052. Nereson adds that *Hamilton*'s marketing and profit-sharing with the originating performers are also among its truly revolutionary innovations.
84 CBS Sunday Morning, '"Hamilton": A Founding Father Takes to the Stage', *YouTube* [video], 9:06, 8 March 2015, available online: https://www.youtube.com/watch?v=0wboCdgzLHg (accessed 13 June 2021).

Chapter 5

1 Michael R. Jackson, *A Strange Loop* (New York: Theatre Communications Group, 2020), 39–40. Performed 24 May–28 July 2019, by Playwrights Horizons in New York City.
2 Douglas Hofstadter, *I Am a Strange Loop* (New York: Basic Books, 2007), xii. This is certainly not to suggest that all playwriting is simply an internal dialogue, with characters being direct manifestations of facets of their author. What dull plays those would be – and after all, what is truly 'internal'? Keep reading!
3 As the concept for this chapter came into being, I was also heavily influenced by the musical *Passing Strange* and plays (with music) *Wise Children* and *Emilia*.
4 Erik H. Erikson, *Identity: Youth and Crisis* (New York: W.W. Norton, 1968), 20.
5 Ibid., 20 and 23.
6 Ibid., 19, emphases in the original.
7 Hofstadter, *I Am a Strange Loop*, xiii and 194.
8 Ibid., 260.
9 Ibid., 272.
10 Butler, 'Performative Acts and Gender Constitution', 402.

11 Suki Ali, 'Reading Racialized Bodies: Learning to See Difference', in *Cultural Bodies: Ethnography and Theory*, ed. Helen Thomas and Jamilah Ahmed (Malden, MA: Blackwell Publishing, 2004), 76.
12 Tim Hodgkinson, *Music and the Myth of Wholeness: Toward a New Aesthetic Paradigm* (Cambridge, MA: MIT Press, 2016), 7.
13 Isabelle Haynes-Hopkins, zoom interview, 2 July 2020.
14 Knapp, *Personal Identity*, 255. Knapp discusses how the motivation for Hedwig's sex-change operation is not driven by a sense of being a woman, but by political necessity to use Sergeant Robinson as a ticket to the West. Hedwig is more of a metaphorical trans character than a human trans character, and in fact, creator John Cameron Mitchell does not consider *Hedwig* to be a trans story at all.
15 W.E.B. Du Bois, 'Strivings of the Negro People', *The Atlantic*, August 1897, available online: https://www.theatlantic.com/magazine/archive/1897/08/strivings-of-the-negro-people/305446/ (accessed 11 June 2021).
16 Homi K. Bhabha, 'The White Stuff (Political Aspect of Whiteness)', *Artforum International* 36, no. 9 (1998): 21.
17 Cheng, *The Melancholy of Race*, 7.
18 Kimberle Crenshaw, 'Demarginalizing the Intersection of Race and Sex: A Black Feminist Critique of Antidiscrimination Doctrine, Feminist Theory and Antiracist Politics', *University of Chicago Legal Forum* 1989, no. 1 (1989): 139–140, available online: http://chicagounbound.uchicago.edu/uclf/vol1989/iss1/8 (accessed 11 June 2021).
19 Du Bois, 'Strivings of the Negro People'.
20 The musical as a genre tends to uphold the cis, white male as an 'integrated' and complete character contained in a single body. There are of course some exceptions and variations. It is worth noting the fragmentation of composer Sergei Rachmaninoff in Dave Malloy's *Preludes* (which contains the fantastic faux operatic aria 'Loop'). In this musical about a three-year dry spell in the composer's career after the disastrous premiere of his first symphony, Rach (represented by a musical theatre performer) is splintered from Rachmaninoff (represented by the onstage music director/pianist of the show). Rach undergoes hypnotherapy to try to overcome depression, reintegrate with his musical self and resume his creative life. However, one might consider this situation an 'identity crisis' (as defined by Erikson) rather than a fundamental disjuncture in

Rachmaninoff's identity. Sondheim's work also plays with dis-integrating the straight white male; see the discussion of *Company* later in this chapter. Other exceptions include *City of Angels* and *Kinky Boots*, and Deaf West Theatre frequently 'doubles' its musical casts by having a deaf actor and a hearing actor share a role together on stage.

21 Butler, 'Performative Acts and Gender Constitution', 402.
22 Lisa Kron and Jeanine Tesori, *Fun Home* (New York: Samuel French, 2015), 17.
23 Alison Bechdel, *Fun Home* (Boston and New York: Houghton Mifflin Company, 2006), 141.
24 Ian MacRae, 'Queering Epistemology and the Odyssey of Identity in Alison Bechdel's *Fun Home*', in *Graphic Novels as Philosophy*, ed. Jeff McLaughlin (Jackson: University Press of Mississippi, 2017), 132.
25 Agnès Muller, 'Image as Paratext in Alison Bechdel's Fun Home', *GRAAT*, no. 1 (March 2007): 16, available online: http://www.graat.fr/bechdel001aaaa.pdf (accessed 11 June 2021). This article was written two years before the first developmental reading of the musical adaptation at the Ojai Playwrights Conference in 2009.
26 Pamela Demory, 'Queer/Adaptation: An Introduction', in *Queer/Adaptation: A Collection of Critical Essays*, ed. Pamela Demory (Cham, Switzerland: Palgrave Macmillan, 2019), 1.
27 Kirle, *Unfinished Show Business*, xix.
28 Jill Dolan, 'Fun Home Makes History', *The Feminist Spectator* [blog], 30 June 2015, available online: http://feministspectator.princeton.edu/2015/06/30/fun-home-makes-history/ (accessed 14 June 2021). *The Color Purple* (2005) also features a lesbian protagonist, but Celie's 'coming out' is not centred in the narrative, and productions often downplay her sexuality.
29 Terry Castle, *The Apparitional Lesbian: Female Homosexuality and Modern Culture* (New York: Columbia University Press, 1993).
30 Jill Dolan, 'Fun Home', *The Feminist Spectator* [blog], 22 October 2013, available online: http://feministspectator.princeton.edu/2013/10/22/fun-home/ (accessed 14 June 2021). The *Slate* article's title has since been changed to '*Fun Home* Won Five Tonys. How Did a Graphic Memoir Become a Musical?' (see below).
31 June Thomas, '*Fun Home* Won Five Tonys: How Did a Graphic Memoir Become a Musical?', *Slate*, 8 June 2015, emphases in the original, available

online: https://slate.com/human-interest/2015/06/fun-home-2015-tony-winner-how-did-a-graphic-novel-become-a-musical.html (accessed 14 June 2021).
32 Dolan, 'Fun Home', emphasis in the original.
33 Kron and Tesori, *Fun Home*, 7.
34 Robin Pogrebin, 'Memoir to Musical: Five-Year Journey', *The New York Times*, 20 November 2013, available online: https://www.nytimes.com/2013/11/21/theater/bringing-fun-home-to-the-stage.html (accessed 14 June 2021).
35 David Gordon, 'Fun Home', *TheaterMania*, 19 April 2015, available online: https://www.theatermania.com/broadway/reviews/fun-home_72584.html (accessed 14 June 2021). The off-Broadway production at the Public Theater utilized a turntable on a museum-like set to shift across timelines.
36 Pogrebin, 'Memoir to Musical'.
37 Kron and Tesori, *Fun Home*, 8.
38 Ibid., 7.
39 Ibid., 12, emphasis in the original.
40 Whitfield, 'Disrupting Heteronormative Temporality', 9.
41 Rebecca Applin Warner, 'Musematic Relationships in Jeanine Tesori's Score for *Fun Home*', in *Reframing the Musical: Race, Culture and Identity*, ed. Sarah Whitfield (London: Red Globe Press, 2019), 153.
42 Ibid., 159.
43 Kron and Tesori, *Fun Home*, 11.
44 Jack Viertel, *The Secret Life of the American Musical: How Broadway Shows Are Built* (New York: Farrar, Straus and Giroux, 2016), xi. Encores! produces concert versions and minimally staged (and thus easily transferrable) productions of Broadway classics. They also have an off-Broadway offshoot (Encores! Off Center), which Jeanine Tesori founded in 2013.
45 Ibid., 239.
46 Ibid., 5.
47 Ibid., 89.
48 Kron and Tesori, *Fun Home*, 41.
49 Ibid., 40.
50 Ibid., 40–1.

51 Ibid., 41.
52 Ibid., 41.
53 Bechdel, *Fun Home*, 118.
54 Ibid., 118.
55 Kron and Tesori, *Fun Home*, 56.
56 Raymond Knapp points out that both 'Ring of *Keys*' and '*Changing* My Major' (emphasis added) implement an unexpected *key change* in the transition to the chorus – a clever musical pun. Raymond Knapp, 'Saving Mr. *[Blank]*: Rescuing the Father Through Song in Children's and Family Musicals', in *Children, Childhood, and Musical Theater*, ed. Donelle Ruwe and James Leve (London: Routledge, 2020), 59–79.
57 Kron and Tesori, *Fun Home*, 57.
58 Warner, 'Musematic Relationships', 162.
59 Suzy Evans, 'Tonys: How Three "Fun Home" Actresses Become Alison Bechdel Each Night', *The Hollywood Reporter*, 13 May 2015, available online: https://www.hollywoodreporter.com/news/tonys-how-three-fun-home-794897 (accessed 14 June 2021).
60 Kron and Tesori, *Fun Home*, 51.
61 Ibid., 66.
62 Roach, *Cities of the Dead*.
63 Muller, 'Image as Paratext', 17.
64 Kron and Tesori, *Fun Home*, 67.
65 James Lovelock, '"What about Love?": Claiming and Reclaiming LGBTQ+ Spaces in Twenty-First Century Musical Theatre', in *Reframing the Musical: Race, Culture and Identity*, ed. Sarah Whitfield (London: Red Globe Press, 2019), 203.
66 Kron and Tesori, *Fun Home*, 70.
67 Ibid., 14.
68 Ibid., 17.
69 Ibid., 31.
70 This number is akin to Coalhouse's 'suicide rag' in *Ragtime* (see Chapter 3), as well as 'Rose's Turn' from *Gypsy*, in which Mama Rose attempts to assemble her identity from disjointed musical fragments of the show.
71 Kron and Tesori, *Fun Home*, 8.
72 Ibid., 66.
73 Ibid., 12.

74 See Chapter 3 for more on the tenuous borders between fact and fiction, past and present.
75 See the discussion in Chapter 1 of 'The Miller's Son' for more on the 'meanwhile'.
76 Kron and Tesori, *Fun Home*, 74.
77 Ibid., 76.
78 Alison's mother also helps launch her daughter on a different life path. In 'Days and Days', Helen opens up to Medium Alison about how her own identity has disappeared in the 'days and days and days' of playing wife; the heteronormative life trajectory is deadening. 'Don't you come back here / I didn't raise you / to give away your days / like me', she concludes. Ibid., 64.
79 Bechdel, *Fun Home*, 3.
80 Warner, 'Musematic Relationships', 164.
81 Kron and Tesori, *Fun Home*, 77.
82 Alysia Abbott, '"We Just Sat and Held Each Other": How It Feels to Watch Your Life Story Onstage', *The Atlantic*, 12 November 2013, available online: https://www.theatlantic.com/entertainment/archive/2013/11/we-just-sat-and-held-each-other-how-it-feels-to-watch-your-life-story-onstage/281369/ (accessed 14 June 2021).
83 Kron and Tesori, *Fun Home*, 77.
84 Sarah Taylor Ellis, 'Fun Home, or Finding a Coherence [sic] Existence in Art', *staylorellis* [blog], 31 October 2012, available online: https://staylorellis.tumblr.com/post/34704036627/fun-home-or-finding-a-coherence-existence-in-art (accessed 14 June 2021). The 'hand [reaching] out and [taking] my own' is a reference to one of Hector's lines in Alan Bennett's *The History Boys*: 'The best moments in reading are when you come across something – a thought, a feeling, a way of looking at things – which you had thought special and particular to you. And now, here it is, set down by someone else, a person you have never met, someone even who is long dead. And it is as if a hand has come out, and taken yours.' See Alan Bennett, *The History Boys* (New York: Farrar, Straus and Giroux, 2004), 56.
85 See Chapter 1 for a discussion of anxieties of integration in *A Funny Thing Happened on the Way to the Forum*.

86 David Benedict, 'Everything's Different, Nothing's Changed', in *Company: A Musical Comedy*, by Stephen Sondheim and George Furth (London: Nick Hern Books, 2019), 5.
87 Joanne Gordon, *Art Isn't Easy: The Achievement of Stephen Sondheim* (Carbondale and Edwardsville: Southern Illinois University Press, 1990), 42.
88 Ben Brantley, 'In Revelatory Revivals, Women Sing Through the Pain', review, *The New York Times*, 25 February 2019, available online: https://www.nytimes.com/2019/02/25/theater/company-caroline-or-change-reviews-london.html (accessed 14 June 2021).
89 Stephen Sondheim and George Furth, *Company: A Musical Comedy* (New York: Theatre Communications Group, 1996), 108.
90 Ibid., 28.
91 Craig Zadan, *Sondheim & Co.*, Second Edition (New York: Harper and Row Publishers, 1986), 117.
92 Sondheim and Furth, *Company*, 50–1.
93 Swayne, *How Sondheim Found His Sound*, 179.
94 For an analysis of the four different endings that Sondheim wrote as the show was in development, see Knapp, *Personal Identity*, 300. The current song plot was established by the 1995 revival, directed by Scott Ellis.
95 Clum, *Something for the Boys*, 226.
96 Adam Feldman, 'Another Gay Bobby?: Neil Patrick Harris to Star in *Company* at the Phil', *Time Out*, 11 December 2010, available online: https://www.timeout.com/newyork/upstaged-blog/another-gay-bobby-neil-patrick-harris-to-star-in-company-at-the-phil (accessed 16 July 2020).
97 Zadan, *Sondheim & Co.*, 125–6.
98 Gordon, *Art Isn't Easy*, 42.
99 Miller, *Place for Us*, 124.
100 Clum, *Something for the Boys*, 222.
101 Ibid., 225.
102 Ibid., 224. Both *A Funny Thing Happened on the Way to the Forum* and *Anyone Can Whistle* are distinctively 'Sondheim' in their own ways, and yet *Company* is still often hailed as the first.
103 Wollman, *Hard Times*, 48.
104 Feldman, 'Another Gay Bobby?'

105 Lindsay Champion, 'In Comes *Company* ... With a Gay Twist! Stephen Sondheim & John Tiffany Team Up for New Reading', *Broadway.com*, 15 October 2013, available online: https://www.broadway.com/buzz/172379/in-comes-companywith-a-gay-twist-stephen-sondheim-john-tiffany-team-up-for-new-reading (accessed 14 June 2021). Furth passed away in 2008, but his estate has been actively involved in revisal concepts, and Sondheim has been a great advocate for maintaining the integrity of Furth's work in new productions.

106 Mark Shenton, 'Company Producer Chris Harper: "Audiences are having the time of their lives – that's why we do it"', *The Stage*, 17 October 2018, available online: https://www.thestage.co.uk/features/company-producer-chris-harper-audiences-are-having-the-time-of-their-lives--thats-why-we-do-it (accessed 14 June 2021).

107 Matt Wolf, 'A Gender Swap Makes Sondheim's "Company" Soar', *The New York Times*, 25 October 2018, available online: https://www.nytimes.com/2018/10/25/theater/sondheim-company-london.html (accessed 14 June 2021).

108 Andrzej Lukowski, '"Company" Review', *Time Out*, 17 October 2018, available online: https://www.timeout.com/london/theatre/company-review (accessed 14 June 2021).

109 Matt Trueman, 'West End Review: "Company"', *Variety*, 17 October 2018, available online: https://variety.com/2018/legit/reviews/company-review-gender-swap-marianne-elliott-1202981961/ (accessed 14 June 2021).

110 Brantley, 'In Revelatory Revivals, Women Sing through the Pain'.

111 Ibid.

112 Matt Wolf, 'A Gender Swap Makes Sondheim's "Company" Soar'.

113 David Levy, 'Fynsworth Alley: Donna McKechnie', *itsdlevy.me* [blog], 14 February 2001, available online: https://itsdlevy.me/2001/02/14/fynsworth-alley-donna-mckechnie/ (accessed 14 June 2021).

114 Peter Filichia, 'Filichia Features: Company: The Return of "Tick-Tock"', *MTI Shows* [blog], 9 December 2016, available online: https://www.mtishows.com/news/filichia-features-company-the-return-of-tick-tock (accessed 14 June 2021).

115 Trueman, 'West End Review: "Company."'

116 Merav Amir, 'Bio-Temporality and Social Regulation: The Emergence of the Biological Clock', *Polygraph* 18 (2006): 52.

117 Ibid., 52.
118 Henry Hitchings, 'Company Review: Marianne Elliott's Glorious Show Savours Sondheim's Subtleties', *Evening Standard*, 17 October 2018, available online: https://www.standard.co.uk/go/london/theatre/company-review-theatre-marianne-elliott-sondheim-a3964531.html (accessed 14 June 2021). See Chapter 1 for a discussion of how some critics have layered a linear trajectory to marriage onto *A Little Night Music*'s 'The Miller's Son' in an attempt to rein in excess.
119 Lauren Sheehan-Clark, 'Limitations of Gender-Swapped Theater: A Closer Look at West End's "Company" Revival', *The Daily Californian*, 21 March 2019, emphasis in the original, available online: https://www.dailycal.org/2019/03/21/limitations-of-gender-swapped-theater-a-closer-look-at-west-ends-company-revival/ (accessed 14 June 2021).
120 Jackson, *A Strange Loop*, 11.
121 Ibid., 55.
122 Sondheim and Furth, *Company*, 7–8.
123 Jackson, *A Strange Loop*, 15.
124 *The Color Purple* again deserves mention as a 'big Black gay musical' on Broadway, but Celie's lesbianism is often downplayed in production. *A Strange Loop* is itself Broadway-bound, although its journey has been stalled due to Covid-19. Broadway, Hollywood and the West End are often problematically seen as the linear, culminating destinations for musical theatre that 'matters'. See Whitfield, 'Introduction', xvii.
125 Ibid., xv. See also Chapter 3 for further discussion of African Americans' spectral labour.
126 Michael R. Jackson, '*A Strange Loop*: A Conversation with Michael R. Jackson', interview by Doug Reside, New York Public Library, 3 August 2020.
127 Lovelock, '"What about Love?"', 187–210.
128 Jackson, *A Strange Loop*, 12.
129 Ibid., 12, emphasis in the original.
130 Jackson, '*A Strange Loop*: A Conversation with Michael R. Jackson'.
131 Jackson, *A Strange Loop*, 14.
132 José Esteban Muñoz, *Disidentifications: Queers of Color and the Performance of Politics* (Minneapolis: University of Minnesota Press, 1999), 31.

133 'Biggest, best creation' is a lyrical reference to Max Vernon's *The View UpStairs*, a queer time-travelling musical in which a contemporary self-involved Black gay man named Wes is transported back to New Orleans 1973. Wes experiences love and loss in a single night as he becomes part of the queer community at the UpStairs Lounge, a fantastically inclusive gay bar. The tragic real-life arson attack on this bar abruptly jets Wes back to the twenty-first century, where Wes realizes that his vision of queer futurity must incorporate the past.

134 Jackson, *A Strange Loop*, 11–12.

135 Ibid., 58–59.

136 Michael R. Jackson, 'Michael R. Jackson Breaks Down His *A Strange Loop* Score', *Playbill.com*, 3 October 2019, available online: https://www.playbill.com/article/michael-r-jackson-breaks-down-his-a-strange-loop-score (accessed 14 June 2021).

137 Jackson, *A Strange Loop*, 48–9.

138 This narrative focus on trauma is of course also applicable to *Ragtime*, analysed in Chapter 3.

139 Playwrights Horizons, 'In Process: Michael R. Jackson on A Strange Loop', *YouTube* [video], 2:27, 24 May 2019, available online: https://www.youtube.com/watch?v=Ujii8_2tj8E (accessed 14 June 2021).

140 *Jackson, 'A Strange Loop*: A Conversation with Michael R. Jackson'.

141 See the discussion in Chapter 4 of the performative strength *Glee*'s Rachel Berry finds in performing the megamusical anthem 'On My Own'.

142 Michael R. Jackson, 'Artist Interview: Michael R. Jackson', interview by Tim Sanford, *Playwrights Horizons*, 17 June, available online: https://www.playwrightshorizons.org/shows/trailers/artist-interview-michael-r-jackson/ (accessed 11 June 2021).

143 Jackson, *A Strange Loop*, 26.

144 Ibid., 40.

145 Ibid., 56.

146 Ibid., 76.

147 Michael R. Jackson, 'Playwright's Perspective: A Strange Loop', *Playwrights Horizons*, 28 February 2019, available online: https://www.playwrightshorizons.org/shows/trailers/playwrights-perspective-strange-loop/ (accessed 14 June 2021).

148 Interestingly, Jack Viertel teaches a song plot course at NYU, which was the basis for *The Secret Life of the American Musical*.

149 Jackson has a penchant for playing with the intersections of fiction and reality; his website offers both 'fake?' and 'real?' biographies for the visitor's perusal, and he delights in the fact that *A Strange Loop* protagonist Usher shares a name with musical artist Usher, just as he shares a name with music icon Michael Jackson. In fact, Michael R. Jackson's website is https://www.thelivingmichaeljackson.com, and his twitter handle is @TheLivingMJ.

150 Jackson, 'Artist Interview: Michael R. Jackson'.

151 Gordon Cox, 'Listen: Michael R. Jackson Has Finally Accepted He's a Composer', *Variety*, 26 May 2020, available online: https://variety.com/2020/legit/news/michael-r-jackson-a-strange-loop-broadway-pulitzer-1234615665/ (accessed 14 June 2021).

152 Michael R. Jackson, 'Diversity in Musical Theater!', *Michael R. Jackson* [blog], 15 August 2015, emphases in the original, available online: https://www.thelivingmichaeljackson.com/diversity-in-musical-theater/ (accessed 11 June 2021).

153 Jackson, *A Strange Loop*, 21, emphasis in the original.

154 In 'Getting off the Trolley', Knapp considers another way in which the 11 o'clock number operates – as a manifestation of musicals' 'second-act problems'.

155 Jackson, *A Strange Loop*, 91.

156 Whitfield, 'Disrupting Heteronormative Temporality', 10.

157 Jackson, *A Strange Loop*, 92.

158 Ibid., 92.

159 Jackson, '*A Strange Loop*: A Conversation with Michael R. Jackson'.

160 Jackson, *A Strange Loop*, 94.

161 Ibid., 96.

Conclusion

1 Suzy Evans, 'A Trip Around the Sun with Taylor Mac's "24-Decade History"', *American Theatre*, 14 October 2016, available online: https://www.americantheatre.org/2016/10/14/a-trip-around-the-sun-with-taylor-macs-24-decade-history/ (accessed 11 June 2021).

2 Alex Needham, 'Taylor Mac on Queering History: "Someone like me doesn't normally get to represent America"', *The Guardian*, 12 September

2017, available online: https://www.theguardian.com/stage/2017/sep/13/taylor-mac-on-queering-history-someone-like-me-doesnt-normally-get-to-represent-america (accessed 14 June 2021).

3   Domenico Cucinotta and Maurizio Vanelli, 'WHO Declares COVID-19 a Pandemic', *Acta Biomed* 91, no. 1 (19 March 2020): 157–60.

4   Arielle Pardes, 'There Are No Hours or Days in Coronatime', *Wired*, 8 May 2020, available online: https://www.wired.com/story/coronavirus-time-warp-what-day-is-it/ (accessed 14 June 2021).

5   The time of capital refers to the paradoxical overlap of the linear, homogenous productive time of labourers as well as the pseudo-cyclical accumulating growth of capital; thus capital is at once measure and system, as well as progress. See Sami Khatib, 'The Time of Capital and the Messianicity of Time: Marx with Benjamin', *Studies in Social and Political Thought* 20 (Winter 2012): 46–69.

6   Amie Tsang, 'Here's How Those Hot Jigsaw Puzzles Are Made', *The New York Times*, 8 April 2020, available online: https://www.nytimes.com/2020/04/08/business/coronavirus-jigsaw-puzzles.html (accessed 14 June 2021).

7   Holly Corbett, 'The Time Bias That Is Forcing Women Out of the Workforce', *Forbes*, 20 December 2020, available online: https://www.forbes.com/sites/hollycorbett/2020/12/20/the-time-bias-that-is-forcing-women-out-of-the-workforce/ (accessed 14 June 2021).

8   And of course, being furloughed in one country means substantial financial support from the government; being furloughed in another means sparing unemployment. Freelancers are often forgotten.

9   Tony Kushner, *Angels in America* (New York: Theatre Communications Group, 1995), 182.

10 Isaac Butler and Dan Kois, 'An Instant Oral History of the Strangest, Starriest *Angels in America* Ever', *Slate*, 8 October 2020, available online: https://slate.com/culture/2020/10/angels-in-america-covid-amfar-oral-history.html (accessed 14 June 2021).

11 Halberstam, *In a Queer Time and Place*, 2.

12 The gender pronoun judy is a playful homage to Judy Garland. 'I was getting introduced onstage and written about, and some people would say "he" and others would say "she" and neither really felt right for the art I was making', Mac explains. 'My friend Justin Vivian Bond started using

the gender pronoun "v", and that made me think I could choose my own. The other part is that I'm an artist, and it's part of my job to make people think outside their norms a little bit. And I wanted a gender pronoun that was fun, and that immediately emasculates you – because you can't roll your eyes and say "judy" without being camp.' See Needham, 'Taylor Mac on Queering History'.

13 *Taylor Mac: A 24-Decade History of Popular Music: 1776–1836: Work in Progress*, Programme, 3. Performed 12, 13 and 16 January 2018, at The Flea Theater in New York City.

14 Ibid., 3. Of course with a steep ticket price of $400, Taylor Mac's 24-hour show was not entirely egalitarian. An anonymous donor made some tickets available at a heavily discounted rate so that fans who could not otherwise afford the performance would be able to attend.

15 Jerry Lieblich, 'An Appropriated History of Appropriation as History', Culturebot, 23 January 2015, available online: https://www.culturebot.org/2015/01/23216/an-appropriated-history-of-appropriation-as-history/ (accessed 11 June 2021).

16 Charles Isherwood, 'An Epic, Sequined Hit Parade', *The New York Times*, 14 January 2015, available online: https://www.nytimes.com/2015/01/15/theater/taylor-macs-a-24-decade-history-of-popular-music-1900-1950s.html (accessed 14 June 2021).

17 Bridge Markland and Dan Borden, '"Oh they love it when things go wrong!": Taylor Mac', *EXBERLINER*, 7 October 2019, available online: https://www.exberliner.com/features/people/taylor-mac-interview/ (accessed 14 June 2021).

18 The song was originally sung by the British military as an insult to ineffectual Yankee troops, but later appropriated by the Yankees as a Revolutionary taunt. America was also founded, we learn, on hating Congress, misinterpreting Thomas Paine's 'Common Sense', making things, loving black hair, forgiving the oppressor and vilifying outsiders. See Marilyn Smith, 'Taylor Mac's "A 24 Decade History of Popular Music" is the Mother of All History Lessons', *EUR*, 18 March 2018, available online: https://eurweb.com/2018/03/18/taylor-macs-a-24-decade-history-of-popular-music-is-the-mother-of-all-history-lessons/ (accessed 14 June 2021).

19 Markland and Borden, '"Oh they love it when things go wrong!"'.

20 Sasha Weiss, 'Taylor Mac Wants Theater to Make You Uncomfortable', *The New York Times*, 2 April 2019, available online: https://www.nytimes.com/2019/04/02/magazine/taylor-mac-gary-broadway.html (accessed 11 June 2021).

21 Taylor Mac, 'A Conversation with Heterogeneity: Ein Gespräch zu "A 24-Decade History of Popular Music"', interview by Thomas Oberender, *Berliner Festspiele Blog* [blog], 9 October 2019, available online: https://blog.berlinerfestspiele.de/a-conversation-with-heterogeneity/ (accessed 11 June 2021).

22 Weiss, 'Taylor Mac Wants Theater to Make You Uncomfortable'.

23 Benjamin, *Illuminations*, 257–8.

24 Brian Teare, 'How to Be a Dandy in the Age of Mass Culture: Notes on Taylor Mac's *A 24-Decade History of Popular Music*', *Kimmel Center for the Performing Arts*, 14 August 2018, available online: https://www.kimmelcenter.org/globalassets/about-us/blog/how-to-be-a-dandy-in-the-age-of-mass-culture.pdf (accessed 11 June 2021).

25 Throughout this text, I invoke not only the 24-hour concert but also various iterations prior to and after the 2016 24-hour marathon at St. Ann's Warehouse; the 24-hour concert is written about in the present tense. This chapter is my own highly subjective patchwork, comprising my own memories alongside other audience members' experiences. Thank you to those scholars, journalists, fans and friends who captured the performances in such rich detail and shared their memories in rapturous writings, photos, videos and conversations.

26 Lieblich, 'An Appropriated History of Appropriation as History'.

27 Mac, 'A Conversation with Heterogeneity'.

28 Weiss, 'Taylor Mac Wants Theater to Make You Uncomfortable'.

29 'They are not minions to us, but to the great spirit of the dandy', Mac clarifies. See Mac, 'A conversation with heterogeneity'.

30 Gareth White, *Audience Participation in Theatre: Aesthetics of the Invitation* (London: Palgrave Macmillan, 2013), 1.

31 Ibid., 1. A recent trend in immersive theatre – such as *Sleep No More* and *The Drowned Man* by Punchdrunk – capitalizes on some audiences' desire for participation, immersion and even intimacy in a theatrical experience; however, these immersive pieces often grant audience members a degree of ghostly anonymity (audiences must wear a mask) and agency

(audience members chart their own individual path through a multi-floor theatrical landscape) that can help to ease initial anxiety and release inhibitions. See Rose Biggin, *Immersive Theatre and Audience Experience: Space, Game and Story in the Work of Punchdrunk* (London: Palgrave Macmillan, 2017). Some audience members have abused this anonymity and agency to sexually assault cast members. See Amber Jamieson, 'Performers and Staffers at "Sleep No More" Say Audience Members Have Sexually Assaulted Them', *BuzzFeed News*, 6 February 2018, available online: https://www.buzzfeednews.com/article/amberjamieson/sleep-no-more (accessed 14 June 2021).

32 Rarely does the audience sit, and the crowd, while very diverse in terms of gender, sexuality and age, is significantly less diverse in race and ethnicity.

33 Teare, 'How to Be a Dandy in the Age of Mass Culture', 3.

34 Weiss, 'Taylor Mac Wants Theater to Make You Uncomfortable'.

35 Mac speaks similarly of his decision to use 'judy' as a stage pronoun: 'It allows me to give people pause — that's the job of the arts'. See Alaina Johns, 'The great judy question', *Broad Street Review*, 20 March 2018, available online: https://www.broadstreetreview.com/cross-cultural/pronouns-and-pifa (accessed 14 June 2021).

36 In fact, within the context of the show, Mac explains how much he hates it when theatremakers promise audience participation will be fun. 'Fuck you, I don't want to have fun', Mac reacts, before adding, 'It's different when I ask you to participate. I *want* you to feel uncomfortable' (emphasis in the original). See Jonathan Mandell, 'Taylor Mac's A 24-Decade History of Popular Music, 1900s–1950s', *New York Theater*, 20 January 2015, available online: https://newyorktheater.me/2015/01/20/taylor-macs-a-24-decade-history-of-popular-music-1900s-1950s/ (accessed 14 June 2021).

37 Muñoz, *Cruising Utopia*, 1.

38 Markland and Borden, '"Oh they love it when things go wrong!"'.

39 Jonathan Kalb, *Great Lengths: Seven Works of Marathon Theater* (Ann Arbor: University of Michigan Press, 2013), 3.

40 Do I sleep on Sunday afternoon? No. I go out to brunch with a friend who made a theatrical pilgrimage from Colorado to attend the show; we prolong the utopian moment together.

41 Chloe Veltman, 'How I Survived Taylor Mac's 24-Hour-Long Musical History Lesson', *KQED*, 12 October 2016, available online: https://www.kqed.org/arts/12186696/how-i-survived-taylor-macs-24-hour-long-musical-history-lesson (accessed 14 June 2021).
42 Weiss, 'Taylor Mac Wants Theater to Make You Uncomfortable'.
43 Hugh Ryan, 'How Taylor Mac's 24-Hour Performance Encapsulated the Experience of the AIDS Crisis', *New York Vulture*, 18 October 2016, available online: https://www.vulture.com/2016/10/taylor-mac-performance-encapsulated-the-aids-crisis.html (accessed 11 June 2021).
44 For Jeannine Murray-Román, *A 24-Decade History of Popular Music* is in fact a manifesto determined 'to make space for those who have been historically displaced, to endure things that go on too long in order to stay committed in direct political actions, and to draw on queer pleasure as a means of sustaining these two processes'. See Jeannine Murray-Román, 'A Manifesto on Making Space in Taylor Mac's *24-Decade History of Popular Music*', *Journal of Dramatic Theory and Criticism* 34, no. 1 (Fall 2019): 9–28.
45 Hans-Thies Lehmann, *Postdramatic Theatre* (New York: Routledge, 2006).
46 Kalb, *Marathon Theatre*, 2.
47 Ibid., 22.
48 Markland and Borden, '"Oh they love it when things go wrong!"'.
49 *Taylor Mac: A 24-Decade History of Popular Music*, Programme, 3.
50 Mac's 24-hour concert has particular resonance for me as one of the last times I saw musical theatre composer Michael Friedman, who died of HIV/AIDS-related complications in 2017.
51 Jill Gentile, 'Time May Change Us: The Strange Temporalities, Novel Paradoxes, and Democratic Imaginaries of a Pandemic', *Journal of the American Psychoanalytic Association* 68, no. 4 (14 September 2020): 650.
52 Ibid., 649–50, emphasis in the original.
53 Ibid., 656.
54 Giorgio Agamben, *Infancy and History: On the Destruction of Experience* (London and New York: Verso, 1993), 99.

Select Bibliography

Adler, Thomas P. 'The Sung and the Said: Literary Value in the Musical Dramas of Stephen Sondheim'. In *Reading Stephen Sondheim: A Collection of Critical Essays*, edited by Sandor Goodhart, 37–60. New York: Garland Publishing, 2000.

Adorno, Theodor W. *Aesthetic Theory*. Translated by Robert Hullot-Kentor. Minneapolis: University of Minnesota Press, 1997.

Agamben, Giorgio. *Infancy and History: On the Destruction of Experience*. London and New York: Verso, 1993.

Ali, Suki. 'Reading Racialized Bodies: Learning to See Difference'. In *Cultural Bodies: Ethnography and Theory*, edited by Helen Thomas and Jamilah Ahmed, 76–97. Malden, MA: Blackwell Publishing, 2004.

Altman, Rick. *The American Film Musical*. Bloomington: Indiana University Press, 1987.

American Scary. Directed by John E. Hudgens. POOB Productions, Z-Team Productions, 2006. DVD.

Amir, Merav. 'Bio-Temporality and Social Regulation: The Emergence of the Biological Clock'. *Polygraph* 18 (2006): 47–72.

Anderson, Benedict. *Imagined Communities*. New York: Verso, 1991.

Aviram, Amittai F. 'Postmodern Gay Dionysus: Dr. Frank N. Furter'. *Journal of Popular Culture* 26, no. 3 (1992): 183–92.

Baltimore, Samuel. 'Do It Again: Repetition, Reception and Identity on Musical Comedy's Margins'. PhD diss., University of California, Los Angeles, 2013.

Baltimore, Samuel, '"With my freeze ray, I will stop-": Carnival Incompleteness in Dr. Horrible's Sing-Along Blog and "Once More, With Feeling"'. *Music and the Moving Image*, 7, no. 1 (Spring 2014): 24–39.

Banfield, Stephen. *Sondheim's Broadway Musicals*. Ann Arbor: University of Michigan Press, 1993.

Baudrillard, Jean. *Simulacra and Simulation*. Ann Arbor: University of Michigan Press, 1994.

Bechdel, Alison. *Fun Home*. Boston and New York: Houghton Mifflin Company, 2006.

Benjamin, Walter. *Illuminations*. Edited by Hannah Arendt. New York: Schocken Books, 2007.

Bennett, Alan. *The History Boys*. New York: Farrar, Straus and Giroux, 2004.

Berlin, Edward A. *Ragtime: A Musical and Cultural History*. Berkeley: University of California Press, 1980.

Bernstein, Robin, ed. *Cast Out: Queer Lives in Theater*. Ann Arbor: University of Michigan Press, 2006.

Bhabha, Homi K. 'The White Stuff (Political Aspect of Whiteness)'. *Artforum International* 36, no. 9 (1998): 21–3.

Biggin, Rose. *Immersive Theatre and Audience Experience: Space, Game and Story in the Work of Punchdrunk*. London: Palgrave Macmillan, 2017.

Bloch, Ernst. *The Utopian Function of Art and Literature: Selected Essays*. Translated by Jack Zipes and Frank Mecklenburg. Cambridge, MA: MIT Press, 1988.

Block, Geoffrey. 'The Broadway Canon from *Show Boat* to *West Side Story* and the European Operatic Ideal'. *Journal of Musicology* 11, no. 4 (1993): 525–44.

Brecht, Bertolt. *Brecht on Theatre: The Development of an Aesthetic*. Translated by John Willett. New York: Hill and Wang, 1964.

Butler, Judith. 'Performative Acts and Gender Constitution: An Essay in Phenomenology and Feminist Theory'. In *Writing on the Body: Female Embodiment and Feminist Theory*, edited by Katie Conboy, Nadia Medina and Sarah Stanbury, 401–18. New York: Columbia University Press, 1997.

Camp. Directed by Todd Graff. IFC Productions, 2003. DVD.

Campt, Tina M. 'Quiet Soundings: The Grammar of Black Futurity'. In *Listening to Images*, 13–46. Durham, NC and London: Duke University Press, 2017.

Carlson, Marvin A. *The Haunted Stage: The Theatre as Memory Machine*. Ann Arbor: University of Michigan Press, 2001.

Castiglia, Chris. 'The Genealogy of a Democratic Crush'. In *Materializing Democracy: Toward a Revitalized Cultural Politics*, edited by Russ Castronovo and Dana D. Nelson, 195–217. Durham, NC: Duke University Press, 2002.

Castle, Terry. *The Apparitional Lesbian: Female Homosexuality and Modern Culture*. New York: Columbia University Press, 1993.

Castles-Onion, Brian. *Losing the Plot in Opera: Myths and Secrets of the World's Great Operas*. Auckland: Exisle, 2008.

Chabon, Michael. *Maps and Legends: Reading and Writing Along the Borderlands*. San Francisco, CA: McSweeney's Books, 2008.
Cheng, Anne Anlin. *The Melancholy of Race: Psychoanalysis, Assimilation, and Hidden Grief*. New York: Oxford University Press, 2001.
Citron, Stephen. *Songwriting: A Complete Guide to the Craft*. New York: W. Morrow, 1998.
Clum, John M. *Something for the Boys: Musical Theater and Gay Culture*. New York: St. Martin's Press, 1999.
Craig, David. 'On Performing Sondheim: A Little Night Music Revisited'. In *Stephen Sondheim: A Casebook*, edited by Joanne Lesley Gordon, 93–106. New York: Garland Publishing, 1997.
Crenshaw, Kimberle. 'Demarginalizing the Intersection of Race and Sex: A Black Feminist Critique of Antidiscrimination Doctrine, Feminist Theory and Antiracist Politics'. *University of Chicago Legal Forum* 1989, no. 1 (1989): 139–67. Available online: http://chicagounbound.uchicago.edu/uclf/vol1989/iss1/8 (accessed 11 June 2021).
Dahlhaus, Carl. *Nineteenth-Century Music*. Berkeley: University of California Press, 1989.
Dawkins, Philip. *The Homosexuals*. New York: Playscripts, 2014.
Decker, Todd R. *Music Makes Me: Fred Astaire and Jazz*. Berkeley: University of California Press, 2011.
Demory, Pamela. 'Queer/Adaptation: An Introduction'. In *Queer/Adaptation: A Collection of Critical Essays*, edited by Pamela Demory, 1–13. Cham, Switzerland: Palgrave Macmillan, 2019.
Diamond, Elin. 'Brechtian Theory/Feminist Theory: Toward a Gestic Feminist Criticism'. *TDR* 32, no. 1 (Spring 1988): 82–94.
Diamond, Elin. *Unmaking Mimesis: Essays on Feminism and Theater*. London: Routledge, 1997.
Doctorow, E.L. 'E. L. Doctorow, The Art of Fiction No. 94'. Interview by George Plimpton. *The Paris Review*, no. 101 (Winter 1986). Available online: http://www.theparisreview.org/interviews/2718/the-art-of-fiction-no-94-e-l-doctorow (accessed 11 June 2021).
Doctorow, E.L. 'False Documents'. In *Jack London, Hemingway, and the Constitution: Selected Essays, 1977–1992*, 149–64. New York: Random House, 1993.
Doctorow, E.L. *Ragtime*. New York: Random House, 1975.

Dolan, Jill. *The Feminist Spectator* [blog]. Available online: http://feministspectator.princeton.edu (accessed 11 June 2021).

Dolan, Jill. *Utopia in Performance: Finding Hope at the Theater*. Ann Arbor: University of Michigan Press, 2005.

Dorsey, Zachary. 'Big Possibility: Moscow, and Musical Theatre's Subjunctive Dramaturgy'. *Studies in Musical Theatre* 10 (2016): 195–207.

Dr. Horrible's Sing-Along Blog. Directed by Joss Whedon. Performed by Nathan Fillion, Felicia Day and Neil Patrick Harris. Timescience Bloodclub, New Video Group, 2008. DVD.

Du Bois, W.E.B. 'Strivings of the Negro People'. *The Atlantic*, August 1897. Available online: https://www.theatlantic.com/magazine/archive/1897/08/strivings-of-the-negro-people/305446/ (accessed 11 June 2021).

Dunson, Stephanie. 'The Minstrel in the Parlor: Nineteenth-Century Sheet Music and the Domestication of Blackface Minstrelsy'. *ATQ: The American Transcendental Quarterly* 16, no. 4 (December 2002): 241–56.

Durkin, Andrew. 'The Self-Playing Piano as a Site for Textual Criticism'. *Text* 12 (1999): 167–88. Available online: https://www.jstor.org/stable/30228031.

Dyer, Richard. *Only Entertainment*. London: Routledge, 1992.

Ellis, Sarah Taylor. 'Establishing (and Re-establishing) a Sense of Place: Musical Orientation in *The Sound of Music*'. *Studies in Musical Theatre* 3, no. 3 (2009): 277–83.

Erikson, Erik H. *Identity: Youth and Crisis*. New York: W.W. Norton, 1968.

Evans, Larry James. 'Rodgers and Hammerstein's *Oklahoma!*: The Development of the "Integrated" Musical'. PhD diss., University of California, Los Angeles, 1990.

Evans, Suzy. 'A Trip Around the Sun with Taylor Mac's "24-Decade History"'. *American Theatre*, 14 October 2016. Available online: https://www.americantheatre.org/2016/10/14/a-trip-around-the-sun-with-taylor-macs-24-decade-history/ (accessed 11 June 2021).

Foley, Helene P. 'Modern Performance and Adaptation of Greek Tragedy'. *Transactions of the American Philological Association* 129 (1999): 1–12. Available online: http://www.jstor.org/stable/284422.

Frankel, Aaron. *Writing the Broadway Musical*. New York: Drama Book Specialists, 1977.

Freeman, Elizabeth. *Time Binds: Queer Temporalities, Queer Histories*. Durham, NC: Duke University Press, 2010.

Frow, John. '"Reproducibles, Rubrics, and Everything You Need": Genre Theory Today'. *PMLA* 122, no. 5 (October 2007): 1626–34. Available online: https://doi.org/10.1632/pmla.2007.122.5.1626.

A Funny Thing Happened on the Way to the Forum. Directed by Richard Lester. United States: United Artists, 1966. DVD.

Gelles, Barrie. 'Glee and the "Ghosting" of the Musical Theatre Canon'. *Popular Entertainment Studies* 2, no. 2 (2011): 89–111. Available online: https://novaojs.newcastle.edu.au/ojs/index.php/pes/article/view/66 (accessed 11 June 2021).

Gentile, Jill. 'Time May Change Us: The Strange Temporalities, Novel Paradoxes, and Democratic Imaginaries of a Pandemic'. *Journal of the American Psychoanalytic Association* 68, no. 4 (14 September 2020): 649–69.

Glee: The Complete First Season. Produced by Ryan Murphy, Ian Brennan and Brad Falchuk. Performed by Matthew Morrison, Lea Michele, Jane Lynch, Cory Monteith and Chris Colfer. Twentieth Century Fox, 2010. DVD.

Gordon, Joanne. *Art Isn't Easy: The Achievement of Stephen Sondheim*. Carbondale and Edwardsville: Southern Illinois University Press, 1990.

Gove, Ben. *Cruising Culture: Promiscuity, Desire and American Gay Literature*. Edinburgh: Edinburgh University Press, 2000.

Grant, M. Shane. '"We're all freaks together": White Privilege and Mitigation of Queer Community'. In *Queer in the Choir Room: Essays on Gender and Sexuality in Glee*, edited by Michelle Parke, 69–83. Jefferson, NC: McFarland & Company, 2014.

Griffin, Sean. 'The Gang's All Here: Generic versus Racial Integration in the 1940s Musical'. *Cinema Journal* 42, no. 1 (2002): 21–45.

Halberstam, Jack. *In a Queer Time and Place: Transgender Bodies, Subcultural Lives*. New York: New York University Press, 2005.

Halberstam, Jack. *The Queer Art of Failure*. Durham, NC: Duke University Press, 2011.

Hamm, Charles. 'The Music of Tin Pan Alley'. In *Music in the New World*, 339–72. New York: Norton, 1983.

Harker, Dave. 'Still Crazy after All These Years: What Was Popular Music in the 1960s?'. In *Cultural Revolution? The Challenge of the Arts in the 1960s*, edited by Bart Moore-Gilbert and John Seed, 186–200. London and New York: Routledge, 1992.

Hart, Mary. 'Satyrs in L.A.'. *Didaskalia* 8, no. 6 (2011). Available online: http://www.didaskalia.net/issues/8/6/ (accessed 11 June 2021).

Hillman, Jessica. 'From Rags to Riches: Ragtime and the Jewish-American Dream'. In *Proceedings of the Association for Theatre in Higher Education*, Denver, CO, 2008.

Hills, Matt. *Fan Cultures*. London: Routledge, 2002.

Hodgkinson, Tim. *Music and the Myth of Wholeness: Toward a New Aesthetic Paradigm*. Cambridge, MA: MIT Press, 2016.

Hofstadter, Douglas. *I Am a Strange Loop*. New York: Basic Books, 2007.

Jackson, Michael R. 'Artist Interview: Michael R. Jackson'. Interview by Tim Sanford, *Playwrights Horizons*, 17 June. Available online: https://www.playwrightshorizons.org/shows/trailers/artist-interview-michael-r-jackson/ (accessed 11 June 2021).

Jackson, Michael R. 'Diversity in Musical Theater!' *Michael R. Jackson* [blog], 15 August 2015. Available online https://www.thelivingmichaeljackson.com/diversity-in-musical-theater/ (accessed 11 June 2021).

Jackson, Michael R. *A Strange Loop*. New York: Theatre Communications Group, 2020.

James, David E. *To Free the Cinema: Jonas Mekas and the New York Underground*. Princeton, NJ: Princeton University Press, 1992.

Joplin, Scott. 'School of Ragtime'. In *Complete Piano Rags*, edited by David A Jansen, xii–xiii. New York: Dover Publications, 1988.

Kafer, Alison. *Feminist, Queer, Crip*. Bloomington and Indianapolis: Indiana University Press, 2013.

Kalb, Jonathan. *Great Lengths: Seven Works of Marathon Theater*. Ann Arbor: University of Michigan Press, 2013.

Keeling, Kara. 'Looking for M – Queer Temporality, Black Political Possibility, and Poetry from the Future'. *GLQ: A Journal of Lesbian and Gay Studies* 15, no. 4 (2009): 565–82.

Khatib, Sami. 'The Time of Capital and the Messianicity of Time: Marx with Benjamin'. *Studies in Social and Political Thought* 20 (Winter 2012): 46–69.

Kirle, Bruce. *Unfinished Show Business: Broadway Musicals as Works-in-Process*. Carbondale: Southern Illinois University Press, 2005.

Knapp, Margaret M. 'Integration of Elements as a Viable Standard for Judging Musical Theatre'. *Journal of American Culture* 1, no. 1 (1978): 112–19.

Knapp, Raymond. *The American Musical and the Formation of National Identity*. Princeton, NJ: Princeton University Press, 2005.

Knapp, Raymond. *The American Musical and the Performance of Personal Identity*. Princeton, NJ: Princeton University Press, 2006.

Knapp, Raymond. 'Getting off the Trolley: Musicals Contra Cinematic Reality'. In *From Stage to Screen: Musical Films in Europe and United States (1927–1961)*, edited by Massimiliano Sala, 157–72. Turnhout: Brepols, 2012.

Knapp, Raymond. 'Saving Mr. *[Blank]*: Rescuing the Father through Song in Children's and Family Musicals'. In *Children, Childhood, and Musical*

Theater, edited by Donelle Ruwe and James Leve, 59–79. London: Routledge, 2020.

Knapp, Raymond, and Mitchell Morris. 'Tin Pan Alley Songs on Stage and Screen before World War II'. In *The Oxford Handbook of the American Musical*, edited by Raymond Knapp, Mitchell Morris and Stacy Ellen Wolf, 81–95. New York: Oxford University Press, 2011.

Knight, Arthur. *Disintegrating the Musical: Black Performance and American Musical Film*. Durham, NC: Duke University Press, 2002.

Koestenbaum, Wayne. *The Queen's Throat: Opera, Homosexuality, and the Mystery of Desire*. New York: Poseidon Press, 1993.

Kron, Lisa, and Jeanine Tesori. *Fun Home*. New York: Samuel French, 2015.

Kun, Josh. *Audiotopia: Music, Race, and America*. Berkeley: University of California Press, 2005.

Kushner, Tony. *Angels in America*. New York: Theatre Communications Group, 1995.

Lang, Anouk. '"The Status Is Not Quo!": Pursuing Resolution in Web-Disseminated Serial Narrative'. *Narrative* 18, no. 3 (2010): 367–81.

Larson, Jonathan. *Rent: The Complete Book and Lyrics of the Broadway Musical*. New York: Applause Theatre and Cinema Books, 2008.

Lehmann, Hans-Thies. *Postdramatic Theatre*. New York: Routledge, 2006.

Lewis, Helen. 'Renting a Queer Space: The Commodification of Queerness in Jonathan Larson's "Rent"'. MA diss., Tufts University, 2007.

Lieblich, Jerry. 'An Appropriated History of Appropriation as History'. *Culturebot*, 23 January 2015. Available online: https://www.culturebot.org/2015/01/23216/an-appropriated-history-of-appropriation-as-history/ (accessed 11 June 2021).

Lim, Bliss Cua. *Translating Time: Cinema, the Fantastic, and Temporal Critique*. Durham, NC: Duke University Press, 2009.

Lovelock, James. '"What about Love?": Claiming and Reclaiming LGBTQ+ Spaces in Twenty-First Century Musical Theatre'. In *Reframing the Musical: Race, Culture and Identity*, edited by Sarah Whitfield, 187–210. London: Red Globe Press, 2019.

Lovensheimer, Jim. 'Texts and Authors'. In *The Oxford Handbook of the American Musical*, edited by Raymond Knapp, Mitchell Morris and Stacy Ellen Wolf, 20–32. New York: Oxford University Press, 2011.

Mac, Taylor. 'A Conversation with Heterogeneity: Ein Gespräch zu "A 24-Decade History of Popular Music"'. Interview by Thomas Oberender,

Berliner Festspiele Blog [blog], 9 October 2019. Available online: https://blog.berlinerfestspiele.de/a-conversation-with-heterogeneity/ (accessed 11 June 2021).

MacRae, Ian. 'Queering Epistemology and the Odyssey of Identity in Alison Bechdel's *Fun Home*'. In *Graphic Novels as Philosophy*, edited by Jeff McLaughlin, 130–49. Jackson: University Press of Mississippi, 2017.

McClary, Susan. *Conventional Wisdom: The Content of Musical Form*. Berkeley: University of California Press, 2000.

McMillin, Scott. *The Musical as Drama: A Study of the Principles and Conventions behind Musical Shows from Kern to Sondheim*. Princeton, NJ: Princeton University Press, 2006.

McMurrer, Jennifer. 'Instructional Time in Elementary Schools: A Closer Look at Changes for Specific Subjects'. *Arts Education Policy Review* 109, no. 6 (2008): 23–8.

Midnight Movies: From the Margin to the Mainstream. Directed by Stuart Samuels. Stuart Samuels Productions, 2005. DVD.

Miller, D.A. *Place for Us: Essay on the Broadway Musical*. Cambridge, MA: Harvard University Press, 1998.

Miranda, Lin-Manuel, and Jeremy McCarter. *Hamilton: The Revolution*. London: Little, Brown Book Group, 2016.

Mordden, Ethan. *The Happiest Corpse I've Ever Seen: The Last Twenty-Five Years of the Broadway Musical*. New York: Palgrave Macmillan, 2004.

Mordden, Ethan. *On Sondheim: An Opinionated Guide*. New York: Oxford University Press, 2016.

Most, Andrea. *Making Americans: Jews and the Broadway Musical*. Cambridge, MA: Harvard University Press, 2004.

Muller, Agnès. 'Image as Paratext in Alison Bechdel's Fun Home'. *GRAAT*, no. 1 (March 2007). Available online: http://www.graat.fr/bechdel001aaaa.pdf (accessed 11 June 2021).

Muñoz, José Esteban. *Cruising Utopia: The Then and There of Queer Futurity*. New York and London: New York University Press, 2009.

Muñoz, José Esteban. *Disidentifications: Queers of Color and the Performance of Politics*. Minneapolis: University of Minnesota Press, 1999.

Murray-Román, Jeannine. 'A Manifesto on Making Space in Taylor Mac's 24-Decade History of Popular Music'. *Journal of Dramatic Theory and Criticism* 34, no. 1 (Fall 2019): 9–28.

Nereson, Ariel. '*Hamilton*'s America: An Unfinished Symphony with a Stutter (Beat)'. *American Quarterly* 68, no. 4 (December 2016): 1045–59.

The Nielsen Company. *Television in Transition: The Initial Impact of the Writers' Strike*. April 2008. Available online: http://www.broadcastingcable.com/file/2329-click_here.pdf (accessed 14 October 2012).

Nyong'o, Tavia. *Afro-Fabulations: The Queer Drama of Black Life*. New York: New York University Press, 2019.

Ostendorf, Berndt. 'The Musical World of Doctorow's Ragtime'. *American Quarterly* 43, no. 4 (December 1991): 579–601. http://www.jstor.org/stable/2713082.

Paris, Leslie. *Children's Nature: The Rise of the American Summer Camp*. New York: New York University Press, 2008.

Parks, Suzan-Lori. *The America Play, and Other Works*. New York: Theatre Communications Group, 1995.

Piro, Sal. 'It Was Great When It All Began'. In *Creatures of the Night: The Rocky Horror Experience*. Redford, MI: Stabur Press, 1990. Available online: http://www.rockyhorror.com/history/howapbegan.php (accessed 3 September 2020).

'Purpose of Songs'. Larry Gelbart Papers (Collection PASC 22). Library Special Collections, Charles E. Young Research Library, UCLA.

Rabkin, Nick, and E.C. Hedberg. *Arts Education in America: What the Declines Mean for Arts Participation*. Report No. 52. February 2011. Available online: https://www.arts.gov/sites/default/files/2008-SPPA-ArtsLearning.pdf (accessed 11 June 2021).

Ragtime. Book by Terrence McNally, music by Stephen Flaherty and lyrics by Lynn Ahrens. Music Theatre International (MTI), 1998.

Rapkin, Mickey. *Theater Geek: The Real Life Drama of a Summer at Stagedoor Manor, the Famous Performing Arts Camp*. New York: Free Press, 2010.

Rapp, Anthony. *Without You: A Memoir of Love, Loss, and the Musical Rent*. New York: Simon & Schuster, 2006.

Reddick, George. 'The Evolution of the Original Cast Album'. In *The Oxford Handbook of the American Musical*, edited by Raymond Knapp, Mitchell Morris and Stacy Ellen Wolf, 179–95. New York: Oxford University Press, 2011.

Rice, T.D. *Jim Crow, American: Selected Songs and Plays*. Edited by W.T. Lhamon Jr. Cambridge, MA: Belknap Press of Harvard University Press, 2009.

Roach, Joseph R. *Cities of the Dead: Circum-Atlantic Performance*. New York: Columbia University Press, 1996.

Robbins, Alexandra. *The Geeks Shall Inherit the Earth: Popularity, Quirk Theory, and Why Outsiders Thrive after High School*. New York: Hyperion, 2011.

The Rocky Horror Picture Show. Directed by Jim Sharman. Twentieth Century Fox, 1975. DVD.

The Rocky Horror Picture Show: The Official Fan Site. n.d. Available online: http://www.rockyhorror.com/ (accessed 11 June 2021).

Rodgers, Richard. *Musical Stages: An Autobiography*. New York: Random House, 1975.

Roell, Craig H. *The Piano in America, 1890–1940*. Chapel Hill: University of North Carolina Press, 1989.

Román, David. *Acts of Intervention: Performance, Gay Culture, and AIDS*. Bloomington: Indiana University Press, 1998.

Román, David. *Performance in America: Contemporary U.S. Culture and the Performing Arts*. Durham, NC: Duke University Press, 2005.

Ryan, Hugh. 'How Taylor Mac's 24-Hour Performance Encapsulated the Experience of the AIDS Crisis'. *New York Vulture*, 18 October 2016. Available online: https://www.vulture.com/2016/10/taylor-mac-performance-encapsulated-the-aids-crisis.html (accessed 11 June 2021).

Savran, David. 'Choices Made and Unmade'. *Theater* 31, no. 2 (2001): 89–95.

Savran, David. *Highbrow/Lowdown: Theater, Jazz, and the Making of the New Middle Class*. Ann Arbor: University of Michigan Press, 2009.

Savran, David. 'Toward a Historiography of the Popular'. *Theatre Survey* 45, no. 2 (November 2004): 211–17.

Sebesta, Judith. 'Of Fire, Death, and Desire: Transgression and Carnival in Jonathan Larson's Rent'. *Contemporary Theatre Review* 16, no. 4 (2006): 419–438.

Shevelove, Burt, Larry Gelbart and Stephen Sondheim. *A Funny Thing Happened on the Way to the Forum*. New York: Applause Theatre Book Publishers, 1991.

Solie, Ruth. '"Girling" at the Parlor Piano'. In *Music in Other Words: Victorian Conversations*, 85–117. Berkeley: University of California Press, 2004.

Sondheim, Stephen. *Finishing the Hat: Collected Lyrics (1954–1981) with Attendant Comments, Principles, Heresies, Grudges, Whines and Anecdotes*. New York: Knopf, 2010.

Sondheim, Stephen, and George Furth. *Company: A Musical Comedy*. New York: Theatre Communications Group, 1996.

Stagedoor. Directed by Alexandra Shiva. Blumhouse Productions, Gidalya Pictures, 2006. DVD.

Stein, Gertrude. 'Plays'. In *Gertrude Stein: Writings 1932–1946*, Vol. 2, 244–69. New York: Library of America, 1998.

Sternfeld, Jessica. '"Everything's Coming Up Kurt": The Broadway Song in the Pop World of Glee'. In *Proceedings of SAM/IASPM National Conference*, Cincinnati, 2011.

Sternfeld, Jessica. *The Megamusical*. Bloomington: Indiana University Press, 2006.

Steyn, Mark. *Broadway Babies Say Goodnight: Musicals Then and Now*. New York: Routledge, 1999.

Swayne, Steve. *How Sondheim Found His Sound*. Ann Arbor: University of Michigan Press, 2005.

Talbot, Brent C., and Margaux B. Millman. 'Discourses Surrounding Marginalized Groups, LGBTQ Issues, and Music Learning and Teaching Practices in Season 1 of Glee'. In *Proceedings of Establishing Identity: LGBT Studies and Music Education*, University of Illinois School of Music, Champaign, IL, 2011. Available online: https://bcrme.press.uillinois.edu/proceedings/Establishing_Identity/14_Talbot_Millman.pdf (accessed 27 October 2011).

Taylor, Diana. *The Archive and the Repertoire: Performing Cultural Memory in the Americas*. Durham, NC: Duke University Press, 2003.

Teare, Brian. 'How to Be a Dandy in the Age of Mass Culture: Notes on Taylor Mac's *A 24-Decade History of Popular Music*'. Kimmel Center for the Performing Arts, 14 August 2018. Available online: https://www.kimmelcenter.org/globalassets/about-us/blog/how-to-be-a-dandy-in-the-age-of-mass-culture.pdf (accessed 11 June 2021).

Todorov, Tzvetan, and Richard M. Berrong. 'The Origin of Genres'. *New Literary History* 8, no. 1 (Autumn 1976): 159–70. Available online: http://www.jstor.org/stable/468619.

Tuan, Yi-Fu. *Space and Place: The Perspective of Experience*. Minneapolis: University of Minnesota Press, 1977.

Viertel, Jack. *The Secret Life of the American Musical: How Broadway Shows Are Built*. New York: Farrar, Straus and Giroux, 2016.

Wagner, Richard. *Opera and Drama*. Lincoln: University of Nebraska Press, 1995.

Wald, Elijah. *How the Beatles Destroyed Rock 'n' Roll: An Alternative History of American Popular Music*. Oxford: Oxford University Press, 2009.

Warner, Rebecca Applin. 'Musematic Relationships in Jeanine Tesori's Score for *Fun Home*'. In *Reframing the Musical: Race, Culture and Identity*, edited by Sarah Whitfield, 151–66. London: Red Globe Press, 2019.

Weber, Carl. 'Brecht's Concept of Gestus and the American Performance Tradition'. In *Brecht Sourcebook*, edited by Carol Martin and Henry Bial, 41–6. London: Routledge, 2000.

Weiss, Sasha. 'Taylor Mac Wants Theater to Make You Uncomfortable'. *The New York Times*, 2 April 2019. Available online: https://www.nytimes.com/2019/04/02/magazine/taylor-mac-gary-broadway.html (accessed 11 June 2021).

Whedon, Joss, and Jane Watkins. *Dr. Horrible's Sing-Along Blog: The Book*. London: Titan Books, 2011.

White, Gareth. *Audience Participation in Theatre: Aesthetics of the Invitation*. London: Palgrave Macmillan, 2013.

White, Hayden V. *The Content of the Form: Narrative Discourse and Historical Representation*. Baltimore: Johns Hopkins University Press, 1987.

Whitfield, Sarah. 'Disrupting Heteronormative Temporality through Queer Dramaturgies: *Fun Home, Hadestown* and *A Strange Loop*'. *Arts* 9, no. 2 (2020): 69. Available online: https://doi.org/10.3390/arts9020069.

Whitfield, Sarah. 'Introduction'. In *Reframing the Musical: Race, Culture and Identity*, edited by Sarah Whitfield, xi–xxxii. London: Red Globe Press, 2019.

Wolf, Stacy Ellen. *Changed for Good: A Feminist History of the Broadway Musical*. New York: Oxford University Press, 2010.

Wolf, Stacy Ellen. *A Problem Like Maria: Gender and Sexuality in the American Musical*. Ann Arbor: University of Michigan Press, 2002.

Wollman, Elizabeth L. *Hard Times: The Adult Musical in 1970s New York City*. New York: Oxford University Press, 2013.

Zadan, Craig. *Sondheim & Co.*, Second Edition. New York: Harper and Row Publishers, 1986.

Index

Note: Page numbers in *italics* refer to Figures.

Abbott, George 16, 117
Actors Fund 76
adaptations 6, 9, 21, 32, 41, 47, 49, 51, 76, 82, 92–3, 96, 100, 102–3, 112, 123–4, 155–7, *see also Fun Home; Little Night Music, A; Ragtime; Ratatouille: The TikTok Musical; Show Boat; South Pacific*
adaptations, film. *See Funny Thing Happened on the Way to the Forum, A; Rent; Rocky Horror Picture Show, The; Sound of Music, The*
Adler, Thomas 30
Adorno, Theodor 110
Aeolian Piano Company 105, 108
Agamben, Giorgio 201
Ahrens, Lynn 82, 93, 104, *see also* Flaherty, Stephen; *My Favorite Year; Once on this Island; Ragtime*
AIDS. *See* HIV/AIDS
alienation effect [*Verfremdungseffekt*] (Brecht) 6–7
'All About Me' (*Dr. Horrible's Sing-Along Blog*) 77
All the Women Are White, All the Blacks Are Men, But Some of Us Are Brave (Crenshaw) 153
Allegro (Rodgers, Hammerstein) 27–8
Alliance of Motion Picture and Television Producers (AMPTP) 67, 73
Amazon Prime 75, 188
American Camp Association 127–8
American dream 91, 93, 97, 99–102 146

American Gothic (Wood) 49
American Horror Story (Murphy, Falchuk) 129
American Idol (Fuller) 127, 139, 140
American Piano Company 108
Amos, Tori 180
Angel of History (Benjamin) 39, 192
Angels in America (Kushner) 31, 189
Anger, Kenneth 52
Animal House (Landis) 55
'Another Day' (*Rent*) 35–6
'Another Hundred People' (*Company*) 170
anthems 10, 33, 35–8, 43, 73, 112, 114, 131, 137, *see also* 'Don't Stop Believin'' (Journey); 'One Day More' (*Les Misérables*); 'Seasons of Love' (*Rent*); 'Strike!' (*Dr. Horrible's Sing-Along Blog*); 'Wheels of a Dream' (*Ragtime*)
anticipatory illumination (Bloch) 4, 41
Apollo Reproducing Piano 109
Are You My Mother? (Bechdel) 156
Aristophanes 151
Aristotle 7, 198
arts education 141–3, *see also* public education system, US
Asian Americans 77, 84, 97, 134
Assassins (Sondheim, Weidman) 28, 125
assimilation 2, 96–7, 99, 114
audience participation 7–8, 11, 21, 38, 43, 48, 49, 50, 53–66, *64*, 126, 176, 185–6, 192–9, *195*, *see also Rent; Rocky Horror Show, The; Rocky Horror Picture Show, The; Strange*

Loop, A; *24-Decade History of Popular Music, A*; White, Gareth
Audience Participation in Theatre: Aesthetics of the Invitation (White) 194
Austin Powers films (Myers, Roach) 55
Avengers, The (Whedon) 76
Averno 117

Barenholtz, Ben 52–3
Barrowman, John 172
Baudrillard, Jean 140–1
　hypermarket 140–1
Beatles, The 135
Beauty and the Beast (Menkin, Ashman, Rice) 100
Bechdel, Alison 154–68, *155*, *167*, 190
　Are You My Mother? 156
　Dykes to Watch Out For (comic strip) 156
　Fun Home (graphic novel) 155–8
'Being Alive' (*Company*) 160, 170–1, 172, 175
Benjamin, Walter 39, 107, 109, 191, 192
　Angel of History 39, 192
　'Work of Art in the Age of Mechanical Reproduction' 107
Bennett, Michael 120, 174
Benson, Amber 79
Beowulf (anonymous) 68
Bergson, Henri 82
Berkeley, Busby 21, 58
Berlin, Irving 86, 97, 116
Bernstein, Leonard 97
B-films 51, 62–3
Billboard Hot 100 117, 136, 140
Billington, Michael 48
biological clock 173–4
Black identity 2, 97, 153, *see also* blackface; Black Lives Matter; Blake, Eubie; 'coon songs'; Du Bois, W.E.B.; jazz; Jim Crow; Johnson, James Weldon; Joplin, Scott; 'Line of Rags, A' (Haworth); Morrison, Toni; Morton, Jelly Roll; Perry, Tyler; ragtime; *Strange Loop, A*
Black composers and performers 2, 9–10, 38, 82, 83, 88, 111, 179, 181–3
Black liberation 5
Black musicals 2, *see also Ragtime; Strange Loop, A*
Black performance practice 18
Black temporality 5
community 179
family relations 87
Glee, depicted in 134
integration 18
queerness and 176–8, 181, 185–6
Ragtime, depicted in 102–6, 112–14
stereotypes 88, 179–80
Strange Loop, A (Jackson) depicted in 176–86
Black Lives Matter 113, 200
blackface 87–8, 181
Blake, Eubie 110
Bloch, Ernst 4, 41
　anticipatory illumination 4, 41
Bloody Bloody Andrew Jackson (Friedman, Timbers) 144, 159
Bono [Paul David Hewson] 135
Book of Mormon, The (Parker, Stone, Lopez) 144
Boublil, Alain 131
Bowie, David 135
Boyle, Danny 48
Brakhage, Stan 52
Brantley, Ben 100, 145, 173
Brecht, Bertolt 6–7, 28, 36, 158, 169, 175
　Verfremdungseffekt [alienation effect] 6–7
Brennan, Ian 129

Breuer, Lee 122
Brexit 193, 201
Brown, Jason Robert 146
Buffy the Vampire Slayer (Joss Whedon) 75, 79
Burgess, Tituss 76
Butler, Judith 151

camp 27, 48–51, 56, 62, 66, 72, 77, 119, 124, 125, 128, 141
Camp (Graff) 10, 119, 120–8, 134, 146
Campt, Tina M. 5
capitalism 4, 7, 41, 47, 78, 99, 180, 201
Carlson, Marvin 102
Carpenter, Charisma 79
Carroll, David 172
Castles-Onion, Brian 29
censorship 51, 66
Chabon, Michael 46
'Changing My Major' (*Fun Home*) 162
Chaplin, Charlie 26
Cheng, Anne Anlin 153
Chernow, Ron 144
Chicago (Kander, Ebb)
    film version (Marshall, 2002) 139
    'Mr. Cellophone' 130
Chicago Tribune 51
Chorus Line, A (Hamlisch, Kleban, Bennett) 178
Christie, Bunny 173
Churchill, Caryl 48
Cinderella (Rodgers, Hammerstein) 159
    'Ten Minutes Ago' 159
Citron, Stephen 30
Clue (Lynn) 55, 57
Clum, John 31, 171
'Coalhouse's Soliloquy' (*Ragtime*) 112–13
Cole, Kai 79
Colfer, Chris 140
Comic-Con 77

commercialization 2, 17, 31, 32, 41, 46, 52, 100, 107, 117, 139, 140
commodification 31–2, 41, 47, 51, 140
communitas 8, 11, 33, 35, 43, 122, 126
community 10, 11, 18, 32, 33, 34, 38–40, 47, 55, 56, 66, 76, 79, 92, 97, 120–8, 133, 135, 141, 179, 188, 190, 191, 194, 198, 200
Company (Sondheim, Furth) 10, 23, 28, 70, 125, 150, 168–75, 176
    'Another Hundred People' 170
    'Being Alive' 160, 170–1, 172, 175
    Doyle, John revival [2006] 171–2
    Elliott, Marianne revival [2018, West End] 172–4
    Kennedy Center revival [2002] 172
    'Ladies Who Lunch, The' 126, 175
    'Little Things You Do Together, The' 169–70
    'Marry Me a Little' 170
    Mendes, Sam revival [1996] 170–1
    'Not Getting Married Today' 175
    queerness in 171–2
    Roundabout revival [1995] 172
    'Someone Is Waiting' 170
concept musicals 23, 169, 175, 176, *see also* Company; Strange Loop, A
consumerism 78, 110
'Cool Ghoul, The'. *See* horror hosts; Zacherle, John
Coolidge, Calvin 87
'coon songs' 87–8, 90
Cop Rock (Bochco) 139
costumes 26, 48, 53, 56–9, 62, 65, 76, 94, 138, 141, 155, 179, 191, 193–4, *see also* Dazzle, Machine; Mac, Taylor; *Rocky Horror Picture Show, The*; *24-Decade History of Popular Music, A*; Zinn, David

counterpoint dialogue 60–2, 72
Covid-19 10, 76, 187–9, 199–201
Craig, David 29
Craig, Rosalie 173, 175
Crazy Ex-Girlfriend (Bloom, McKenna) 144
Crenshaw, Kimberle 153
crip time 5
Cry-Baby (Waters) 57
cult classics 53, 55–6
Cumming, Alan 172
Curry, Tim 49, 57
Cyclops, The (Euripides) 68

dance 1–3, 5–7, 11, 14–17, 21, 23, 24, 27, 41, 45, 48, 54–5, 65, 70, 72, 78, 81, 94, 113, 119, 121, 123, 128, 130, 132, 133, 134, 140, 141, 156, 159, 174, 176, 182, 186, 189, 190, 196
Daniele, Graciela 95
Dawkins, Philip 13
Day, Felicia 74–6, see also *Dr. Horrible's Sing-Along Blog*; *Guild, The*
Geek & Sundry 76
Dazzle, Machine 193
De Shields, André 76
Deren, Maya 52
Diamond, Elin 60
disidentification 16, 178–9, 180–1, 183–4, 186
Disney 75–6, 100, 128, 177, 179, 181, see also *Beauty and the Beast*; *High School Musical* trilogy; *Lion King, The*; *Little Mermaid, The*; *Ratatouille*
divorce trope (Knapp) 113–14
Doctorow, E.L. 9, 81, 82, 92–3
   'False Documents' 91
   Ragtime 9, 81, 82, 83, 86, 90–2, 99, 105–6, 112
Dolan, Jill 7–8, 40, 156–7
'Don't Stop Believin'' (Journey) 136–8, 140

Doogie Howser, M.D. (Bochco, Kelley) 69
Dorsey, Zachary 6
double consciousness 152–3
Downey, Jr., Robert 127
Doyle, John 171–2
Dr. Horrible's Sing-Along Blog (Whedon, Whedon, Whedon, Tancharoen) 9, 46, 47–8, 67–79
   Commentary! the Musical 72–3, 74, 77
   'My Freeze Ray' 70–3, 131
   'Strike!' 70, 73–4
Drabinsky, Garth 92
drag 26, 31, 34, 48, 51, 123, 177, 190, 192–3, 199, see also Camp; *Dr. Horrible's Sing-Along Blog*; *Funny Thing Happened on the Way to the Forum, A*; Mac, Taylor; *Rent*; *Rocky Horror Picture Show, The*; *Strange Loop, A*; *24-Decade History of Popular Music, A*
dreams 7–8, 15, 111–13, 118, 125, 131–3, 166, 176, 185, 199
Du Bois, W.E.B. 152–3
Duo-Art player pianos 108
Dyer, Richard 41
Dykes to Watch Out For (Bechdel comic strip) 156
dystopian imagery 46, 170

Ebb, Fred 146
'ecstatic time' 4–5, 8
11 o'clock numbers 28–30, 159, 164–5, 184–6, see also 'Memory Song' (*A Strange Loop*); 'Miller's Son, The' (*A Little Night Music*); 'Welcome to Our House on Maple Avenue' (*Fun Home*)
Eliot, T.S. 170
Elliott, Marianne 172–4
Emmy Awards 75, 140

entertainment 2, 9, 20, 32, 41, 46–7, 55, 74, 75, 99, 108, 145, 180, 191
entertainment, incidental 17, 20
Erikson, Erik 150
Esparza, Raul 172
Euripides 68
Evans, Daniel 172
'Everybody Ought to Have a Maid' (*A Funny Thing Happened on the Way to the Forum*) 20–1, 23, 25

Facebook 117
Falchuk, Brad 129
'False Documents' (Doctorow) 91
Falsettos (Finn, Lapine) 31
Fame [television series] (Gore, De Silva) 139
fan art 9, 46, 74–6
fan culture 2, 9, 32–3, 42, 47, 51, 56–7, 82, 146
  Hamilfans 146
  Rentheads 32–3, 40, 42
fans 6–8, 26–7, 33, 40, 48, 52–6, 62–6, 74–79, 115, 125, 128, 135, 146–7
farce 16, 19, 22, 26
Farese, Louis 60
Feldman, Adam 172
Ferber, Edna 96
Fiddler on the Roof (Bock, Harnick, Stein) 3, 95
film musicals 58, 135, 137, 139, 144, *see also Chicago*; *High School Musical* trilogy; *Into the Woods*; *Misérables, Les*; *Moulin Rouge*; Musically Enchanced Reality Mode (MERM); *Rocky Horror Picture Show, The*
Finn, William 31
Firefly (Joss Whedon) 75
Fitzgerald, Ella 116
Five Lesbian Brothers 157, *see also* Kron, Lisa

Flaherty, Stephen 82, 93, 104, *see also* Ahrens, Lynn; *My Favorite Year*; *Once on this Island*; *Ragtime*
'Flying Away' (*Fun Home*) 166
Follies (Sondheim, Goldman) 28, 168
  'I'm Still Here' 125
Ford, Henry 91, 92
Fosse, Bob 120
Foster, Stephen 87
Foucault, Michel 174
Franco, James 196
French Woods 127
Freud, Sigmund 91, 150
Friedman, Michael 42, 144, 199
Fun Home (Bechdel graphic novel) 155–7
Fun Home (Tesori, Kron) 10, 113, 149, 154–68, *155*, 171, 176, 178, 179, 185
  'Changing My Major' 162
  'Flying Away' 166
  'Ring of Keys' 161–2, 163, 164
  'Telephone Wire' 162–3, 166
  'Welcome to Our House on Maple Avenue' 164
'*Fun Home*: Is America Ready for a Musical about a Butch Lesbian?' (*Slate* article) 157
Funny Thing Happened on the Way to the Forum, A (Sondheim, Gelbart, Shevelove) 9, 15, 16–30
  'Everybody Ought to Have a Maid' 20–1, 23, 25
  film adaptation [Lester, 1966] 21
  'When I Kiss Him, I'll Be Kissing You' [renamed 'That'll Show Him'] 19
Furth, George 23, 169, 170, 171
futurities 5, 118, 189, 199, 201

Gaiman, Neil 186
Gaines, Boyd 172
Galati, Frank 93

Gardner, John 68
  Grendel 68
Geek & Sundry (Day) 76
Geeks Shall Inherit the Earth, The (Robbins) 118
Gelbart, Larry 16–17
Gellar, Sarah Michelle 79
Gendrault, Philippe 200
genre 9, 45–8, 51–2, 55, 67–79, 104–5
Gentile, Jill 200
Gershwin, George 97, 110, 116
Gershwin, Ira 97, 116
Gesamtkunstwerk (Wagner) 3, 15, 17, 96
Gilbert, W.S. 146, 191
Glee (Ryan, Falchuk, Brennan) 10, 66, 115, 119, 124, 129–44, 146
'Gliding' (*Ragtime*) 100–1
Glover, William 50
Golden Age musicals 2, 17–18, 113, 116, 144, 158
Golden Globe Awards 140
Goldman, Emma 91, 100
Goldman, James 168
Gospel at Colonus, The (Breuer, Telson) 122–4
  'How Shall I See You Through My Tears' 122–4
gospel plays 179, 184, *see also* Perry, Tyler
Graff, Todd 121, 127, 128
Grant, M. Shane 135
Grease (Jacobs, Casey) 139
  live telecast [2016] 144
Great Lengths: Seven Works of Marathon Theater (Kalb) 197
Greif, Michael 36
Grendel (Gardner) 68
Grine Milyoner, Der [*The New Millionaire*] (Perlmutter, Wohl, Thomashefsky) 101
Groff, Jonathan 145
Guild, The (Day) 74–5, 76

Hair (MacDermot, Rado, Ragni) 50, 145
Hal Leonard (music publisher) 142
Halberstam, Jack 4, 14–15, 33, *see also* queer temporality
Hamilton (Miranda) 116, 144–7
  'I Know Him' 145–6
  'Room Where It Happened, The' 146
  'What Comes Next?' 145
  'You'll Be Back' 145
Hammerstein II, Oscar 3, 17, 23, 27, 56, 96, 116, 159, 182
Happiest Corpse I've Ever Seen, The: The Last Twenty-Five Years of the Broadway Musical (Mordden) 116
Harold & Kumar Go to White Castle (Leiner) 69
Harper, Chris 173
Harris, Neil Patrick 69–70, 77, 140
haunting 9, 82, 102–3
Haworth, D.
  'Line of Rags, A' 88–90, *89*
Hedwig and the Angry Inch (Mitchell, Trask) 70, 151–2, 151
Heredia, Wilson Jermaine 33
heteronormativity 2, 4, 14, 18, 26, 49, 50, 56, 58, 70, 78, 113, 157, 164–6, 168, 171, 174–5
High School Musical trilogy (Ortega, Barsocchini) 139–40
HIV/AIDS 4, 5, 15, 28, 30–6, 31, 38–42, 180, 189, 192
Hofstadter, Douglas 149, 150–1, 182
Homosexuals, The (Dawkins) 13–15
Hopper, Antwayn 178
horror hosts 62–5, *see also* Lustgarten, Edgar; Zacherle, John
Houdini, Harry 91, 99
How I Met Your Mother (Bays, Thomas) 69

'How Shall I See You Through My Tears' (*The Gospel at Colonus*) 122–4
Hull High (Grant) 139
Hulu 75
Huntley, Paul 155
hypermarket (Baudrillard) 140–1

'I Cain't Say No' (*Oklahoma!*) 162
'I Know Him' (*Hamilton*) 145–6
'I Know It's Today' (*Shrek The Musical*) 166
'I want' songs 131, 146, 147, 159, 164–5, 183, 185, *see also* 'My Shot'; 'On My Own'; 'Today'; 'Welcome to Our House on Maple Avenue'
'I'll Cover You' (*Rent*) 39–40
'I'm Still Here' (*Follies*) 125
identification 3, 14, 15, 16, 26, 32, 33, 47, 56, 65, 66, 117, 119, 161, 162, 178–80
identity 1–2, *see also* Black identity; Jewish identity; queer identity
In the Heights (Miranda) 146
incidental entertainment. *See* entertainment, incidental
'Inner White Girl' (*A Strange Loop*) 131, 180
Instagram 79, 117
'Integration of Elements as a Viable Standard for Judging Musical Theater' (Knapp) 23
Interlochen Center for the Arts 127
Into the Woods (Sondheim, Lapine) film version [Marshall, 2014] 144
It Gets Better Project 118
iTunes 68, 125

Jackson, Jr. James 178
Jackson, Larry 52
Jackson, Michael R. 176–86
 Strange Loop, A 149, 150, 176–86
 'Why I Can't Get Work' 182

Jacobs, Ken 52
jazz 2, 81, 83, 85, 177
Jesus Christ Superstar (Lloyd Webber, Rice) 139
Jewish identity 9, *see also* American dream; Berlin, Irving; Bernstein, Leonard; *Fiddler on the Roof*; Gershwin, George; Houdini, Harry; Kern, Jerome; 'Lebn Zol Kolumbus'; *Melting Pot, The* (Zangwill); *Ragtime*; Tin Pan Alley
 assimilation 2, 99, 100–2
 composers 97
 creators of *Ragtime* 93
 Glee, in 130
 immigration 2, 91, 95–6
 integration 18
 klezmer 95
 popular music and 83, 86
Jim Crow 88
Jodorowsky, Alejandro 52
Johnson, Boris 200
Johnson, James Weldon 86
Jones, Dean 172
Joplin, Scott 81–2, 90, 103, 110
 'Maple Leaf Rag' 90
 'Wall Street Rag' 90
Joseph and the Amazing Technicolor Dreamcoat (Lloyd Webber, Rice) 139
Journey 136–8, 140
 'Don't Stop Believin'' 136–8, 140
 'Lovin' Touchin' Squeezin'' 136

Kalb, Jonathan 197
Kander, John 146
Kane, Sarah 48
Kendrick, Anna 126
Kenilworth, Walter Winston 85
Kern, Jerome 96, 97
Kert, Larry 172
Kirle, Bruce 18

Kiss of the Spider Woman (Kander, Ebb, McNally) 100
'Kiss the Girl' (*The Little Mermaid*) 181
Kittrell, Konnie 128
klezmer 95, 101
Knapp, Margaret M. 23
Knapp, Raymond 27, 113, 137
   divorce trope 113–14
   marriage trope 113–14
   Musically Enhanced Reality Mode (MERM) 137
Koestenbaum, Wayne 26
Kron, Lisa 154, 157–8, 165, *see also* Five Lesbian Brothers
   Fun Home (with Tesori) 154–68
Kushner, Tony 31, 189

Lacamoire, Alex 145
'Ladies Who Lunch, The' (*Company*) 126, 175
landscape 6, 54–6, 58–60, 65, 93, 137, 142, *see also* Stein, Gertrude
Lapine, James 31
Larson, Jonathan 27, 32
   Rent 30–43
Leacock Hoffman Victoria 34
'Lebn Zol Kolumbus' [Long Live Columbus!] (*Der grine Milyoner* [*The New Millionaire*] (Perlmutter, Wohl, Thomashefsky) 101–2, *101*
Lee, L. Morgan 178
Legally Blonde: The Musical (O'Keefe, Benjamin) 139
Lehmann, Hans-Thies 198
Lehmann-Haupt, Christopher 91
leitmotif 39, 158, 176, 184
Lerner, Alan Jay 116
Les Misérables (Schönberg, Boublil) 117, 131, 137
   film version [Hopper, 2012] 144
   'On My Own' 130–3, 136, 137
   'One Day More' 131
Lester, Richard 21
Lewis, Helen 31–2
Lieblich, Jerry 191, 193
Lim, Bliss Cua 82
'Line of Rags, A' (Haworth) 88–90, *89*
Lion King, The (John, Rice, Taymor) 176, 178, 179, 181
Little Mermaid, The (Menken, Ashman, Slater) 181
   'Kiss the Girl' 181
Little Night Music, A (Sondheim, Wheeler) 9, 15
   'Miller's Son, The' 15, 27–30
'Little Things You Do Together, The' (*Company*) 169–70
Livent (Live Entertainment Corporation of Canada) 100
Lloyd Webber, Andrew 139, 143
Loewe, Frederick 116
Losing the Plot in Opera (Castles-Onion) 29
Love! Valour! Compassion! (McNally) 31, 92
'Lovin' Touchin' Squeezin'' (Journey) 136
Lucas, Sydney 155, 161
Luhrmann, Baz 58, 139
Lustgarten, Edgar 63
Lyles, John-Michael 178
Lynch, Jane 140

Mabou Mines 122
Mac, Taylor 10, 187, 189–99
   24-Decade History of Popular Music, A 10, 189–99, *195*
Madonna [Madonna Louise Ciccone] 142
Maguire, Gregory 68
Make American Great Again (MAGA) 201
Malone, Beth 155, 163
Maltin, Leonard 63

'Maple Leaf Rag' (Joplin) 90
marathon theatre 197, 199, *see also* Kalb, Jonathan; Mac, Taylor; *24-Decade History of Popular Music, A*
marginalization 2, 5–11, 16, 33, 51, 55, 74, 84, 115, 119, 153, 177, 178, 183, 190, 194
Marjory Stoneman Douglas High School 42
Markopoulos, Gregory 52
marriage trope (Knapp) 113–14
'Marry Me a Little' (*Company*) 170
Mars, Bruno 142
Marshall, Rob 139
Martin, Barb 118
Marvel Studios 76
Master Class (McNally) 92
McClary, Susan 84
McDonald, Audra 104
McKechnie, Donna 174
McMillin, Scott 41
  Musical as Drama, The 5, 24
McNally, Terrence 31, 82, 92–3, 96, 104, *see also Ragtime*
  Love! Valour! Compassion! 31, 92
  Master Class 92
McNulty, Charles 47
Meat Loaf [Michael Lee Aday] 49
Mekas, Jonas 52
Melting Pot, The (Zangwill) 97, *98*
'Memory Song' (*A Strange Loop*) 184–6
Mendes, Sam 170–1
#MeToo movement 200
Mexican Americans 84
Michele, Lea 127
Michener, James A. 96
midnight movies 52–3, 54, *see also* Anger, Kenneth; audience participation; Barenholtz, Ben; Brakhage, Stan; counterpoint dialogue; cult classics; Deren, Maya; horror hosts; Jackson, Larry; Jodorowsky, Alejandro; Markopoulos, Gregory; Mekas, Jonas; Rice, Ron; *Rocky Horror Picture Show, The*; Romero, George A.; shadowcasts; Smith, Jack; Warhol, Andy; Waters, John
Miller, D.A. 14, 171
'Miller's Son, The' (*A Little Night Music*) 15, 27–30
Minnelli, Nina 56–7, *see also* Sins o' the Flesh
Miranda, Lin-Manuel 146
  In the Heights 146
Mitchell, Brian Stokes 104
modern time consciousness 3
Moderwell, Hiram 85–6
Mommie Dearest (Perry) 56
Mordden, Ethan 116
More, Thomas 8
Morgan, J.P. 92
Morissette, Alanis 180
Morris, William 8
Morrison, John-Andrew 178
Morrison, Matthew 142
Morrison, Toni 84
Morton, Jelly Roll 110
Moulin Rouge (Luhrmann) 58, 139
'Mr. Cellophane' (*Chicago*) 130
Muller, Agnès 156
Muñoz, José 4, 8, 178, *see also* disidentification, *see also* 'ecstatic time'
Murphy, Ryan 129, 139, 140
Musical as Drama, The (McMillin) 5, 24
musical comedy 2, 15–17, 23, 83, 101, 116, 141, 145
Musically Enhanced Reality Mode (MERM) 137–8
My Fair Lady (Lerner, Loewe) 116
My Favorite Year (Flaherty, Ahrens) 93

'My Freeze Ray' (*Dr. Horrible's Sing-Along Blog*) 70–3, 131
Myspace 132

narrative 1–3, 5–7, 14–28, 30, 36, 38, 41–2, 45–6, 48, 53, 54, 59–60, 64–5, 68, 74, 83–4, 92, 93, 97, 102, 113–14, 116, 119, 121–3, 130, 135, 138, 140–1, 146–7, 151–3, 157, 159, 175, 177, 180, 186, 190–1, 200
National Association for Music Education 143
National Health Service (NHS) 201
Nesbit, Evelyn 91, 99
Netflix 75, 143, 187
'New Music' (*Ragtime*) 102–3
New York Theatre Workshop 31
New York Times, The 91, 145, 172, 173, 192
Next to Normal (Kitt, Yorkey) 47
Night of the Living Dead (Romero) 53
Nightengale, Eric 121
Nip/Tuck (Murphy) 129
No Child Left Behind (NCLB) 118–19
'Not Getting Married Today' (*Company*) 175
Nuart Theatre 55, 58, *64*
Nugent, Ted 196
NYU (New York University) 182

O'Brien, Richard 48, 51, 55, 60
Occupy Wall Street 200
Oklahoma! (Rodgers, Hammerstein) 3, 17
   'I Cain't Say No' 162
   'People Will Say We're in Love' 26
   'Surrey with the Fringe on Top, The' 196
Oliver! (Bart) 139
'On My Own' (*Les Misérables*) 130–3, 136, 137
Once on This Island (Flaherty, Ahrens) 93

'One Day More' (*Les Misérables*) 131
Only Entertainment (Dyer) 41
Opacic, Ralph 142
opera 26, 29–30, 31–2, 54, 63, 68, 105, 156
'Origin of Love, The' (*Hedwig and the Angry Inch*) 151–2
Owens, Larry 178

parallel fiction 68, *see also* Beowulf; *Cyclops, The*; *Dr. Horrible's Sing-Along Blog*; Euripides; Gardner, John; *Grendel*; Maguire, Gregory; Psittacus Productions; *Wicked*; *Wizard of Oz, The*
Parks, Suzan-Lori 84–5
Passing Strange (Stew) 159
People (magazine) 69
'People Will Say We're in Love' (*Oklahoma!*) 26
performance 1, 2, 3, 7–9, 15, 16, 18, 32, 41, 48, 50, 54, 58–9, 74, 83, 84, 90, 103, 104, 105–11, 114, 119–21, 119, 124, 129, 131–8, 141, 150, 158, 164, 167, 172
performativity 2, 6–9, 7, 11, 15, 30, 40, 48, 53–6, 78–9, 83, 97, 99, 106, 133, 134, 138, 142, 147, 150–1, 180–1
Perlmutter, Arnold 101
Perry, Katy 142
Perry, Tyler 179–81, 184, *see also* gospel plays; *Strange Loop, A*
Phair, Liz 149, 179, 180, 182
   'Strange Loop' 182
Pike, James 86–7
Pink Flamingos (Waters) 53
Piro, Sal 60, 63
Plato 151
player pianos (pianolas) 8, 9, 105–11, *109*, *see also* Aeolian Piano Company; American Piano Company; Apollo

Reproducing Piano; Duo-Art player pianos; Standard Pneumatic Action Co.
Playwrights Horizons 177
Polycarpe, Jordan *143*
popular music 47, 84, 86, 104, 115–17, 124, 130, 135, 146, 189–93, *see also* jazz; ragtime
Porter, Cole 116
Portman, Natalie 127
power ballads 136–8
Prince, Harold 168, 170–1
Prop 8: The Musical (Shaiman) 69–70
Psittacus Productions 68
public education system, US 141–4, *see also* arts education
Public Theater 145, 157, 161, 168
Pulitzer Prize 32, 47, 68, 122, 176, 190

queer identity 2, 13–16, 26, *see also* Camp; Dolan, Jill; ecstatic time; *Fun Home*; *Funny Thing Happened on the Way to the Forum, A*; *Glee*; Halberstam, Jack; Harris, Neil Patrick; HIV/AIDS; Mac, Taylor; marginalization; 'Miller's Son, The' (*A Little Night Music*); Muñoz, José; *Rent*; *Rocky Horror Picture Show, The*; *Rocky Horror Show, The*; show queens; Stein, Gertrude; Waters, John
  commodification of in *Rent* 31–2
  Company (Sondheim, Furth), in 171–2
  Dr. Horrible as countercultural hero 69
queer audiences 48, 49, 51, 53, 65–6
queer communities 10, 39, 135
queer futurity 4–5
queer narratives 14–15, 156–7
queer space 53, 192–3

queer temporality 4, 8–9, 14–15, 25–38, 43, 53, 54, 189, 192–3, *see also* Halberstam, Jack
'queer time' 4
queering of popular music 189–97
race and 176–8, 181, 185–6
Rentheads 32–3, 40, 42
Strange Loop, A (Jackson) 176–8, 181, 185–6
quirk theory (Robbins) 118

Radio City Music Hall 42
ragtime 9, 81–3, 85–90, 92, 93–6, 102, 104–5, 106, 110, 111–13, *see also* Black identity; Blake, Eubie; Joplin, Scott; 'Line of Rags, A' (Haworth); Morton, Jelly Roll; Stark, John
Ragtime (Doctorow novel) 9, 81, 82, 83, 86, 90–2, 99, 105–6, 112
  film adaptation [Forman, 1981] 92
Ragtime (Flaherty, Ahrens, McNally) 9, 92–7, 99–105, 112–14
  'Coalhouse's Soliloquy' 112–13
  'Gliding' 100–1
  'New Music' 102–3
  'Wheels of a Dream' 112, 114
  'Your Daddy's Son' 112
Rapkin, Mickey 117–18, 121, 126
Rapp, Anthony 36
Ratatouille: The TikTok Musical 76
Ray, Matt 197
recitative 35, 40
Reefer Madness (Gasnier) 56
Rent (Larson) 9, 15, 30–43
  'Another Day' 35–6
  film adaptation [Columbus, 2005] 32, 41
  'I'll Cover You' 39–40
  'Seasons of Love' 36–43
  'Will I?' 40
Rent: School Edition 32
repetition 5–6, 15, 22, 24, 26, 35–40, 45, 54–5, 85, 150–1, 176, 186

reprise 20, 22, 26, 35, 38–41, 43, 55–6, 103, 114, 145
Rice, Ron 52
Riedel, Michael 33, 40
'Ring of Keys' (*Fun Home*) 161–2, 163, 164
Rise and Fall of Ziggy Stardust and the Spiders from Mars, The (Bowie) 135
Robbins, Alexandra 118
   quirk theory 118
Rock of Ages (D'Arienzo) 136
Rocky Horror Picture Show, The (Sharman, O'Brien) 9, 46, 47–8, 49, 50–66, 51, 67
Rocky Horror Show, The (O'Brien) 1, 48–51
   'Time Warp' 1, 45, 49, 54–5, 64–6, 142
Rodgers, Richard 3, 17–18, 23, 27, 56, 96, 116, 146, 159, 182
Roell, Craig 108–10
Roland. *See* horror hosts; Zacherle, John
Romero, George A. 53
Romy and Michele's High School Reunion (Mirkin) 55
'Room Where It Happened, The' (*Hamilton*) 146
Rupert, Michael 172
Ryan, Hugh 198

Savran, David 31, 83
scholar-fan 64–5
Schönberg, Claude-Michel 131
science fiction/fantasy 9, 46–8, 50, 77, 79, 115, 134
'Seasons of Love' (*Rent*) 36–43
Seaview Productions 76
Secret Life of the American Musical, The (Viertel) 158
Seurat, Georges 125, 168
Sgt. Pepper's Lonely Hearts Club Band (The Beatles) 135

shadowcasts 8, 9, *see also* Sins o' the Flesh
Shaiman, Marc 69
Sheehan-Clark, Lauren 175
Shepard, Sam 48
Shevelove, Burt 16
Shock Treatment (Sharman, O'Brien) 55
Show Boat (Ferber novel) 96
Show Boat (Kern, Hammerstein) 96
   Livent revival 100
show choirs 129, *see also* arts education; *Glee*; public education system, US
show queen 2, 9, 13–15, 115, 116, 117, 120, 123, 124, 130, 134
showstoppers 1, 15, 16, 20, 21, 23, 25–6, 33, 35, 36, 125–6, 131, 133, 138, 145, 200, *see also* 'Another Day'; anthems; communitas; 'Don't Stop Believin''; 'Everybody Ought to Have a Maid'; 'I'm Still Here'; 'Ladies Who Lunch, The'; 'On My Own'; 'Seasons of Love'; 'You'll Be Back'
Shrek the Musical (Tesori, Lindsay-Abaire) 166
   'I Know It's Today' 166
Simas, Rick 96
Sinatra, Frank 116
Sins o' the Flesh (Los Angeles performance troupe) 55–9, 57, *see also* Minnelli, Nina; shadowcasts; Stockton, Liz
Six (Marlow, Moss) 116
Skeggs, Emily 155, 159, 162
Smiles of a Summer Night (Bergman) 28
Smith, Darius Marcel 180
Smith, Jack 52
Smith, Morgan 117
Socha, Alexandra 159
'Someone Is Waiting' (*Company*) 170

Something for the Boys: Musical Theater and Gay Culture (Clum) 31
Sondheim, Stephen 16, 23, 26, 27–8, 120, 125, 170, 171–3, 183, 190
   Assassins (with Weidman) 28, 125
   Company (with Furth) 10, 23, 28, 70, 125, 126, 150, 160, 168–75, 176
   Follies (with Goldman) 28, 125–6, 168
   Funny Thing Happened on the Way to the Forum, A (with Gelbart, Shevelove) 9, 15, 16–30
   Into the Woods (with Lapine) 144
   Little Night Music, A (with Wheeler) 9, 15, 27–30
   Sunday in the Park with George (with Lapine) 28, 125, 168
   Sweeney Todd (with Wheeler) 28, 125
Sontag, Susan 50
Sophocles 122
   Oedipus at Colonus 122
Sound of Music, The (Rodgers, Hammerstein) 116, 139
   live telecast [2013] 144
   sing-a-long showings of film 55–6
South Pacific (Rodgers, Hammerstein) 96, 116
   'Wonderful Guy, A' 159
Southerland, Thom 104
spectatorship 2, 3, 5, 6, 9, 32, 33, 43, 45–79, 81, 119, 122, 157, 190
Spotify 117
Stagedoor Manor 118, 121, 125–8
Standard Pneumatic Action Co. 106
Stark, John 90
Steggert, Bobby 172
Stein, Gertrude 54, 59–60, 198, *see also* landscape

Stephen Sondheim: A Life (Secrest) 172
stereotypes 13, 16, 88, 90, 115, 134, 177–81
Stockton, Liz 56–7, *see also* Sins o' the Flesh
Stonewall 28, 171
Strange Loop, A (Jackson) 10, 149, 150, 176–86
   'Inner White Girl' 131, 180
   'Memory Song' 184–6
   queerness in 176–8, 181, 185–6
   'Today' 183–4
'Strange Loop' (Phair) 182
strange temporalities 1, 3–7, 9, 15–16, 25, 45, 82, 198, 201, *see also* Black temporality; crip time; futurities; haunting; queer temporality
streaming platforms 75–6, 143
'Strike!' (*Dr. Horrible's Sing-Along Blog*) 70, 73–4
Stritch, Elaine 126
subculture 50–2, 65, 118
Sullivan, Arthur 146, 191
summer camps 119–28, *see also* Camp; French Woods; Graff, Todd; Interlochen Center for the Arts; Kittrell, Konnie; Nightengale, Eric; Rapkin, Mickey; Stagedoor Manor; Zilberberg, Raymond
Sunday in the Park with George (Sondheim, Lapine) 28, 125, 168
'Surrey with the Fringe on Top, The' (*Oklahoma!*) 196
survival 8, 10, 123–6, 142, 179, 185
Sweeney Todd (Sondheim, Wheeler) 28, 125
Symposium (Plato) 151
synchronization 9, 53–4, 56, 59–60, 63

syncopation 6, 9, 53, 59–60, 63, 65, 81, 83, 88–90, 92, 94, 105, 111, 112, 161, 163, 164

Tales of the South Pacific (Michener) 96
Tancharoen, Maurissa 67, 73, 77
Tarento, Danielle 104
Teare, Brian 193
'Telephone Wire' (*Fun Home*) 162–3, 166
Telson, Bob 122
'Ten Minutes Ago' (*Cinderella*) 159
Tepper, Jennifer Ashley 144
Tesori, Jeanine 154, 158, 163, 166–7
  Fun Home (with Kron) 154–68
  Shrek The Musical (with Lindsay-Abaire) 166
  Violet (with Crawley) 166
Testa, Mary 76
Theater Geek: The Real Life Drama of a Summer at Stagedoor Manor (Rapkin) 117, 121
Theater Journal 96
theatre geeks 10, 115, 117–18, 121–5, 128, 143
Thomashefsky, Boris 101
Tiffany, John 172
TikTok 76, 117
time collapses 6, 28, 35, 162–3, 166, 168
'Time Warp' (*The Rocky Horror Show*) 1, 45, 49, 54–5, 64–6, 142
Tin Pan Alley 86, 116
'Today' (*A Strange Loop*) 183–4
TodayTix 76
Tony Awards 14, 16, 32, 42, 70, 154
Topo, El (Jodorowsky) 52–3
Trachtenberg, Michelle 79
transphobia 79
Tumblr 117, 125
TV musicals 130, *see also Crazy Ex-Girlfriend*; *Glee*; *Grease*; *Sound of Music, The*

24-Decade History of Popular Music, A (Mac) 10, 187, 189–99, *195*
Twitter 117

Universal Pictures 62
Up Against the Clock: Career Women Speak on the Choice to Have Children (Fabe, Winkler) 174
Urie, Michael 172
utopianism 5, 7–8, 11, 40–1, 43, 46, 66, 70–3, 111, 114, 128, 147

Van Matre, Lynn 51
Veasey, Jason 178
Verfremdungseffekt [alienation effect] (Brecht) 6–7
Viertel, Jack 158–9
  Secret Life of the American Musical, The 158
Vimeo 78
Violet (Tesori, Crawley) 166
Viva Laughlin (Bowker, Lowry) 139

Wagner, Richard 15, 17, 96, *see also Gesamtkunstwerk*
Wall Street Journal 50
'Wall Street Rag' (Joplin) 90
Warhol, Andy 52
Warner, Rebecca Applin 158, 162, 167
Washington Post 174
Washington Times 117
Waste Land, The (Eliot) 170
Waters, John 53
web series 8, 67–8, 72, *see also Dr. Horrible's Sing-Along Blog*; *Geek & Sundry*; *Guild, The*; *Ratatouille: The TikTok Musical*
'Welcome to Our House on Maple Avenue' (*Fun Home*) 164
Welte-Mignon 108
'What Comes Next?' (*Hamilton*) 145
Whedon, Jed 67, 73

Whedon, Joss 67, 72–3, 75, 76, 79
  Buffy the Vampire Slayer 75, 79
  Firefly 75
Whedon, Zack 67, 73, 74
Wheeler, Hugh 28
'Wheels of a Dream' (*Ragtime*) 112, 114
'When I Kiss Him, I'll Be Kissing You' [renamed 'That'll Show Him'] (*A Funny Thing Happened on the Way to the Forum*) 19, 22
White, Gareth 194
Whitfield, Sarah 184
Who, The 135
'Why I Can't Get Work' (Jackson) 182
Wicked (Schwartz, Holzman) 68
'Will I?' (*Rent*) 40
Williams, Wendy 184
Willson, Meredith 116
Wilson, Edwin 50
Wizard of Oz, The (Baum) 68
Wizard of Oz, The (musical adaptation) 139
Wodehouse, Artis 110
Wohl, Herman 101

Wolf, Matt 173
'Wonderful Guy, A' (*South Pacific*) 159
Wood, Grant 49
World Health Organization (WHO) 187
Writers Guild of America (WGA) 67, 73

Xbox Live 76

'You'll Be Back' (*Hamilton*) 145
Young, Neil 124
'Your Daddy's Son' (*Ragtime*) 112
youth musical theatre 10, 115–44, *see also* arts education; *Camp*; *Glee*; summer camps; US public education system
YouTube 73, 75, 78, 117

Zacherle, John 62–4
Zangwill, Israel 97
  Melting Pot, The 97, *98*
Zilberberg, Raymond 126
Zinn, David 155, 157

www.ingramcontent.com/pod-product-compliance
Lightning Source LLC
Chambersburg PA
CBHW052217300426
44115CB00011B/1722